"For anyone who cares about the church in the modern world—especially the issues of institutional health for the sake of the church and global mission—this is an important work. Many of the personalities told in this story have had a national or international presence and impact. Here we see their institutional home, through all the vicissitudes of social issues and economic fluctuations. A tale well-told."

—SCOTT W. SUNQUIST,
president, Gordon-Conwell Theological Seminary

"*Great is Thy Faithfulness* is an engaging story of God's faithfulness to a relatively small school—which has made a significant impact—born from a small denomination who never wavered from a deep commitment to Scripture and the message of the gospel. For 125 years, the Lord has used Trinity to his glory and the growth of his church both in the United States and around the world. The Trinity story is a testament to the faithfulness of God and the deep commitment of godly leaders who have remained 'entrusted with the gospel.' "

—KEVIN KOMPELIEN,
president, EFCA

"Trinity International University has a living legacy in training global leaders for the evangelical church. This compelling narrative—marking 125 years of the school's history—documents Trinity's enduring commitment to proclaiming the biblical gospel and teaching historic, ecumenical orthodoxy. Here leading church historians and other scholars from the Trinity community recount their institutional history as a story of God's faithful provision and enduring grace—not just for Trinity, but for people all over the world whose lives are changed by its ministry."

—PHILIP RYKEN,
president, Wheaton College

Great

IS THY

Faithfulness

Great
IS THY
Faithfulness

THE TRINITY STORY

125 YEARS OF
TRINITY INTERNATIONAL UNIVERSITY

John D. Woodbridge
David M. Gustafson
Scott M. Manetsch
Bradley J. Gundlach

Foreword by
David S. Dockery

Afterword by
D. A. Carson

LEXHAM PRESS

Great Is Thy Faithfulness: The Trinity Story—125 years of Tninity International University

Lexham Press, 1313 Commercial St., Bellingham, WA 98225
LexhamPress.com

Print ISBN 9781683596325
Digital ISBN 9781683596660
Library of Congress Control Number 2022937323

Lexham Editorial: Todd Hains, Claire Brubaker, Abigail Stocker, Mandi Newell,
    Kelsey Matthews, Allisyn Ma, Jessi Strong, Katie French
Cover Design: Joshua Hunt, Brittany Schrock
Typesetting: ProjectLuz.com

Contents

PRAYER FOR ALL ENTRUSTED WITH THE GOSPEL   IX

FOREWORD   XI
David S. Dockery

CHAPTER 1

Humble Beginnings (1897–1915)   1
David M. Gustafson

CHAPTER 2

On the Move to Merger (1916–1960)   31
David M. Gustafson

CHAPTER 3

A Gift to Evangelicalism (1963–1974)   61
Scott M. Manetsch

CHAPTER 4

A Christian Liberal Arts College (1957–1996)   96
Bradley J. Gundlach

CHAPTER 5

Decades of Consolidation (1975–1996)   150
Scott M. Manetsch

CHAPTER 6

Trinity Blossoms as a Christian University (1996–2019)   181
David M. Gustafson

CHAPTER 7

Thanksgiving to the Lord for His Great Faithfulness   229
John D. Woodbridge

AFTERWORD   233
D. A. Carson

POSTSCRIPT   241
Nicholas Perrin

NOTES   245

Prayer for All Entrusted
with the Gospel

IN THE NAME of the Father and of the Son and of the Holy Spirit.
Amen.

THE STEADFAST LOVE of the LORD never ceases;
his mercies never come to an end;
they are new every morning;
great is your faithfulness. *Lamentations 3:22–23*

I WILL SING of the steadfast love of the LORD, forever;
with my mouth I will make known your faithfulness
to all generations. *Psalm 89:1*

ALMIGHTY AND GRACIOUS GOD, the Father of our Lord Jesus
Christ, you commanded us to pray that you would send out laborers into your harvest. Of your infinite mercy, give us true teachers and ministers of your word. Put your saving gospel in their
hearts and on the lips that they may truly fulfill your command
to preach nothing contrary to your holy word, that we, so being
warned, instructed, nurtured, comforted, and strengthened by your
heavenly word, may do those things which are well pleasing to you
and profitable to us; through Jesus Christ, your Son, our Lord.
Amen.

Foreword

God's faithfulness has shaped the life and work of the institution now called Trinity International University since its founding in the nineteenth century. This wonderful place has been used of God to prepare generation after generation of men and women who have served the Lord in the marketplace, in government, in healthcare, in education, and in the legal community, among so many other spheres in this country and around the world. Primarily, however, the influence of Trinity through the years has been in service to churches, parachurch organizations, colleges and seminaries, mission agencies, and other nonprofits.

THE TRINITY HERITAGE

Trinity's heritage can be traced back more than twelve decades to 1897, when a Swedish Evangelical Free Church hosted a ten-week Bible course in the basement of a Chicago church. This class developed into the Swedish Bible Institute of Chicago. Joining together with the Norwegian-Danish Bible Institute and the Evangelical Free Church Bible Institute and Seminary, the unified merger of these Scandinavian schools became known as the Trinity Seminary and Bible College. In the early 1960s, the institution moved to its current location and was renamed Trinity College and Trinity Evangelical Divinity School. President Wilbert Norton and Dean Kenneth Kantzer were instrumental in leading these efforts to envision a new day for all programs at Trinity. These two administrators typify the many faithful leaders who have served at Trinity over the decades.

In the 1990s, the institution was once again renamed and reorganized through the combined administrations of Ken Meyer and Greg Waybright.

The little Scandinavian Bible College was transformed a century after its founding into a complex and comprehensive learning community consisting of Trinity College, Trinity Graduate School, Trinity Law School, and Trinity Evangelical Divinity School, with a campus in Deerfield, Illinois, as well as south Florida and southern California. The Carl Henry Center for Theological Understanding, the Center for Bioethics and Human Dignity, the Center for Transformational Churches, the Hiebert Center for World Christianity and Global Theology, and the Law School's Center for Human Rights now flourish as major aspects of this work. For more than 120 years, Trinity has educated women and men to think, live, and serve in a manner consistent with the gospel of Jesus Christ. These alums have joined with faculty and staff through the years to provide leadership and guidance for Trinity to become an influencer of North American and global evangelicalism.

Shaped by a shared mission and core values, Trinity has prioritized graduate theological education with a focus on serving both the church and academy. Dean Kantzer's vision for theological education has attracted some of the finest evangelical scholars in the world to the Trinity faculty. Together they have advanced the shared work of teaching, research, and scholarship in ways characterized by the highest academic standards combined with evangelical faithfulness. The listing of faculty members who have served at Trinity Evangelical Divinity School through the decades reads like a "who's who" in the evangelical world.

Since the days of President Wilbert Norton in the middle of the twentieth century, Trinity has also been committed to liberal arts–based undergraduate programs, which are enhanced by professional and graduate programs with a focus on serving society and engaging culture. The global reputation of this dynamic academic community can be attributed to the quality faculty, staff, and students who have served and studied at Trinity. Through the years, those serving at Trinity have been able to draw from this heritage as a source of hope to face the future. Details of this heritage are carefully portrayed in this well-written volume, coauthored by John Woodbridge, David Gustafson, Scott Manetsch, Bradley Gundlach, and D. A. Carson. The oversight for the project provided by Woodbridge is certainly worthy of commendation.

ACADEMIC QUALITY AND
CONFESSIONAL COMMITMENTS

For more than 120 years the men and women associated with Trinity have been characterized as "a people of the Book," viewing holy Scripture as a special form of God's revelation, a unique mode of divine disclosure. The confession of the total truthfulness or infallibility of the verbally inspired Bible has been an important safeguard, a necessary commitment for the Trinity community to remain tethered to a faithful Christian orthodoxy. The doctrine of scriptural authority, a commitment to the good news of the gospel, leadership in global missions, pace-setting efforts in the area of serious evangelical scholarship, and the undergirding emphasis on cooperative collaboration with other believers who proclaim "one faith, one hope, one Lord" have been hallmarks of the best of Trinity's heritage through the years. The Trinity motto, "Entrusted with the gospel," reflects the mindset of those who have served as board members and administrators as well as members of the faculty and staff.

In God's providence, Trinity has served as a strategic leader in these areas for the larger evangelical community. Helping to foster Christian unity across denominational lines has also been a distinctive feature of the Trinity community. This emphasis on unity has always been combined with a dedication to biblical orthodoxy, a historical Christianity shaped by the pattern of Christian truth, a faithful intercultural, multigenerational, multiethnic, and transcontinental evangelicalism that stands or falls on first-order issues.

Even as some other institutions have lost their theological compass during the twelve decades of Trinity's history, Trinity, by God's grace, has remained faithful to the pattern of Christian truth concerning the truthfulness of God's written word, the holy Trinity, the deity and humanity of Jesus Christ, the uniqueness of the gospel message, the enabling work of God's Spirit, salvation by grace alone through faith alone, the importance of the church and the people of God who are both gathered and scattered, the hope of Christ's return, the sacredness of life and family, and a concern for the least, the last, and the lost. This commitment to confessional integrity is in accord with the Nicene affirmations that the church is "one, holy, catholic, and apostolic."

Committed to academic excellence, Christian faithfulness, and lifelong learning, those who have been a part of Trinity International University through the years have taken seriously the calling that is theirs. Entrusted with the gospel of Jesus Christ, serving together to advance a distinctive mission through grace-filled relationships, called to serve the global church through the development of servant and shepherd leaders, these men and women have shared a kingdom-focused vision for the renewal of church and culture. Those who have been called to serve at Trinity through the years have recognized the special responsibility that has been theirs to ensure that this institution remains mission-faithful, a responsibility that increases in importance with each passing year.

As previously noted, Trinity now includes an undergraduate college and a graduate school, a law school and a divinity school, with campuses in Illinois, Florida, and California. The reality, however, is that the institution has been put together through the years without an apparent overarching design. This has made missional, academic, and fiscal challenges quite real.

The authors of this fine institutional history relate Trinity's story of God's remarkable faithfulness to the school through both good and trying days. They do so in an engaging way in the pages that follow. With the Lord's help Trinity survived both hard financial bumps and educational and theological challenges along the way. The school's doors almost closed on several occasions. In God's good providence, a few last minute rescues saved the school. Trinity also kept in a healthy balance disparate influences such as Scandinavian pietism, American revivalism, evangelical confessionalism, social activism, and global theological trajectories, in addition to the push and pull from very real regional and programmatic differences.

Trinity International University has earned a reputation for its dedication to serious academic scholarship formed by its commitments to the truthfulness of holy Scripture and the transformational power of the gospel message. Recognizing their place as heirs of the sixteenth-century Reformation, pietism, and Puritanism, as well as the Awakenings, the men and women of Trinity have been shaped by the great historic Christian confessions and the larger evangelical tradition.

As noted, Trinity has characteristically been a place in which the great variety of this evangelical tradition can be celebrated. While this is certainly true, those who have served at Trinity have also recognized that there is not unlimited variety without boundaries or without a convictional core. In fact, the Trinity community has embraced an understanding of the clearly articulated confessional commitments that have been affirmed and adopted through the years.

A hallmark at Trinity through the years has been an unflinching belief in the full inspiration and truthfulness of Scripture together with the great affirmations of the early church regarding the Trinity and Christology. Unlike so many other institutions, Trinity has, in God's kind providence, been able to avoid swinging the pendulum too far in reaction to errors on the left or on the right, thus rejecting a fundamentalist reductionism on the one hand and a liberal revisionism on the other. Even while being sensitive to emphases on localism, populism, and volunteerism, all of which have frequently acted to spur renewal and mobilization for ministry and missions, Trinity has waved the banner high for a holistic orthodoxy while maintaining the importance for serious scholarship and academic engagement. These shared commitments have paved the way for Trinity to serve the global Christian movement and to celebrate the amazing work of God around the world.

THE EVANGELICAL FREE
CHURCH OF AMERICA

Trinity is decidedly not a church. Yet, since the beginning days in the nineteenth century, it has recognized its role as an academic arm of the churches. Working constructively with the Evangelical Free Church of America, the body of believers who have helped to build and sustain the institution through the years and who have largely influenced the work of the governing board, has remained a high priority at Trinity. Still, those who have served at Trinity have emphasized gospel commonalities more so than denominational distinctives.

Through the decades, onlookers were able to observe a commitment to the oneness and the universality of the church, recognizing the essential characteristics of holiness and apostolicity. The Trinity community, while struggling at times through the years to find consistency in these areas, has nevertheless understood that these commitments must be supported by the right kind of virtues: a oneness that calls for humility and gentleness, patience and forbearance with one another, and a diligence to preserve the unity of the Spirit in the bond of peace.

These perspectives, coupled with an expanded vision for the work of the global church and renewed dedication to racial reconciliation, have represented the best aspects of the Trinity community since 1897. Observing the directionless and confused state that can be seen across many aspects of higher education, theological education, and legal education, Trinity, guided by a purposeful governing board, has emphasized the importance of shared core values and church connectedness.

FACULTY, STAFF, AND STUDENTS

Trinity faculty members, through the quality of their scholarship, have helped to create a place for Trinity in the larger academy, seeking to build bridges within that academy rather than walls. They have done these things in a manner that has been faithful to the lordship of Jesus Christ, exemplifying the great commandment, seeking justice and showing love and mercy, prioritizing worship and service as central to all of the pursuits on the various Trinity campuses, while working with other faithful followers of Christ to advance the Great Commission given to the church by the resurrected Christ.

Trinity has been an exemplar for many other institutions in promoting and enhancing an understanding of intellectual discipleship, helping others see what it means to live out a genuine love for God not only with heart and soul but with the mind as well. In doing so, key voices across the Trinity community have continued to caution against some cold intellectual approach to the Christian faith unaccompanied by affections. Such balance has helped the Trinity faculty to avoid a kind of intellectual aloofness or uncommitted intellectual curiosity.

Trinity's holistic approach to education has helped to prepare men and women to serve both church and society in ways that have encouraged others to know and love the resurrected and exalted Christ, the Lord of the church. In doing so, Trinity has modeled what it means to think Christianly, which is so vital for the church's teaching and apologetic tasks, helping followers of Christ to better understand what Christians are called to be, to believe, and to do. Such work has helped to ensure Trinity's church connectedness, touching the heart of the church's life and mission.

Through the years, it has been the Trinity faculty who have continued to exemplify excellence in teaching and scholarship. They have prioritized and emphasized classroom teaching. At the same time, Trinity faculty members through the decades have become some of the most widely published scholars in the entire evangelical world, not only serving students well but producing hundreds of books and resources, now available in the Woodbridge Reading Room in the Rolfing Library. Trinity faculty members have earned a reputation for effective teaching and far-reaching and influential scholarship.

This institutional history, which recounts the faithfulness of God in such remarkable ways at Trinity, points readers to the contributions of particular faculty members who have made such a difference in the life of the Trinity community. In doing so, this account allows Trinity alums and friends to celebrate the various perspectives represented on the Trinity faculty, which has truly been one of the many strengths of this great institution. Not only have Trinity faculty made a difference through the years, but their students have had a huge influence in the work of Christian higher education and theological education by serving on the faculties of major institutions in North American in addition to numerous international settings.

In ways difficult to comprehend by those who serve at institutions with one primary denominational affiliation, the faculty at Trinity have not only come from an Evangelical Free Church background, but from Lutheran, Presbyterian, Anglican, Wesleyan, Baptist, Anabaptist, Holiness, and nondenominational traditions. In the midst of this great variety has been a unified commitment to the Trinity mission, to academic excellence, and to confessional faithfulness. The efforts to advance the Trinity mission, to educate men and women to engage in God's redemptive work in the world, has been understood in light of the shared theological commitments articulated in the institution's confessional statement. Trinity has stressed the importance of preserving and passing on the Christian tradition while encouraging honest intellectual inquiry and intellectual seriousness. The Trinity faculty has not seen these confessional commitments as burdens to bear but as convictions that have been used of God to bind together a Christ-centered learning community, evangelical by conviction and tradition.

Whether in the college, the law school, the graduate school, or the divinity school, exploring every discipline from a confessional perspective that proclaims Jesus as Lord has shaped and sharpened the focus of the work. Administrators and staff members have joined with faculty to embrace truth where it has been made known in God's word and God's world, following the lead of faithful Christian educators who have proposed that all that is good or true or beautiful or beneficent, be it great or small, perfect, fragmentary, natural, supernatural, moral or material, finds its source and meaning in God. Such an educational ideal is rooted in the conviction that God, the source of all truth, has revealed himself fully in Jesus Christ.

The story that is found in these pages is one of faithfulness. First and foremost, the Trinity story is a picture of God's faithfulness to an academic community for more than a century. It is also a picture of this academic community and its efforts to live and serve faithfully before a watching world. Apart from God's faithfulness, the Trinity story would have ceased years ago. Seeing the history of the institution through this lens enables us to see that the work at Trinity has significant consequences not only for this life but for all eternity.

The overall purposes for a comprehensive learning community such as that found at Trinity have always pointed to a focus on students. All activities, efforts, and programs have been put together by administrators, faculty, and staff to serve the long-term interests of students in the spirit of Christian servanthood. For more than twelve decades, Trinity has been blessed to see multiple generations of kingdom leaders come forth from the Trinity campus. Students have learned to express and articulate their convictions clearly while learning to appreciate, respect, understand, and evaluate the thoughts of others, resulting in the habit of lifelong learning. Trinity alums will no doubt read the pages that follow with heartfelt thanksgiving for the preparation they received during their days on the Trinity campus. Whether students were moving from the Trinity campus toward the marketplace or toward a vocational ministry call, Trinity has seen its calling to prepare students to think and live Christianly in society, enabling them to be faithful, wise, and flourishing kingdom citizens in the world.

The ideals and aspirations of the Trinity community have been carried out on a day-to-day basis by the members of the Trinity staff, women and men who have rarely received the notoriety of the Trinity faculty. The story of the Trinity heritage found in this volume is also their story. While faculty have worked to encourage academic excellence and lifelong learning with the dynamic Trinity learning community, it has been the staff, often behind the scenes, who have cared for and served students as they wrestled with the great ideas of history and the pressing issues of the day.

Trinity staff have regularly provided resources and examples for both undergraduate and graduate students to encourage their faith and shape their intellectual pursuits. While the work on the Trinity campus through the years has prioritized the life of the mind, it has quite often been the loving labors of staff members who have emphasized the institution's holistic call for the formation and transformation of head, heart, and hands in shared learning and service.

Accolades have often come to the brilliant Trinity faculty members who have provided noteworthy lecture series or who have written award-winning books. At other times, attention has come to administrators or to members of the governing board when key decisions have been made to advance the work and mission of Trinity International University. Yet, it should never be forgotten, especially in a volume such as this one, that this work has been the team-oriented efforts of loyal staff members who daily, generally without fanfare, make things happen for all who have studied and served at Trinity.

All that has taken place in, with, and among the Trinity community has been done with a focus on students. One of the wonderful strengths of the Trinity community has been the rich variety of students. What was once a student body who predominantly came with a Scandinavian cultural connection has now become a gathering of students who represent large intercultural and international sectors. The students not only have come from Midwest farmlands but also from the inner city. They represent Asian, African, and Latino heritages. Students have come to Trinity from the East Coast and the West Coast, from Canada and South America, and from every region around the world as Trinity in the twenty-first century has truly become Trinity *International* University.

All programs, activities, and academic offerings have been carried out to serve the long-term interests of Trinity students in the spirit of Christian servanthood. Faculty and staff have attempted to guide students in the development of priorities and practices to contribute to their overall well-being and effectiveness in all areas of life. Students have been encouraged to think deeply about the issues of truth, values, worldview, and the bearing of subject matter on people's lives so that they are equipped for their God-called place in the world.

While education on the Trinity campus has emphasized the improvement of the mind, students at Trinity have been blessed by an educational approach that has also stressed the importance of character and faith development. In addition, relational priorities and professional competency have been seen as essential for a full-orbed understanding of education at Trinity.

GOD'S FAITHFULNESS

While the story of Trinity points readers over and over to the faithfulness of God, it must be acknowledged that on many days at Trinity, the work has been carried out in a frugal manner with minimal resources. Trinity has never experienced financial abundance, nor it has enjoyed the privileges of the finest resources or facilities found at other institutions. Still, the Lord has over and over been faithful to the Trinity community, providing what has been needed for each day. Trinity has been blessed with selfless board members who have attempted to steward the institution well. Dedicated staff members and administrators have worked tirelessly for the good of the institution. Brilliant and gifted faculty have invested deeply in the lives of students while serving church and society well. Faithful donors, serving as God's instruments, have invested in the Trinity mission through the years, often in sacrificial ways.

This book also acknowledges that each generation at Trinity has been able to stand on the shoulders of those who have served previous generations. It is a joy to read these accounts that have been told so well by these outstanding Trinity historians. Many who read this volume will count it a privilege to have been able to be a part of Trinity International University, an institution admired, appreciated, and loved by so many all around the world.

I know that the authors pray that the book will serve the larger Trinity constituency well in order that the next generation of Christian leaders who will be educated at Trinity will be prepared to make a difference for the cause of Christ and his kingdom. Those who currently serve at Trinity, following the leadership of President Nicholas Perrin, will continue to carry forward this heritage, doing so with faithfulness for years to come. They will seek the good of all concerned, while teaching, learning, and serving together for the glory of the God with heartfelt gratitude for the faithfulness of God, as testified at each commencement service with the singing of Thomas O. Chisholm's inspiring hymn:

> Great is Thy Faithfulness, O God my Father,
> There is no shadow of turning with Thee;
> Thou changest not, Thy compassions they fail not;
> As Thou hast been, Thou forever wilt be.
> Great is Thy Faithfulness!

DAVID S. DOCKERY, chancellor,
Advent 2020

Chapter 1

Humble Beginnings
(1897–1915)

David M. Gustafson

The year was 1897. The twentieth century was about to dawn. A small
group of Swedish immigrants in Chicago gathered together for a ten-
week course of Bible knowledge and other subjects. The Swedes wanted to
be better equipped to serve the Lord in gospel ministry and mission. Their
professors were Swedes as well. From these humble beginnings emerged
Trinity International University (TIU). In 2022, 125 years later, Trinity
has nearly thirty thousand graduates from multiple ethnic backgrounds
and nations serving the Lord around the world.[1]

The Trinity story reveals God's marvelous faithfulness to the school
over the years. Without the Lord's gracious providential care, Trinity could
not have survived, flourished, or remained biblically faithful to its mission.

Trinity continues to take seriously the school's motto: "Entrusted with
the gospel." Nor is this any gospel, but the gospel of Jesus Christ according
to holy Scripture. It is the gospel Saint Paul described as the "power of
God for salvation" (Rom 1:16). Through many joys and challenges, Trinity
has trained generation after generation of students for gospel ministry in
churches and in the marketplace.

The first president of Trinity was Rev. Peter Johan Elmquist (1851–1924),
a Swedish immigrant to America. While serving as superintendent of mission
of the Swedish Free Mission—known simply then as "the Free" (de fria) and
known today as the Evangelical Free Church of America (EFCA)—Elmquist

1

founded the school. He served as its president from 1897 to 1908. In time, this Swedish school merged with another Scandinavian Bible Institute from the Norwegian/Danish Free Church tradition.

HISTORICAL ROOTS OF THE EVANGELICAL FREE CHURCH OF AMERICA

During the Protestant Reformation of the sixteenth century, Lutheranism became well-established in Scandinavia. Martin Luther (1483–1546) taught the supreme, final authority and infallibility of the Scriptures, salvation by grace alone through faith alone in Christ alone, and the priesthood of all believers.

Peter Johann Elmquist, founder of Trinity

In the mid-eighteenth and early nineteenth centuries, the influence of Moravian missionaries from Herrnhut, Germany, shaped a movement in Sweden, Norway, and Denmark known as Readers—pietistic Lutherans who gathered in small groups to read the Bible, sermons of Luther, and devotional writings such as *True Christianity* by Johann Arndt (1555–1621).

The Readers emphasized conversion as the "one thing needful." They claimed to possess a living faith in contrast to dead orthodoxy—an expression they used to describe the state churches that had declined in spiritual earnestness and harbored nominal Christians, including clergy.[2] Some Readers known later as "Mission Friends" preached in home meetings and to larger groups. This led to the formation of regional mission societies and in a few instances to the creation of independent congregations or free churches.

In the late nineteenth century, Mission Friends in Scandinavia came under Anglo-American religious influences. In addition to Baptist and Methodist impulses from England and America, Scandinavia was affected by "Moody fever."[3] American evangelist Dwight L. Moody (1836–1899) of Chicago became an international hero not merely in Great Britain and the United States but also in Sweden, Norway, and Denmark. This occurred despite the fact that he never visited any of the Scandinavian countries. Moody's influence came first through his sermons in periodicals and books that were translated from English and published in the Swedish and Dano-Norwegian languages. These publications became popular among Mission Friends. The publications prepared the path for Moody's Scandinavian disciples, who returned from Chicago to the Nordic countries to plant and renew free churches.

Swedish immigrant Fredrik Franson (1852–1908) joined Moody's church in Chicago. He served as the church's first missionary. He became a proponent of Moody's theology and evangelistic methods, spreading them in America, Sweden, Norway, and Denmark.[4] In cooperation with Franson, Cathrine Juell of Norway and Nils Peter Lang of Denmark brought Moody's teachings, writings, and methods from Chicago to their respective countries.

Concurrent with Anglo-American religious influences entering Scandinavia, the great migration of Swedes, Norwegians, and Danes to America reached its peak at the end of the nineteenth century.[5] More came to Chicago and Minneapolis than anywhere else. Mission Friends who immigrated to the United States drew richly from their Scandinavian pietistic traditions of Carl O. Rosenius (1816–1868), Gustaf A. Lammers (1802–1878), and P. P. Waldenström (1838–1917), as well as from the American revivalist doctrines and methods of Dwight Moody. This was particularly true of Free Mission Friends.

Fredrik Franson

The early years of the Scandinavian free church movement in America were filled with evangelism, tent meetings, and revivals led by people such as Franson, John G. Princell, and Ludwig J. Pedersen. Revival fires burned brightly as Free preachers visited Swedish, Norwegian, and Danish immigrant neighborhoods and towns. The evangelists preached the gospel under the most advantageous and adverse circumstances. Hundreds of young

Scandinavian immigrants came to mission meetings to hear the gospel. Some of the Christian workers were trained ministers, and others were laymen without any formal theological education. Some were female evangelists who went from place to place with their guitars and Bibles to sing and preach about the saving power of God.

Many of the immigrants came under the conviction of the Holy Spirit, converted to faith in Jesus Christ, and formed local churches in the communities where they settled—in Illinois, Minnesota, Wisconsin, Iowa, Nebraska, Texas, Colorado, the Dakotas, New York, Massachusetts, and Washington. The ministry of the free preachers grew as they labored with great personal sacrifice.[6] E. A. Halleen describes the times, saying:

> Sinners under conviction would come under a peculiar power. They would sometimes fall down as men slain in battle. They would remain that way for a long time, during which intermittent groanings and piercing shrieks would be heard. Then would follow a season of earnest prayer for mercy and pardon. After some time of such agonizing they would obtain deliverance. The gloomy cloud that covered their faces disappeared. "Hope in smiles brightened into joy." The converted would rise shouting deliverance, and would give a personal testimony of their new experience. They addressed the surrounding group in language truly eloquent and impressive. It was astonishing, to say the least, to thus hear men, women and children declare the wonderful power of salvation. This had a tremendous influence upon the unconverted. It was bound to. Churches, schoolhouses and homes were therefore crowded at nearly every service. No matter where the services were held crowds would congregate.

E. A. Halleen and
Gustaf F. Johnson

And all expected something to happen at these services; and it usually did. Because of this expectancy no one felt he could afford to stay away from the services. The pioneer messengers thus had marvelous opportunities to reach the unconverted. The outsiders would in most cases outnumber the Christians. Those were harvest days indeed—days of divine visitation.[7]

An example of a dynamic free preacher was Gustaf F. Johnson, who engaged in evangelistic work in his home state of Texas, along with his coworker John Herner. Thousands of Swedish immigrants lived in the area surrounding Austin, the capital. Johnson experienced there some of his greatest successes in evangelistic ministry. In fact, he became known as "Texas Johnson." As a result of the revivals that took place under his ministry, several Free Churches were established.

One such revival occurred during a mission meeting held at Brushy, Texas, in the summer of 1896. On a Sunday morning, Johnson preached a sermon from Genesis 35:18, which says: "And as her soul was departing (for she was dying), she called his name Ben-Oni; but his father called him Benjamin." The listeners never forgot this message. When the meeting was over, many of the listeners went home with "wounded and bleeding hearts," only to return to the afternoon meeting.[8]

Johnson preached then from another text, and not having spoken long, all of a sudden, a man cried out loud, "I want to be saved." The preacher then said, "When the Holy Spirit begins to lead the meeting, then I end." In a little while, the mission house had turned into a hall of tears. From the door to the platform, people were on their knees praying and weeping. People were stopped in their sins; the Holy Spirit had taken over the meeting."

In his own account, Johnson describes the revival as a time of heartfelt spiritual repentance and confession:

At seven o'clock I was so tired that I said to my coworker: "We need to go and get a glass of milk and a sandwich at the farmhouse nearby and rest for a few minutes." Just before eight o'clock we went back to the mission house to start the evening meeting. However, no start was needed because the afternoon meeting was still going! Even beside the tombstones of the nearby cemetery, young men and women were kneeling in prayer. One young man knelt by his father's grave and cried out: "My father's Savior, save my soul!" A young woman beside her mother's grave exclaimed, "My mother's God, forgive me of my sins!" The prayer meeting continued until midnight. When we gathered together the next day at three o'clock in the afternoon, the number who had come to confess faith in God was one hundred and fifty souls. This meeting is still talked about. Many of those who were saved that day are alive today.[9]

This revival continued, and the number of believers multiplied. Free churches soon formed in the Texas towns of Deckar, Austin, Kimbro, and Brushy.

THEOLOGICAL EDUCATION AMONG FREE MISSION FRIENDS IN AMERICA

The Free Mission Friends in America held to the major beliefs of the infallible Bible's final authority, the Trinity, Christ's atoning work on the cross, and salvation by grace alone through faith alone. They looked to the bodily return of Jesus Christ in glory as their "blessed hope." They held to the autonomy of the local church and to spiritual unity among all Christians, and they opposed sectarian views that promoted one denomination over another. They believed in cooperation in their common mission and work of evangelism at home and abroad.[10]

In the early days, Free Mission Friend preachers and evangelists traveled in pairs, often with one seasoned preacher and an associate in training. Evangelistic meetings were held in schoolhouses, farmhouses, community halls, churches, and barns. It was customary in this setting for younger preachers to claim the tutelage of a seasoned preacher as credentials for ministry. At the time, only a few Free Mission churches in America had full-time, resident pastors.[11] All other free congregations were served by itinerant preachers and evangelists.

The Free Mission preachers and evangelists gathered annually for regional and national mission meetings at various locations. These meetings welcomed people from the local community and often concluded with a Moody-style "after-meeting" in which "anxious souls" would walk forward to meet with the preacher or evangelist, who encouraged them to accept Christ as their Lord and Savior.

The mission meetings also served as a means of theological education for those who were called to become preachers and evangelists. Theological discussions were particularly formative, as four to five theological questions were raised and then addressed by several preachers at the meeting. A secretary captured the discussion and forwarded the transcript for publication, for example, to *Chicago-Bladet*, the popular periodical of the Free Mission Friends. This periodical was later purchased by the Swedish Evangelical Free Church.

MEETING A GROWING NEED: THE SWEDISH BIBLE INSTITUTE OF CHICAGO

Beginning with his first year of residence in the United States, P. J. Elmquist was active in the revival work of the burgeoning Free Mission Friends.[12] In 1894, he was elected vice president of the Swedish Free Mission's executive committee. At the 1896 annual conference held at the Oak Street Swedish Free Mission in Chicago, known later as First Evangelical Free Church, Elmquist was called by the annual conference to the new full-time position of superintendent of mission of the Swedish Free Mission.

Although the Swedish Free Mission began in the 1880s with a simple vision to cooperate in mission and evangelism "with as little ecclesiastical machinery as possible,"[13] greater organization developed over time as it became necessary. Evangelists were working as home missionaries in Utah, Montana, Colorado, and the Dakotas, and itinerant preachers, such as Johnson, were starting new congregations in Minnesota, Illinois, Nebraska, Wisconsin, Iowa, and Texas. At the same time, Free Mission Friends were closely tied to the newly opened Christian Children's Home in Nebraska and the Canton Mission in south China.

The growth of home missions led to the decision to employ Elmquist as superintendent of mission to coordinate the various activities of the Free Mission work. Elmquist saw new churches form and membership increase in other congregations. He labored to organize structures that would promote the Free Mission's work. With the formation of new Free Churches in several states, the number of preachers increased. Moreover, a growing number of congregations wished to call resident pastors rather than receive visits by itinerant preachers and evangelists. All of this prompted the Swedish Free Mission to provide theological education for pastors and missionaries.

In 1897, Elmquist apprised the annual conference of the critical educational void. He had received several letters from various congregations asking him to send them preachers, but he was grieved that he was unable to recommend anyone.

Until this time, preachers who received formal theological education had attended schools such as Ansgar College in Knoxville, Illinois, a fledgling school of the Ansgar Lutheran Synod.[14] Some preachers attended the Swedish department of Chicago Theological Seminary, the school of the American Congregationalists. Most female evangelists attended Ellen Modin's school in Minneapolis, known as the Scandinavian Mission Alliance Women's Bible Institute. A few older preachers had attended mission schools in Sweden such as the Mission School at Kristinehamn. Most preachers, however, attended two- or three-week courses for preachers and missionaries at the Evangelist Training Course led by Fredrik Franson at various locations such as Chicago, Minneapolis, and Omaha, as well as Princell's Bible course held at St. Paul. Until this time, formal education for pastors, missionaries, and evangelists *within* the simple structure of the Swedish Free Mission had not been considered.

A good percentage of Free Mission preachers had little or no formal theological education. For example, G. A. Young "had no college education" but was described as "a gifted and powerful public speaker and ... naturally studious, a lover of books."[15] Johannes S. Norén claimed to have attended "the school of the Holy Spirit for 50 years, and read through the Bible 26 times."[16] Only a few of the early free preachers were trained at secondary schools that had an emphasis in Swedish grammar, rhetoric, logic, Greek, and Latin. Some younger preachers heard from older church members that education would dampen their enthusiasm for ministry, or that Jesus might return while their noses were buried in the books, and so they should get busy doing the Lord's work.

Then, at a mission meeting on June 9, 1897, in Boone, Iowa, Elmquist said:

> We have another year of ministry behind us, during which we have experienced God's rich blessing. Those who have labored throughout this year have done so with zeal and strength. Not a few, over the past year, have given themselves to Jesus, from which God's work progressed. During a short time (4 months), according to the

calling that I received to this work, I have been traveling almost continuously, during which time I have visited, in part, places in Iowa, Illinois, Minnesota, and Montana. Generally, I have had meetings daily, in part to preach and in part to meet with congregations. Some new congregations have been established on occasions when I was present. Of course, through written correspondence I had offered advice and information that I was glad to give. Overall, there has proven to be a great need for preachers, particularly those who are gifted at teaching and who could stay with the congregations in order to lead and care for them. I suggest that during this meeting we discuss what can be done in order to remedy this situation, in hopes of making the situation better than what presently exists. In many places, we see the need to introduce better arrangements in order to carry out more systematically the work at home, as well as abroad.[17]

At this meeting, Johnson and other itinerant preachers and evangelists presented glowing reports from the home mission field. From several regions, the need for good laborers was heard, "especially for such laborers who are gifted by God as shepherds and teachers and who are able to assume responsibility for the care of a congregation." After this, there was discussion about the establishment of an instruction course to educate laborers for the home mission field. A lively discussion followed, during which it became clear that theological and practical ministry courses were desperately needed and were warmly recommended by most who were present.

After the meeting, the school committee reported: "We deem it is useful and necessary for the ministry that at some time during the year to offer an instruction course for the purpose of, in some measure, to improve the preaching ministry among us. We propose to entrust this to Brother Elmquist, that in the best way, in regards to both time and place, etc., to arrange this course as early as this year."[18] The report was accepted. The Swedish Free Mission's school course would be held for a ten-week term in the fall of 1897. The school was open to men and women.[19]

Elmquist arranged space for the school at the Oak Street Swedish Free Mission, located at 205 Oak Street, situated on the north side of Oak Street and west of Wells, Chicago. Classes would meet free of charge in the smaller rooms but also in the large hall of this storefront building. *Chicago-Bladet* published announcements for the Free Mission School and Bible Course. One announcement read: "Herein, notice is given that the previously discussed school and Bible course is set, if God wills, to be held at the Mission's building at 205 Oak Street, Chicago, Ill., and begins Friday, 1 October [1897] at 10:00 a.m., and will continue for ten weeks."[20] The school offered courses in biblical studies, including hermeneutics and exegesis, Swedish language, church history, natural sciences, anthropology, and logic.

The announcement further stated:

SKOL-
och
BIBEL-KURS

Moreover, it is the intention to hold and lead many practical classes in penmanship, essay composition, public speaking (practice in preaching), and practical mission work. A most sincere invitation to this School and Bible Course is given, in part, to those who are already in the ministry, and in part, to those who are gifted and possess a sense of personal call to preach. The instruction is free. In order to get room and board as inexpensive as possible, we are taking steps with particular apartment managers, and we hope that the cost will not exceed $10 per month. Note that in order to participate in the course, letters of application must include testimony and attestation of good character from a congregation or particularly well-known persons. Send such materials as soon as possible to the undersigned below.

Announcement of the School and Bible Course, *Chicago-Bladet*, 1897

We hope that it is possible for us to arrange for Prof. J. G. Princell who has practical experience as an educator to join with some others to share in the instruction. We plan to arrange a number of special lectures that will be given repeatedly by several capable people during the course. Our desire is that some men will support this effort and fill this great need, in respect to exercising their teaching gifts among us. May now and then, henceforth, all God's children in general who have an interest in the Free Work, let their interest for this matter be known, in part, through prayer for this and for us, and in part, by extending a hand to us and to send in financial means, for it is entirely common that we will face extra expenses, if not for one, for the other, with regards to expenses for this course. It can be expected that here and there, there are less well-to-do preachers who serve their congregations and who wish to participate in the course but who lack the requisite means to do so. Such congregations ought, in order for their preacher to be able to attend, take up an extra collection. Surely the congregation that does so will itself win. Knowing that many believers in Jesus who have waited long for something to be done in order to improve the preaching ministry among us, who are interested in this matter and pray for us, we hope that this effort will serve to the glory of the name of God, because we enter this work in the name of the Lord Jesus, desiring all that is due him. Welcome.[21]

It was signed: "As per the committee's direction, Your brother in the Lord, P. J. Elmquist, Chicago, Ill."

With Elmquist's vision and leadership, the assistance of Axel Nordin, pastor of the Oak Street Free Mission, and Princell, the course began with twenty-two students enrolled, eighteen men and four women.[22] Among the male students, a number were middle-aged pastors active in ministry, and one was a missionary to north China.

Students and faculty of the first course in 1897

Princell instructed students in biblical subjects, Elmquist taught Swedish grammar and general studies, and Nordin lectured on practical subjects related to congregational life. Nordin also participated in sessions on Saturday mornings that included practical exercises for students such as preaching and leading meetings.

The term ended in December with a farewell event at the Oak Street Free Mission hall. Students gave testimonies and offered gratitude for the instruction they received and friendships they formed. Among those who participated, several returned to their previous work as pastors and evangelists.

FEATURED ALUMNA

Amanda Gustafson (Mrs. Victor Carlson)

Among the first class of students in 1897 to complete the Swedish Free Mission School and Bible Course was Amanda J. Gustafson (1870–1956) of Minneapolis, originally from Sweden.[23] After completing the course, Amanda continued studies at Moody Bible Institute. She was ordained as an evangelist in the Swedish Free Mission and spent nine years traveling as an evangelist, becoming "famed as an eloquent speaker."[24] It was said of her that "she could preach as well as anyone and better than many."[25]

In one account Nathaniel Carlson described the thoughtful and caring ministries of Amanda and other women like her:

> In those early days of our work, the zeal and fervor for evangelism and winning fellow men and women to Christ deeply touched both the learned and uneducated, preacher and peasant both among men and women. Many of our devoted and gifted young women went out full time to evangelize and do home missionary work, much as we now send women to our foreign missionary fields.

Young Amanda Gustafson

Oftentimes they could go a step farther in winning their way into homes and communities by going into homes where sickness and want was found, nursing, helping and cheering the sick mother in the home, tidying up the house and making up meals for the family, washing the dishes, etc., and then comforting the sick one and the family by the reading of God's word and with prayer for them. People thus ministered to were quite willing and sometimes eager to come and hear what these "missionaries" would have to say in public, to receive the spoken word and consequently seek the Lord for salvation.

Many of these ladies developed into good speakers who could expound the word of God to eagerly listening audiences.

Our own Mrs. Victor Carlson, of Minneapolis, then known as Amanda Gustafson, who with Christina Matson as her partner travelled widely over our field. ... I will never forget a service in our farm home when these two ladies held a meeting there; I was then in my early teens and was carried away with the speaking and singing they presented. ... It was during and after such visits of preachers and missionaries that the yearning awakened in my heart to someday and in some way become one of God's messengers in the Gospel work, and especially so when someone who could play and sing came to us.[26]

In his account, Nathaniel Carlson describes opposition that these female evangelists encountered. On one occasion, when Amanda Gustafson and Christina Matson were holding a

Young Amanda
with guitar

meeting at a schoolhouse in Orrock, Minnesota, some hooligans hurled eggs through an open window, with one egg landing on "Miss Matson's head, as she was on the platform and made a good target." Carlson says that at this very moment she "was preaching with the Lord's prayer as her subject, and significantly had come to the very sentence of 'Forgive us our trespasses as we forgive those who trespass against us.' " Despite such opposition, during the following winter "souls were saved." This resulted in the founding of the Scandinavian Free Church of Orrock, which erected a church building in 1902.[27]

Amanda remained active in the Evangelical Free Church throughout her life and was prominent among Swedish Free Church women. She organized the Minnesota district of the Women's Missionary Society and served as president of the national society.[28] She remained a supporter of the Free Church's Bible Institute and Seminary, being one of three alumni in 1947 to attend its fiftieth anniversary.[29]

Mature Amanda

At the Swedish Free Mission meeting in 1898, it was decided to hold the School and Bible Course again that fall. In 1898, the fall term of the School and Bible Course began in October under the same arrangements as the previous year. Twenty-seven students enrolled, four female and twenty-three male.[30]

In the following year, although there was approval at the mission meeting at Rockford for the course again that fall, demands on free churches for home and foreign missionary work were pressing, and they felt they could not afford to support the school at the time.[31] This sentiment continued the following year. Some churches had taken on new commitments to overseas missionaries, while others helped to organize state and district associations for home missions that demanded equal funding. Thus, the Free Mission Friends did not press the matter of the school at the time.

Elmquist was thankful that as a result of the courses held previously, more than twenty students had entered work for the first time as preachers, evangelists, and missionaries, and were bearing fruit in their respective fields.[32] Nonetheless, he continued to receive letters with requests for preachers, and in most cases, he had no names to recommend, except a few here and there. This continued to weigh heavily on his mind. Looking ahead, he thought about the future and how it would go with the Swedish Free Mission if additional preachers could not be sent to the various places that requested them—to say nothing of the places that were spiritually dead and had nobody who could even cry for help. Yet he knew these were places where preachers of the gospel—evangelists and pastors—should be sent. Nevertheless, at the moment the prospects seemed dark and the situation discouraging. Later, he told the story:

> Then, early in the morning, on November 3, 1900, as I traveled by train between Des Moines and Boone, Iowa, I was reading through several letters that had come to me, perhaps 5 or 6, that all contained requests for preachers. Since I did not know anyone to recommend or send, I felt discouraged and my thoughts sank. I knew that something must be done to meet these needs, and what should be done, could be done. Then, quite suddenly, I heard a voice within me that, more or less, said: "Go and gather ten thousand dollars as a foundation to fund a Swedish, non-denominational Bible Institute—whose doors are always open to all young men and women who believe in Jesus, who possess an inner urging and the gifts to go out as preachers, evangelists, and missionaries—an institute where such can receive the necessary training in Bible knowledge and other subjects required for preaching the gospel."[33]

This experience led Elmquist to ask: How can this happen? When he met Young near Boone, Iowa, he told him of this new idea and asked him what he thought of it, and how it might happen. Young said, "Start by asking someone to give $100 as a pledge to the fund and continue until you have 100 people and you will have your ten thousand dollars."[34] This was a good proposal, but Elmquist replied: "And in any case, if someone wants to give something other than $100, then I will receive it gratefully—$50 from two or $25 from four—for this is as good as someone who gives $100, and a whole lot better than those who give nothing!"

As Elmquist thought about where he would start—uncertain about whom he would speak with—he made it a matter of prayer to God, asking for insight, wisdom, and direction, knowing that if it was God's plan for there to be a Bible institute, the Lord would show him how to go about it.

Then, one evening after he finished speaking while on a preaching tour, an older woman asked to speak with him. She mentioned that she was a widow and had no children or close relatives. She and her husband, when he was alive, had wanted to give money to a "much-needed and useful project in the Mission."[35] She said:

I have pleaded with God for light and guidance about what to do. And just this morning as I was praying about this important matter, I cried out and asked Him for assurance that I might know how to proceed. I was told just today that you were coming here and when I heard it, the thought immediately came to my mind: I want to speak to him. And as I saw you here in the church, it was as if someone said to me: Speak with him and ask his advice on the matter and follow his counsel.

Elmquist recalled:

When she presented this story, it became clear to both her and me at nearly the same time that this day was certainly different, and by meeting each other, we received our answers, and shared complementary experiences. I told her that before I would give her any advice that I should tell her of my thoughts and concerns earlier that day. Then I spoke briefly about my prayers for preachers, my plans, thoughts, worries, and prayers to God for guidance and light on the matter. ... When I told her this, we were both moved to tears and she said, "This is the Lord's ways; this is his leading. For this reason, I would like to give what is left of my estate after my death to a Swedish, non-denominational Bible Institute. This bequest will be between four to five thousand dollars, and is given with the only condition that the school be established in Chicago,

Ill., because I lived there, and I am quite interested in the spiritual work among the Swedish people in that place, and from there activities can spread out to our people everywhere in the country and to the peoples of other countries."[36]

Thus the foundation for the Bible institute began.

During his visits to Iowa and Nebraska, Elmquist talked about his vision for a Bible institute, and others soon became interested. Already in the fall of 1900 he was busy in Chicago with plans to make what had started as the School and Bible Course into a free-standing Swedish Bible Institute. He gathered the necessary information and forms so that the school might be legally incorporated. He wrote: "What the [Moody Bible] Institute is for the English-speaking population, our [Swedish] Bible Institute will be for Scandinavians."[37] Moreover, he was busy planning a ten-week course that would begin in January of 1901.

On 12 January 1901, the school incorporated as the Swedish Bible Institute of Chicago.[38]

The corporate charter stated that the purpose of the school was "to provide instruction in the Bible's contents and study, as well as other subjects that may be found needful and desirable for the education and training of evangelists, missionaries, and teachers in churches and Sunday schools."[39] Although the school was independent and nondenominational, its board was composed of leaders of the Swedish Free Mission, its president gave reports to the Free Mission's annual conference, its financial support came almost entirely from Free Mission Friends, and it served mostly the needs of Free Churches and affiliated missions.[40]

With the new organization, the third Bible course began in January. Elmquist wrote an article that appeared in *Chicago-Bladet*, in which he cast his vision for the school:

> One of the most pressing needs for the Swedish Free Mission in this country is a Swedish, free, non-denominational Bible Institute, where those who are called by God are able to receive practical training to serve congregations. Also we need an army of young people with a basic knowledge of the whole Bible who thoroughly long after the salvation of souls, and who are willing to go to the

Oak Street Free Mission Church of Chicago,
location of the first course

so-called difficult fields and dark regions in order to speak about
Jesus and his love. We need those who are driven by the love of
Christ, not by party-zeal, who are willing to go where duty and
the Spirit of God call them, more than it comes to ensuring themselves and their own personal comfort.[41]

As interest in a more thorough course of study increased, Elmquist
and the school board decided to offer a three-year curriculum. The first
academic year, 1902–1903, would begin in October and continue for thirty
weeks, which included fall, winter, and spring terms.

At the end of this first academic year, the board of directors decided to
call Princell as a full-time teacher. His appointment would give students
greater depth in biblical studies. Moreover, his earlier role as a part-time
teacher proved difficult given his pastoral responsibilities in Minnesota.
The board also called Elmquist to the school with a full-time salary, and
he accepted the invitation. Therefore, he resigned as superintendent of
missions and devoted himself fully to the work of the school.

The additions of Princell and Elmquist serving full time at the Swedish Bible Institute brought an academic and institutional seriousness to the school. Princell taught courses in biblical studies and philosophy. He had studied years earlier at Augustana Seminary, the old University of Chicago,

Professor J. G. Princell

and German-American College in Philadelphia, where he graduated from the Lutheran seminary.[42] As a seminarian in Chicago in the 1860s, he worked alongside D. L. Moody in the Young Men's Christian Association. Moreover, Princell had published books and journals, served as a Free Church pastor, and had worked as associate editor of *Chicago-Bladet*.

Elmquist taught courses in his areas of specialization, namely, the Swedish language, natural science, and history. In addition, Charles J. Anderson was called to teach courses in music part time. A total of nineteen students attended courses, with two female and seventeen male students.

In the following years, Josephine Princell served at the school as well. Trained as a teacher at Kungliga Seminariet (Royal Teacher's School) in Sweden, she assisted in teaching Swedish- and English-language classes.[43] Since most students would minister in the Swedish language, they were taught proper Swedish grammar, spelling, penmanship, vocabulary, composition, and Bible reading.

Professor A. Francke, a professional song teacher in Chicago, was hired to teach music and voice. Regarding the

Josephine Princell

music classes, Elmquist said: "For instruction in singing and music—subjects of great importance and significance for preachers, especially for traveling evangelists and missionaries—a brother, who is a well-known and accomplished teacher in these subjects, namely A. Francke, has been employed during most of the school year. Both good teaching and good training have been provided to our students in these beautiful, glorious arts."[44] The general courses taught by Elmquist, along with courses in music, showed that from the beginning of the school he saw the importance of training students in the humanities as well as in the biblical subjects.

Class of 1904–1905, Swedish Bible Institute, Chicago

In order to develop funding for the school, Elmquist continued to seek donors to give one hundred dollars, or even twenty-five dollars, to the school foundation. In addition, the executive committee developed the School Aid Society, in which members gave two dollars per year.[45] Letters were sent to potential members with an invitation to join. By 1905, nearly five hundred people had participated. The plan provided the school with an annual stream of revenue.

In 1908, Elmquist resigned as president of the Swedish Bible Institute. He had carried the burden of the school for eleven years and decided to step aside from his role as president and teacher. He believed it was time to pursue new opportunities and for others to take over the leadership.

Immediately the school board was concerned about who might succeed him. On Princell's recommendation, the board called Professor K. Newquist from Minneapolis to teach.[46] Karl Newquist had studied at Ahlberg's school in Örebro, Fjellstedt's school in Uppsala, and Bethel Seminary in Stockholm, Sweden. Moreover, he studied at Yale University and Augustana Theological Seminary in the United States.[47] He had served as an editor of the Swedish-language journals *Chicago-Bladet* and *Veckobladet* in Minneapolis.

Swedish Bible Institute, 1911

Then, on November 6, 1908, the board called Princell to become the institute's second president. He accepted this invitation. With this addition, the school now had two full-time teachers with formal theological education.

The Swedish Bible Institute remained independent until 1909, when its corporation dissolved so that the school might become a legal entity of the Swedish Evangelical Free Church of America.[48] Furthermore, in 1910, it was decided at the annual meeting that the school should move to Minneapolis. Therefore, the institute relocated that fall, and classes were held at the newly renovated Twelfth Avenue Swedish Free Church, known later as First Evangelical Free Church of Minneapolis, where E. A. Halleen served as pastor.[49] The Bible Institute of the Swedish Evangelical Free Church continued in Minneapolis until 1914. Tragically, Princell's health began to fail. He slipped on a patch of ice and injured one of his hips. He was hit by a car. He caught double pneumonia and died a year later.

FEATURED ALUMNUS
H. G. Rodine

Hugo Gustaf Rodine (1892–1971) from Polk, Nebraska, was converted to faith in Christ at the age of seventeen. Within a year after his conversion, God began to speak to him about leaving the farm and going away to school.[50] The inward struggle went on for weeks and months before he finally surrendered. He later recalled: "It simply did not seem within the realm of possibility that I ever could become a missionary or minister. I told the Lord my many obvious difficulties and tried to reason and argue, but it did no good."[51]

Rodine began his studies in 1911 at the Bible Institute of the Swedish

Young Rodine

Evangelical Free Church in Minneapolis, graduating in 1914. He recalled: "It was an exceptional privilege to be enrolled in 'Princell's School,' as it was affectionately known, and to graduate ... under the guidance of this outstanding teacher, preacher, and leader."[52] Near graduation, he accepted a call to serve during the summer in evangelistic work with the Evangelical Tent Mission in Nebraska.

Following Hugo's marriage to Ruby Nordin, the couple moved to Portland, Oregon, where he served as pastor of the Evangelical Free Church. While serving at Portland, Hugo and Ruby were called as missionaries to Canton, China. They began in 1917 and continued for ten years, despite Hugo's bout with typhoid.

When the couple returned to America, Hugo served as pastor for congregations in Albert City, Iowa; Holdrege, Nebraska; St. Paul and Kerkhoven, Minnesota; and Turlock, California.

In 1946, he became the first full-time secretary of overseas missions of the Evangelical Free Church of America. He worked to open mission fields in Japan, the Philippines, Singapore, and Germany. In twelve years, he saw the mission grow from 43 missionaries in four fields to 158 missionaries in seven fields.

His legacy is recognized in the name of Trinity's H. G. Rodine Global Ministry Building, dedicated in 2003.

Mature Rodine

THE NORWEGIAN-DANISH EVANGELICAL FREE CHURCH SCHOOL IN RUSHFORD, MINNESOTA

As the Evangelical Free Church of America supported the Swedish Bible Institute, so in 1910, the Norwegian-Danish Evangelical Free churches opened their school in Rushford, Minnesota, and six years later moved the school northwest to Minneapolis. The Swedish and Danish-Norwegian Bible institutes would ultimately merge as constituent parts of Trinity.

For the Norwegian-Danes, the challenges and costs of opening and operating their own school outweighed the benefits of a twenty-five-year affiliation with Chicago Theological Seminary funded almost entirely by American Congregationalists. The liberal trend toward downplaying if not denying the divinity of Christ and the final authority of Scripture had reached a climax at the beginning of the twentieth century, prompting these churches to open this school based on their evangelical convictions.[53]

Since 1884, the majority of Norwegian-Danish Evangelical Free Church preachers received theological training at the Dano-Norwegian department of Chicago Theological Seminary. The Congregationalists were eager to form a relationship with Scandinavians in hopes that they would join forces with them.[54] The Congregationalists had considerable wealth and gave generously to home missions in order to reach the immigrant populations in America. The Congregationalists were eager to see immigrants from Norway, Denmark, and Sweden become "good Christians, good Americans, and good Congregationalists."[55] In these efforts, Congregationalists assisted in organizing both Scandinavian Congregational churches and Norwegian-Danish Evangelical Free churches.[56]

Between 1884, when the Dano-Norwegian department opened, and 1906, when Chicago Theological Seminary underwent a "tradition-shattering reorganization," the school took a turn in the direction of liberal theology.[57] During these years, however, the vast majority of Danish-Norwegian Evangelical Free Church pastors maintained their evangelical convictions from their pietist, revivalist past. Moreover, the Norwegian-Danish Free congregations were closely tied to the Scandinavian Alliance Mission, founded by Fredrik Franson, who was as influential among these churches as he was among the Swedish.[58] The Norwegian-Danish Free churches held unwaveringly to the Bible as the rule of faith and doctrine. They believed fervently in the atoning work of Christ on the cross for the forgiveness of sins. They preached passionately about the personal return of Jesus Christ and labored for the salvation of souls before his glorious return.[59] Thus, both those who were not educated at Chicago Theological Seminary and those who were voiced concerns over the school's movement toward liberal theology. Regarding the pastors who attended this school, "they deeply grieved when the liberal trend became more and more evident."[60]

In 1908, action by the Norwegian-Danish Free churches was taken up at their Western Association's annual meeting, held at Winona, Minnesota, when a committee formed to study the question of founding a new school. Then, at the annual meeting held in Milwaukee in 1909, the Western and Eastern Free Church associations voted to establish "A Bible School for Free Christians."[61] The Eastern Association of Norwegian-Danish Evangelical Free churches was represented at the meeting and pledged full support. In the report C. A. Helmer Andrewsen states:

> It is just a little more than a year since this question first came up, if there was need for a Bible school for our young people in our free evangelical work, and unanimously the thought was immediately endorsed when presented at the annual meeting in 1908. ... The school's task must be to help the students know their Bible, believe it, and live it! "The word of the Lord endures forever." The school must always be a free evangelical Bible school open to young men and women, no matter to what denomination they may belong. ... Parents, send to the school your sons and daughters who desire a higher level of education within a distinctly Christian environment, and with a course of study that will provide thorough instruction in the Bible and Christian doctrine and history. Young men and women, you who desire preparation for missionary work whether at home or out in the mission field among the spiritually lost, or just wish to become more skilled as the Lord's witnesses and disciples in daily life, come to the school and receive the help that can prepare you. And young men, you who feel called to preaching or desire it and would like to discern if God really has called you to it, come and receive an education that can serve as a foundation for further theological study at the seminary in Chicago.[62]

Moreover, Andrewsen reported the purchase of property in Rushford, Minnesota,[63] located in a beautiful part of town on a small hill, noting that the building was surrounded by a grove of shade trees. The school had five classrooms (one of them large enough to seat one hundred students), an office, a large entrance, a good furnace, a pipeline from the city's waterworks, and indoor plumbing. He commented: "It seems strange that we should acquire such a solid and practical building for a school on such favorable terms. We must consider it as God's leading, and rejoice in it as a 'wink from the Lord' that he is pleased with our work and an indication of his further help."[64]

Norwegian-Danish Bible Institute at Rushford, Minnesota

The school was incorporated under the laws of the state of Minnesota as a religious educational institution for young men and women, providing a general course of high school academic instruction, particularly to prepare students for missionary and evangelistic work, and to provide a course of theological instruction and studies designed to equip young men for Christian ministry.[65]

In May 1910 Ludwig J. Pedersen (1868–1950) agreed to assume the role of president. He resigned his pastorate in Boston and took up his new position, serving as the school's first president that fall. Pedersen had emigrated with his parents from Norway as a boy and settled near Minneapolis. He attended Chicago Theological Seminary, graduating in 1899.

Students and faculty of the Norwegian-Danish Bible Institute

On September 28, 1910, the school opened with two teachers, Pedersen and Miss Grace Skow, and eleven students—four males and seven females. As courses and instructors were added, the school grew to eighty students in a short time.[66]

To the three-year Bible course, a music course was added in 1911, a three-year academic and business course in 1912, and a four-year theological course in 1914.[67] A teacher's course was offered to prepare young women for public school teaching. There was also a music department that offered practical instruction in instrumental and vocal music. Besides Pedersen and Skow, George Herrigstad, Professor E. M. Paulson, a former missionary to China, and Rev. Carl B. Bjuge, a graduate of Chicago Theological Seminary and Carleton College, made up the teaching faculty. Instruction was offered in English and the Dano-Norwegian language.

FEATURED ALUMNA
Christine Villadsen

Christine Villadsen (1888–1918) began as a student in 1910, the first year the school opened. She was the first graduate of the Bible Institute and Academy at Rushford, Minnesota.[68] She was originally from Norway but lived most of her life in Chicago, where she was a member of Salem Evangelical Free Church.[69] Following completion of the two-year Bible program, she applied to serve as a missionary with the Scandinavian Alliance Mission, known later as TEAM.[70] She traveled to China in autumn 1913 and worked there in cooperation with the China Inland Mission.[71] In 1918, students and teachers of the Bible Institute and Academy were deeply shocked by news that Christine had been martyred on January 14 on the mission field.[72]

Young Christine Villadsen

Christine was headquartered at Tinchow and worked at Sunshui (Sanshui, Shao-shui) in the province of Shensi, engaging actively in sharing the gospel.[73] She was murdered by outlaws while trying to protect Chinese Christians.[74] In defending the village women and children who were fleeing to her school to save themselves from the bandits, she was killed.[75] She was thirty years old. A month earlier, she had been captured along with another missionary, Jessie Gregg of the China Inland Mission, but they were released without harm. On January 14, 1918, Christine did not escape with her life. She is buried at Pinhsien.[76]

Pastor C. T. Dyrness of Salem Evangelical Free Church and board member of the Scandinavian Alliance Mission wrote of Christine:

> Our sister has laid down her life in the struggle to bring the gospel to the Chinese people, and she has the pleasure and honor of being counted among the martyrs. ... Over a year ago she received her own station at Sunshui where she worked with much zeal and success.

But then she was driven away from there—a work that she loved with her life and soul, a work that was crowned with the salvation of many souls. This is strange in our eyes. But the Lord sees and acts in wisdom, and he is never at fault in what he allows and what he does.[77]

Mature Christine Villadsen

In 1911, the seminary curriculum at Rushford offered courses in analytical studies of the Bible, Greek, homiletics, elocution, poetical writings in the Bible, church history, historical development of theology, pastoral theology, and Christian psychology, as well as anthropology and logic. Moreover, the Bible Institute course for men and women included studies in Old and New Testament books, Bible doctrine, biblical types and prophecies, Bible geography, church and mission history, the life of Christ, world history, Danish-Norwegian grammar, anthropology and logic, and penmanship.

As with most new schools, the Bible Institute and Academy suffered from two constant challenges, namely, the faculty was overworked and the budget was underfunded.[78] The pressure on Pedersen was evident. In a letter to him dated June 12, 1912, Ingvald Andersen, secretary of the board, writes: "We all feel grateful to you for the two years' service that

L. J. Pedersen

you have given to the school under such difficult and trying circumstances, as it naturally must have been in starting up a new school of this character, and we are also aware of the still more difficult position this last year, as you, as well as we, were disappointed in not securing another teacher as we had hoped, and thus this double responsibility fell upon you."[79]

Despite these challenges, the Bible Institute and Academy at Rushford had the full support of the Norwegian-Danish Evangelical Free Church Association. Further, the new school's theological center was also securely rooted in the evangelical convictions of the Norwegian-Danish pioneers. Pedersen wrote:

> We stand for the old time religion, faith in God, Christ and the Bible. As our churches are born in revivals, they must be maintained by the same spirit, since we believe church membership should consist of only converted people. ... Hence, there is a great need of a revival. Our congregations are not held together by ritualism and formalities but by the preaching of the Word and the unity of Spirit. Hence, we must seek the fullness of the Spirit more than anything else. Learning and education have their place and should be appreciated, but these are not by any matter of mention sufficient for the revival, up-building, and progress of the church. We must be wholly dedicated to God in order to become instruments of the Holy Spirit through which He can work and thus glorify God through the ministry of the church and the preaching of His word.[80]

The Free Church Swedes of the Evangelical Free Church and the Free Church Danes and Norwegians of their body held similar convictions about the infallible, final authority of the Bible, asking, "Where stands it written?" They rejoiced to hear the faithful preaching and exposition of the word of God. They engaged in the winsome proclamation of the gospel. They recognized the need for personal conversion to Christ, the fullness of the Spirit, and a living faith of holiness and discipleship. They were committed to Christ's Great Commission at home and abroad. They prayed for spiritual revival from God to energize and refresh their churches and ministries.

Chapter 2

On the Move to Merger
(1916–1960)

David M. Gustafson

T he Norwegian-Danish Evangelical Free Church Association and the Swedish Evangelical Free Church of America maintained their respective schools in the first half of the twentieth century. During these years, both schools raised their academic standards at a time when education levels in the United States were rising significantly. It was common, for example, for Scandinavian immigrants in the 1880s and 1890s, as well as for Americans in general, to attain a fourth-grade level of education with skills in reading, writing, and arithmetic. In 1910, 9 percent of Americans had a high school diploma. In 1920, the number grew to 16 percent, and by 1930 it reached 30 percent.[1]

For this reason, both the Norwegian-Danish and Swedish Free Church schools offered high school education with theological seminary programs in their respective high school academies. However, by 1940, 50 percent of all young adults were earning high school diplomas from public high schools. The original reasons for the Free Church's academies were no longer pertinent. As educational levels increased, the seminary programs moved from offering diplomas of completion, to high school diplomas, to bachelor of divinity degrees, and later to master of divinity degrees. At the time, the two Free Church schools were step by step on the move to a merger.

THE NORWEGIAN-DANISH BIBLE INSTITUTE: A MOVE TO MINNEAPOLIS

With growth of the Norwegian-Danish Bible Institute and Academy at Rushford, it was necessary that the board of directors look for a larger facility. Sooner than expected, the school's building was too small to accommodate the students enrolling in its programs. In 1916, a well-suited property became available in Minneapolis at 243 20th Avenue South. The school building was situated beside the Mississippi River across from the University of Minnesota. At the annual meeting of the Western Association of the Norwegian-Danish Free Church held at Minneapolis, delegates pledged the three thousand dollars required for the down payment to purchase the property.[2] Then, at the annual meeting of the national Free Church held on Staten Island, New York, of the same year, delegates ratified the decision to relocate the school 135 miles northwest to Minneapolis.[3] The school opened the fall term of 1916 with sixty-two students.[4]

In 1917, the faculty of the Norwegian-Danish Bible Institute and Seminary was strengthened with the addition of Thorvald B. Madsen (1887–1962), who held a diploma from Nyack Missionary College in New York and a BA from Colby College in Maine.[5]

T. B. Madsen

Nevertheless, these were trying times for the school. In 1918, the Spanish flu pandemic not only brought numerous deaths in various churches but also reduced the Bible institute enrollment in the fall of that year.[6]

In 1919, the pressure of financial challenges grew so intense that President Pedersen resigned due to discouragement. However, as pastors and delegates pleaded with him to continue, he reconsidered his resignation and carried on with the work.[7] The situation improved, and three years later the school purchased an adjacent house and lots for a new dormitory. In August 1923, the school board decided to build a men's dormitory. It was dedicated the following March.[8]

and Academy" was changed to "Trinity Seminary and Bible Institute."[21] The new name was approved by fifty-two delegates. Five ballots were cast for other names.[22] Regarding the new name, Madsen reported:

> The Annual Conference of the Free Church assembled at Muskegon, Michigan, made an important decision, namely to settle upon a name of the Seminary at Minneapolis. ... The Evangelical Free Church school is now definitely Biblical-theological. The name decided upon at Muskegon was "Trinity Seminary and Bible Institute." "Trinity" is a confession of faith.[23]

Trinity Seminary and Bible Institute, Minneapolis

For the Norwegian-Danish Evangelical Free Church Association, the name "Trinity" signified adherence to the orthodox view of the Trinity as stated in its confession, which reads: "We believe in the triune God: Father, Son and Holy Spirit, one God in three persons, in accordance with the apostolic faith."[24] In addition, Madsen reported that the name "Trinity" was neither unique to the Evangelical Free Church nor exclusive to any particular denomination. He notes: "The term was seemingly, at an early date in this country mostly appropriated by the Congregationalists and the Episcopalians, but not necessarily peculiar to, or the special property of any group. Of later decades it has been used generously by both Methodists, Baptists, and possibly other denominational groups."[25] He added that the term "seminary" signified theological studies, which continued to be offered in the school's seminary course.

Moreover, Madsen stated that the new name was "Biblical-theological" because it maintained the words "Bible Institute." As mentioned earlier, the 1912 statement of the Norwegian-Danish Evangelical Free Church Association confessed, "We believe, that the Bible, the Old and New Testament, is the Word of God and is the only infallible rule and guide for faith, life, and doctrine."[26] From the beginning, the school was founded "to help the students know their Bible, believe it, and live it." This had not changed.[27]

In 1942, the chairman of the school board enthusiastically reported to the annual conference in New Haven, Connecticut, "We are happy to be able to report that the work at our school this year has been carried on in a better and more effective way than perhaps for many years in the past. The number of students has increased; their efficiency has been noticeable and progressive, a good spirit prevailing between the faculty and students."[28]

FEATURED ALUMNA
Rev. J. R. Johns

Rev. John R. Johns (MA, PhD) taught at Trinity from 1942–1946. He was born in Swansea, a large coal-mining center in Wales. At the age of thirteen he began working as a laborer in the coal mines. It was there in Swansea that the great Welsh revival broke out in 1904, and Johns was deeply moved by its influence. He was then called by God to Christian ministry, and so he completed coursework at the University of Wales and Trefecca Theological College. After completing his ministerial requirements with the Welsh Presbyterian Church in 1909, he served as a missionary-pastor among the Welsh peoples of western Canada.

J. R. Johns

Two years later, he began as a pastor of an English-speaking congregation in Winnepeg and later served churches in Newark, New Jersey, and Minneapolis. He continued his studies at the University of Manitoba and the University of Indiana. During his years of teaching at Trinity, he lectured on the philosophy of preaching and Christian ethics. His experience of the Welsh revival affected his evangelical convictions and his dedication to prepare preachers as expositors of the Scriptures.[29]

Following World War II, a number of veterans took advantage of federal grant money for education. Madsen reported, "With a revised schedule and the influx of GI students the attendance increased to about 140."[30]

School song of Trinity Seminary and Bible Institute

THE SWEDISH EVANGELICAL FREE CHURCH
SCHOOL: A RETURN MOVE TO CHICAGO

With the absence of Princell in 1914 and his death the following year with no one to replace him, the fledgling Swedish Bible Institute faced a crisis. It was at a low ebb without a principal teacher and president.[31] Therefore, the school did not open as usual for the 1914–1915 academic year. Nonetheless, in January 1915, E. A. Halleen and Gustav Edwards, preachers of the Swedish Evangelical Free Church, taught a short Bible course at the Swedish Evangelical Free Church of Minneapolis.

Later that year, delegates at the annual conference of the Swedish Evangelical Free Church held at Turlock, California, considered the future of the school. The idea surfaced to pursue affiliation with the Moody Bible Institute of Chicago. If such an affiliation were possible, the school board would make arrangements with this school on a temporary basis.[32] The board of directors of Moody Bible Institute approved the proposal. In fact, the arrangements were quite generous to the Free Church.[33] Moody Bible Institute offered to provide classrooms and other facilities free of charge on the condition that the Swedish Free Church would engage and pay its own instructors to teach its courses in the Swedish language.

Faculty and students of the Free Church Bible Course, Minneapolis, 1915.
At center are Rev. Gustav Edwards (left) and Rev. E. A. Halleen (right).

Moreover, the Swedish Free Church students, as well as Swedish students from other churches, were welcome to take the English-language courses. With this arrangement, the Free Church school, or so-called Swedish department or Swedish-English Course of Moody Bible Institute, began in the fall of 1916.[34] The affiliation between the Swedish Evangelical Free Church and Moody Bible Institute clearly demonstrated their revivalist heritage.

The Free Church's school board decided to approach Edwards, who was serving as pastor of Lake View Evangelical Free Church of Chicago, to lead the Swedish department.[35] Edwards accepted the call.

Gustav Edwards (1874–1948) had worked as an evangelist in Sweden for three years. He then left his native country to be a missionary to north China. After serving there for six years with the China Inland Mission, he received permission for further theological study in Chicago.[36] In 1915, he graduated from Wheaton College with a bachelor of philosophy. In 1916, he completed a bachelor of divinity from the Swedish department of Chicago Theological Seminary.[37] In 1916, he started teaching at Moody Bible Institute, with five students enrolled during the term.[38]

Gustav Edwards

The Swedish department of Moody Bible Institute, 1917

At the end of the 1917–1918 academic year, Edwards reported that thirty students had received instruction in the Swedish department during the year. The Swedish-English Course included those subjects offered at Moody Bible Institute in Bible, theology, practical ministry, evangelism, and missions, plus courses for Swedish students in New Testament Greek, history, the English language, the Swedish language and literature, and homiletics.[39]

Anna J. Lindgren
(TIU Archives)

Two courses of study were offered in the Swedish department—a two-year Bible course and a three-year program. Students who stayed the extra year earned both a diploma from Moody Bible Institute and a diploma from the Swedish Evangelical Free Church.

With an increase of students in the Swedish department, an additional teacher was hired on a part-time basis, named Anna J. Lindgren.[40] She was a graduate of Detthowska Teacher's School in Stockholm. She was a former schoolteacher in Sweden and a graduate of Moody Bible Institute.[41] It was said that her "intellectual training and gifts were only exceeded by her spiritual depth and Christ-possessed personality that left an impression upon the lives of her students that lingered much longer than her well-taught lessons in Swedish grammar, Swedish composition, and Swedish

The Bible Institute of the Swedish Evangelical Free Church
at Moody Bible Institute, winter term, 1922

literature."[42] Regrettably, in 1922 she had to give up her work as an assistant instructor due to health concerns.

In the following year, Edwards announced that the enrollment of the school exceeded eighty students, many of whom were missionary candidates who came from Sweden to spend a year or two at the school before going out to their respective mission fields.[43]

The school continued to grow so that at times there were as many as one hundred students enrolled in the Swedish department. After Lindgren's departure, Edwards sought to employ another instructor.

Meanwhile, the need was recognized for wider educational offerings, since the majority of students enrolled in the Swedish department were not high school graduates.[44] In 1923, at the annual conference of the Swedish Free Church, upon recommendation of the school board, a call was extended to A. L. Wedell, then principal of Hilmar Union High School in Hilmar, California.[45] Wedell accepted the invitation and began teaching at the Swedish department that fall.[46]

Wedell was engaged as an instructor partly with the expectation that he would inaugurate a high school department since such a broader education was not available at Moody Bible Institute.[47] Moreover, Wedell sensed a decreasing need for some Swedish subjects taught at the school. He felt that the Free Church should not be limited by its affiliation with Moody Bible Institute. Largely as a result of the vision for a high school academy, delegates of the Swedish Free Church at its annual conference in 1925 approved the purchase of a large mansion as a school building located at the corner of Hermitage and Berteau Avenues in the Ravenswood neighborhood of Chicago.[48]

Edwards made plans for a three-year seminary course, also to be offered at the Free Church's newly acquired school building. Thus, there were plans for three academic programs. First, the Free Church school would launch a four-year high school academy that would have a distinctly Christian influence. Second, the Free Church school would launch a three-year seminary course for prospective pastors and missionaries that had as its prerequisite a four-year high school diploma.[49] Third, the Free Church would continue its affiliation with Moody Bible Institute to offer the two-year Bible Course with the Swedish department, ensuring a smooth transition for students.

Bible Institute and Academy
on North Hermitage Avenue, Chicago, 1926

In January 1926, the mansion at 4211 North Hermitage Avenue was ready for occupancy for the newly organized high school academy.[50] Gradually this department attracted more and more high school–age students from various churches in Chicago, especially students whose parents desired them to enjoy the benefit of a Christian education.

With an increase in the number of courses offered at the academy, it was necessary to add instructors. Harry Lindblom, pastor of Lake View Free Church, was the first instructor in the science department.[51] Myrtle E. Johnson taught English and mathematics. The curriculum of the academy was educationally sturdy. It included four years of English, four years of Swedish, two years of mathematics, three years of science and history, two years of Latin, and one year of Greek.[52] In spring 1928, the academy was accredited by the University of Illinois.[53]

For several years, it appeared that the high school academy had taken priority over the Bible Institute and the seminary. For this reason, there was a renewed vision to strengthen the latter. In 1931, additional part-time instructors were added, namely, Halleen and Harry P. Lundell.[54]

As the Bible institute and seminary programs were strengthened, the enrollment increased. Student enrollment of the Bible Institute and Academy peaked in the academic year 1932–1933, with 105 students.[55]

However, the economic depression that affected the entire country had its effect on the school's enrollment. In the following year, only fifty-six students were enrolled. Slowly the enrollment began to increase, which again made it difficult to have a four-year high school, a two-year Bible Course, and a three-year seminary program under one roof.

Faculty and students of the Bible Institute and Academy
in Chicago. Second row at center are Prof. A. L. Wedell,
Rev. Gustav Edwards, and Rev. Harry Lindblom, 1932

To compound the problem, the Bible Institute and Academy was facing financial challenges due to the downturn in the economy. Furthermore, a number of Free Church leaders, pastors, and laypeople were becoming less and less supportive of the high school academy.[56] The reason was clear. The academy served almost entirely high school students from Chicago. This was not the case, however, with the Swedish Bible Institute and seminary course, which drew students from around the country and served the Free Church more directly.

At the same time, the percentage of Swedish Bible Institute and seminary students at the school was on the rise. The challenge of three educational programs in one facility, the continuing financial pressure of funding all three, and the decreasing need for providing high school education for incoming students as a result of improved public education all combined to prompt the Swedish Free Church to make a decision regarding the academy.[57]

Furthermore, it was decided that Wedell's influence would be used more strategically as an instructor in the seminary rather than a principal of the high school. After all, he had received an MA from Northwestern University in Greek and a bachelor of divinity (BD) from McCormick Presbyterian Theological Seminary.

A proposal at the 1938 annual conference of the Free Church held in Chicago was to discontinue the high school. With the closing of the academy, Wedell was made president of the school, and Edwards became dean. Together they threw their energies into developing the two programs of the school with a new name: Bible Institute and Seminary.[58]

During the next two years as president of the school, Wedell saw interest improve on the part of the Free Church as a whole. The Bible Institute and Seminary enrolled more than eighty young men and women in a single year.[59] After a successful start, Wedell delivered what would be his last report to the annual conference in June 1940. He said, "Much blessing has attended this first year of the school since the elimination of the Academy, not only in the increased enrollment but in the spirit of the students."[60] That fall semester, an unanticipated illness led to his sudden death.

With Wedell's passing, Halleen, president of the Swedish Evangelical Free Church, was called on to teach the Bible subjects, J. C. Olson taught homiletics, and Frank W. Anderson along with John Dahlin took over other courses.[61] At the end of the 1940–1941 school year, Edwards, once again president, reported: "Eighty-eight students had been enrolled."[62] He also reported that the financial condition of the school was better than it had been for years. Moreover, in 1941 the first student from the overseas mission field of China arrived. Theodore Choy came from Hong Kong to enroll in the seminary course.

FEATURED ALUMNUS
Theodore ("Ted") Choy, Cai Xihui (蔡錫惠)

Theodore Choy (1916–1992), from Shantou, Guangdong, China, graduated in 1939 from Canton Bible Institute of the Swedish Free Mission (later Evangel Seminary in Hong Kong). Earlier he had dedicated himself to full-time Christian service during a revival meeting led by famous Chinese evangelist John Song.[63] Choy traveled to Chicago with his missionary teachers,

Theodore Choy

who were returning on furlough, and enrolled as a student at the Swedish Free Church Bible Institute and Seminary.[64] After graduation from the seminary course, he entered Wheaton College for further biblical and theological studies. His studies were interrupted, however, when he joined the US Marine Corps as a specialist interpreter in northern China. While there, he also served at Youth for Christ meetings for Chinese young people.

After World War II, Choy returned to Wheaton, where he completed his bachelor's degree and met his wife, Leona. In 1948, the couple traveled to Hong Kong, where he took a position as pastor of the Swatow Christian Church

in Kowloon (香港潮人生命堂). In 1951, he accepted a teaching position at a seminary in Singapore. A year later, he and his wife returned to the United States, where he began studies in the School of Religion of the University of Iowa, receiving his master's in 1955.

As an international student, Choy sympathized with others who had come to study in the United States. He and his wife joined International Students Inc., concentrating on Chinese students. Based in Washington, DC, the organization also helped to cofound the Chinese Christian Church. In 1962, along with Moses Chow, Ted and Leona founded Ambassadors for Christ, a campus ministry to Chinese university students, scholars, and professionals throughout North America.[65]

In their later years of ministry, the Choys made regular visits to China to teach the Bible and provide Christian literature, mostly to Christians in house churches. Ted's ministry experience and extensive biblical knowledge made him a valuable resource to Chinese Christians in China and the United States.

During the following year, Edwards worked to hire new faculty members. The first instructor to be added was Dr. Carl R. Steelberg, an alum of the Swedish department at Moody Bible Institute. The second instructor added was Millicent V. Johnson, who had served as a missionary in

Chapel of the Bible Institute and Seminary. From left, Dr. Carl R. Steelberg, Dr. Gustav Edwards (standing), Millicent V. Johnson, and Rev. Roy A. Thompson.

Canton and Hong Kong in south China, attended Moody Bible Institute, and was a graduate of Wheaton College.[66] She taught courses in missions and Christian education.

With a growing student body, the Swedish Free Church school board proposed resolutions at the 1943 annual conference held in Minneapolis for soliciting funds for a new school building.[67] A committee was formed to raise the funds. By the 1944 conference, $80,000 of the $95,000 had been raised in gifts and pledges.[68] In the meantime, the Women's Missionary Society of the Swedish Free Church had collected more than $10,000 to purchase a building at 4526 North Paulina Street to be used as a women's dormitory.[69]

In 1944, the Bible Institute and Seminary had ninety-seven students enrolled.[70] The school board appointed Steelberg to become dean and Rev. Roy A. Thompson to become executive secretary to oversee matters of business administration. These arrangements were considered temporary until a new president could be secured.[71]

THE MERGER: THE NORWEGIAN-DANISH AND SWEDISH EVANGELICAL FREE CHURCH SCHOOLS BECOME ONE

In 1945, at the annual meeting of the Norwegian-Danish Evangelical Free Church Association at Bethany Church in Madison, Wisconsin, the conference elected a committee to investigate the possibility of merging Trinity Seminary and Bible Institute in Minneapolis with the Bible Institute and Seminary of the Swedish Evangelical Free Church in Chicago.[72] A resolution for a merger from both groups was approved. In light of this merger, students were welcome to attend the campus of their choice, whether in Chicago or Minneapolis.[73] Of course, the merger of the two schools was part of a wider plan to merge the two Free Church bodies, which happened in 1950, forming the Evangelical Free Church of America, known simply as the EFCA.

FEATURED ALUMNUS
Carl R. Steelberg

Carl R. Steelberg (1905–1983) graduated from the Swedish department of Moody Bible Institute in 1925. He returned to his hometown of Denver to complete his AB at the University of Denver and his ThM and ThD at Illif Graduate School of Theology.[74]

Carl R. Steelberg

After serving evangelical churches in Colorado, Steelberg was invited to join the faculty of the Swedish Free Church's Bible Institute and Seminary in 1941, making him the first faculty member to hold an earned doctorate. He taught courses in church history, Greek, homiletics, Bible survey, evangelism, and ethics. Moreover, he and his wife, Drusilla, housed a number of students in their home for years, easing the acute dormitory shortage at the school.

Steelberg served as dean of the seminary until 1950.[75] He also served as interim pastor of Evangelical Free churches in Chicago, in Bay City, Michigan, and in McKeesport, Pennsylvania. Between 1954 and 1975 he supervised the Sunshine Gospel Mission in Chicago, a rescue mission founded in 1905 by Moody Church.

Later, David J. Hesselgrave, professor of missions at Trinity, wrote about Steelberg's ministry:

In the 1940s the seminary of the Evangelical Free Church was small. It had its weaknesses, but its strength lay in a spiritual and knowledgeable faculty. My professor of Bible and theology, Carl R. Steelberg, was one of the most knowledgeable Bible scholars I had ever met. Moreover, despite my youthfulness, he demonstrated confidence in me by recommending me as teacher of a large Sunday school class of professionals in a church on Chicago's far south side. ... Despite my immaturity and limitations, the response of the class was most exhilarating. In short, my seminary experience awakened in me a profound appreciation for biblical revelation and for the importance of communicating its changeless message as opposed to the ever-changing machinations of mortal men.[76]

A united school board was elected, with Rev. Bernhard Rom as chairman and Thompson as secretary. Madsen was elected to serve as acting president of the school, while David R. Anderson was made dean of the Minneapolis school and Steelberg was to serve as dean of

C. Raymond Ludwigson

the Chicago school. Madsen traveled from Minneapolis to Chicago to work on a plan to consolidate the two campuses. In 1948, it was decided to sell the Minneapolis property and hold classes in Chicago beginning in the fall of the following year.[77] In addition, the school would be named "Trinity Seminary and Bible College." A committee was elected to develop funds for the united school and Rev. Arnold T. Olson became campaign manager of the "Trinity Advance."[78]

Dr. C. Raymond Ludwigson was chosen to become president of the united school. The choice of Ludwigson as president was given considerable thought. He was an accomplished scholar and clearly within the pietistic, evangelical tradition of the two Free Church bodies. In 1949, *The Evangelical Beacon*—the periodical of the Evangelical Free Church—reported:

The merging of the schools makes possible the merging of our faculties, so that the best we have had in both schools is carried over into the new institution. The merger, too, made possible the securing of the kind of president we needed in order to make possible the attainment of the highest objectives in our educational program. God has been exceedingly good to us as Free Church groups to give us the kind of leader we shall have in Dr. C. Raymond Ludwigson, who has been equipped both intellectually and spiritually for the tremendous job he is undertaking. Though coming originally from another denomination, he is already so thoroughly imbued with the "Free Church spirit" that he has become one of us even before he has an opportunity to become a member in any official sense.[79]

Ludwigson was an evangelical scholar who held to a "simple faith in the Bible as the very word of the living God."[80] He demonstrated an irenic, nonsectarian spirit in his association with Lutherans, Baptists, Disciples, Presbyterians, Congregationalists, and free churches. He possessed a passion for mission at home and abroad.[81]

Ludwigson was a graduate of Moody Bible Institute, Wheaton College, and the Lutheran Theological Seminary in Maywood, Illinois, where he had completed a bachelor of divinity and master of sacred theology degrees. He completed the PhD at the University of Iowa.

In the summer of 1947, as a professor at Wheaton College, Ludwigson was invited to speak at the annual conference of the Free Church Youth Fellowship, held at Medicine Lake in Minneapolis.[82] Ludwigson's Bible teaching prompted organizers of the Free Church Youth Fellowship Conference the following year to invite him to return as a speaker. *The Evangelical Beacon* reported:

> Dr. Ludwigson accepted and will team with Billy Graham of Charlotte, N. C., on the first three days and with other leading speakers on the other three nights. ... [Ludwigson] will be on the grounds for the entire week. God has used him in a marked way among the students at Wheaton College, and the FCYF committee feels very happy over his coming.[83]

At the 1948 annual conference of the (Swedish) Evangelical Free Church of America, a resolution was "unanimously adopted urging the Board of Education to extend a call to Dr. Ludwigson as an instructor of the school.[84] The resolution was backed by a pledge of partial financial support. This offer opened the door for Ludwigson to join the faculty part time at the Chicago campus in the fall of 1948 while fulfilling his teaching responsibilities at Wheaton College.[85]

Then the announcement came in November 1948 that Ludwigson would become president of the united Evangelical Free Church school.[86] He made plans to begin his new role as president the following September.[87] The school board approved Ludwigson's plan, which included raising the school's educational standards. This plan meant adding a two-year Bible college program that provided general junior college subjects and Bible training and would serve as the prerequisite for admission to the three-year seminary course.[88] Madsen, who had served as acting president of the schools during the merger negotiations, continued in this capacity until September 1949. In addition, David Anderson, Steelberg, and William Hallman remained as full-time faculty members of the united school.[89]

Ludwigson's vision for the school profoundly influenced the philosophy of education and curriculum.[90] He envisioned sending into "Free Churches and into all the world leaders who are consistently spiritual and scholarly."[91] In his inauguration address, based on 1 Thessalonians 2:4, Ludwigson said:

> As a call to the entire Evangelical Free Church of America in carrying out this trust of the gospel, I can only say when it comes to the faculty of our school: Give us the best, the very, very best.

Architect's drawing for the new academic building
on West Berteau Avenue, Chicago

The effect of such a faculty will soon be felt in the more effective carrying out of the trust of the gospel. Along with the faculty, a student body is of course a necessity and while all are not alike in personality, in gifts, and in talents, we ask again for the best, the very, very best.[92]

In spring 1949, Ludwigson announced: "When school time comes again in September, the doors of our new Free Church administration and classroom building in Chicago will open for the first time to the incoming student body. The new building will offer modern classrooms and equipment, a newly furnished library with stacks for 7,000 books, new offices, a large auditorium for chapel, and more dormitory space for ministerial students."[93]

The academic year of "the united Trinity in Chicago" began September 13, 1949.[94] Fifty-one students moved from Minneapolis to Chicago, 41 returned from Chicago, and 43 enrolled for the first time, comprising a total student body of 135, with 65 men and 70 women.[95] Despite higher admission standards, student registration reached a level higher than the previous

Lecture Hall of the academic building.
Dr. Ludwigson is front and center.

mark of 95 at the Chicago school.[96] Yet, the number of 135 was short of the projected 170 students.[97] However, by the second semester, student enrollment had increased to 163 students, with 99 men and 64 women.[98]

Since the new administration and classroom building would not be ready for occupancy until January 1950, it was necessary to secure other facilities in addition to the property at North Hermitage and Berteau and the houses that the school owned that functioned as dormitories.[99] The elders of the nearby Ravenswood Presbyterian Church graciously opened their doors to the auditorium for chapel services and the basement and kitchen for a dining hall, and did so free of charge until Trinity could occupy the new facility.[100] In January 1950, the new classroom and administrative building opened for use.

During the first academic year of the united school, Ludwigson emphasized the biblical theme "entrusted with the gospel" (πιστευθῆναι τὸ εὐαγγέλιον), from 1 Thessalonians 2:4. Then he reported: "After much prayer and consideration by the united student body and faculty of our Free Church School, this text was chosen to be the school verse."[101] He commented further:

> The truth expressed in this verse will have a great effect upon all of us as we allow it to enter into our thinking and activity. To be put in trust with the Gospel is no small thing and, day by day, to be aware of this will allow the Holy Spirit to make us very conscientious and responsible in all that we do for our Lord. The verse expresses a gracious allowance on the part of God to permit us as sinful creatures to be entrusted with so great a message.[102]

In his inaugural message, he chose to preach from this text, further commenting:

> We have been called to evangelize. This is the essential substance of our trust. ... The very message that we proclaim is basically evangelistic and has the great object in the eternal purpose of God to save the souls of men. All teaching becomes evangelism by virtue of the very nature of the message of the gospel. ... God is not willing that any should perish but that all should come to repentance, and the evangelization of lost men and women is

basic in the eternal purpose of God according to which we are placed in trust with the gospel. ... The task of those entrusted with the gospel is the evangelization of the lost ... first, last, and always.[103]

Ludwigson, as well as the united school board, sought to address any fears over raising the school's educational standards, especially the fear that this might somehow lower the school's spiritual standards.[104] They assured the Free Church constituents that intellectual rigor would not become a substitute for evangelical spirituality.[105]

Any such fear was set aside on February 14, 1950, when the student body was stirred by a spiritual revival—a phenomenon felt also at Wheaton College and nearby at Northern Baptist Theological Seminary.[106] Wes Carlson, a student from Maple Plain, Minnesota, told of his experience, describing how "the Lord had laid bare the sin that had been accumulating [in me]." Carlson recalled that after hearing confessions of sin by other students that he soon came "under the heavy hand of the Holy Spirit" and acknowledged his sin too. Carlson concluded his account of the spiritual revival, saying: "Truly God had really met us in a way which was unmistakable."[107]

Ludwigson gave his account of the meeting as well, saying: "The Lord has been pleased also to give to us a revival. ... Great decisions were made and according to the testimonies of some students, struggles within their own hearts that had gone on for years came to an end."[108] Moreover, Ludwigson reported that students made decisions to enter the mission field. He said, "In many cases all was laid on the altar and the Holy Spirit caused many reservations to vanish."[109]

Despite all of the positive progress at the school, Ludwigson increasingly felt the weight of his role as president. He faced the challenge of a new curriculum with higher educational standards. He faced the challenge of arranging for dormitories, chapel, kitchen, and dining hall when the new administrative and classroom building was delayed in its completion. He faced the challenge of bringing faculty and students together from the two previous schools. In fact, one of the typical expressions for the first year of the united school, written in the school yearbook, was: "But it was *this* way last year."[110]

The Revival of 1950 as Recalled by Marge Anderson, a Trinity Student from St. Paul, Minnesota

Last summer when the Trinity catalog was made up for the fall and spring semesters ... , February 14 was set aside as a day of prayer. ... Many of the students had had a feeling for three or four days before the day of prayer that the Lord was going to deal with them through the services that day. Consequently, many of us didn't even want to attend school that morning. We were fearful of what the Lord was going to require of us; our spirit of pride wouldn't permit us to confess our secret and open sins and come before Him with a clean slate. The morning started out with a united prayer service of the entire school. In the second hour we divided up into three groups and the faculty was available for special consultation and prayer. ... The third hour was chapel. We were presented with a wonderful challenge of the work the Lord had for us either in the foreign or home field—and especially giving us the story of China and the possibilities there. The hour after chapel we met again in three different groups. At 11:45 we were all to congregate in the chapel to observe communion. Dr. Ludwigson had a message for us but before he started he gave an opportunity to testify of the blessings of the morning to anyone who felt led to do so. The working of the Lord then became manifest. Students stood up all over the chapel and confessed sins. We didn't realize that such sin existed in the lives of students. But as they confessed, we realized that we, too, were guilty of the same and even greater sins. God was gracious, and for over two hours—almost three hours [students confessed their sins]. ... Our communion service had to be postponed until the following day when Dr. Ludwigson also got to his message—based on Hebrews 10:17—"and their sins and iniquities will I remember no more."[111]

Furthermore, Ludwigson was burdened by the school's lack of finances.[112] When H. A. Faugerstrom, a Free Church superintendent from Nebraska, visited the school, he noted that Ludwigson was "one busy man, who puts in fearfully long hours."[113] Faugerstrom concluded his remarks, saying: "He needs your prayers. He has one gigantic task in this period of transition in bringing the school program into a coordinated whole. The financial burden is tremendously heavy just now. We must hasten to relieve the pressure thereof."[114]

The budget deficit had climbed with additions of faculty members such as Rev. H. Wilbert Norton, Dr. Stanley Lindquist, and Rev. Robert Culver. In total, the faculty had increased from ten to fifteen full-time and part-time instructors. This was necessary, of course, to expand the two-year course for Christian workers into a four-year course with a bachelor's degree with majors in Bible, missions, and Christian education, and to offer two years of Hebrew Old Testament study and three years of Greek New Testament study.[115]

Despite the financial challenges, students were prepared for ministry and Christian service, both inside and outside the classroom. The purchase of a new tour bus allowed the Trinity choir to travel on weekends and summers to hold concerts.[116] Moreover, students fulfilled their practical Christian service assignments in churches under the direction of Norton.[117]

Stanley Lindquist (left) and Gunnar Urang (right)

As a result of this work, Ludwigson reported that a new church had been organized in Libertyville, Illinois. The work was initiated by Lindquist and continued by Norton and Trinity student George Tweed.[118] Ludwigson reported a similar work led by Trinity student John Svaan in Arlington Heights, Illinois. By December 1952, a small group of Christians there had decided to affiliate with the Evangelical Free Church and began holding Sunday services at the North School auditorium. The church grew in part due to Trinity students and members of the new congregation visiting three thousand homes.[119]

Ludwigson also reported the enrollment of international students at Trinity. Among them were Rosendo Apeles from the Philippines; Isabella Wong from China; Hoy Fa Tan from Java, Indonesia; Marta Andersson from Sweden; and Anton Netland from Norway.[120] Ludwigson also announced new faculty arriving to teach, such as Dr. J. Barton Payne, professor of Old Testament.

Rosendo Apeles, student from the Philippines

Dr. Ludwigson balanced a number of roles as president, giving leadership to faculty, teaching courses, traveling, speaking, preaching, supporting students in extracurricular activities, fundraising, securing accreditation for a teacher certification with the state of Illinois, and writing. While he faced challenges on every hand, there can be little doubt that the financial pressures tried him the most.[121] It was said that no one who knew him well was surprised when in 1955 he resigned to return to Wheaton College as a full-time professor of the Bible.[122]

With his resignation, the united school chose Madsen to serve as acting president. Madsen had filled this role prior to hiring Ludwigson and had served as vice president under him. In 1955, when Madsen became acting president, the total student body of the college and seminary totaled 181, and within a year it increased to 258, an increase of nearly 40 percent.[123] The school soon hired Bennett Anderson as vice president for development to give serious attention to fundraising and general promotional work of the school.

Isabella Wong, student from China

When Madsen took over as acting president, Norton became the dean of education. The school soon announced that five new majors would be offered in the four-year BA program. It was now possible to major in elementary education, French, Spanish, and music and the humanities, in addition to Bible, missions, and Christian education.

In his report to the 1957 EFCA conference, Madsen announced that other colleges and universities, including the University of Illinois, accepted the credits of Trinity Seminary and Bible College, and that the elementary teaching program had been approved by the State Teachers Certification Board. He announced that the US Armed Forces received Trinity graduates for the chaplaincy program. Finally, it was reported that a long-range planning committee of the school was making preparation for additions to the school's facility, as well as plans to expand the faculty in order to prepare for accreditation with the North Central Association.[124]

H. Wilbert Norton, 1963

Following the school report, it was announced that Norton would become the school's president. Norton (1915–2017) was energetic and unusually gifted in his ability to stir people to Christian commitment. His tenure as president of Trinity proved productive.

Norton was a graduate of Wheaton College and Columbia Bible College. Following his studies, he served as a missionary in Africa with the Evangelical Free Church mission in the Belgian Congo between 1940 and 1949. While on furlough in Chicago from 1945 to 1947, he helped launch the mission conference that became InterVarsity's Urbana conference. He joined the faculty of Trinity in 1950. Five years later he completed a PhD in church history at Northern Baptist Theological Seminary. He set about right away to develop a full-fledged liberal arts curriculum for the college.

In 1959, the EFCA conference discussed purchasing additional property to expand the campus of Trinity in the Ravenswood neighborhood of Chicago. There was also a proposal to purchase property at a location other than where the school was situated. The campus was composed of several buildings including homes in the neighborhood that served as dormitories. After extended discussion following the report from a site committee, the conference delegates passed a resolution that granted authorization "to purchase or sell land and property adjacent or not adjacent to the present location."[125]

The passing of the resolution presented the EFCA with a decision, namely, to expand the campus facilities at the Ravenswood location or to consider relocating the campus elsewhere.[126] A decisive factor was the wisdom, or even the possibility, of building a larger campus in the Ravenswood neighborhood where the school was landlocked. The other option was to purchase a larger property.[127]

Then came the Sunset estate, a far more expansive and suitable property than anyone had dared to hope for.[128] This was a seventy-nine-acre parcel of land owned by the Welch family in Bannockburn, located twenty-two miles northwest of the Ravenswood location.

Sunset Estate in Bannockburn

President Norton was sitting in his office when the phone rang. It was his friend and real estate broker Carlson. "Look," Carlson said, "I understand Trinity is looking for property. I just got a beautiful farm here." The tone of his voice suggested that this was something that the president ought to see at once. Having seen so many "beautiful farms" that turned out to be bitter disappointments, among them one in Highland Park owned by the president of the National Tea Company, President Norton was not really unhappy that he had other plans. When Dr. Norton returned to his office the following week, a phone call assured him that the property was still available and his friend, Carlson, was clearly excited about the potential of "Sunset Estate" out in Bannockburn. "Well," Norton replied, "that's fine, but I don't want to see it alone. Let me see if I can set up something with one of the members of the committee." So a few days later Dr. Norton found himself comfortably settled in Carl Gunderson's car on the way to "Sunset." What Gunderson did not know was that Will Norton, in his established fashion, had made a very specific covenant with God. He had prayed, "Now, Lord, if you have anything in this for us, help Gunderson to answer affirmatively to my question, Should the other members of the committee see this property?" ... Dr. Norton was engulfed by a wave of emotion as Gunderson turned his Cadillac into the "Sunset" driveway. It was a glorious October afternoon with the Illinois maples in gorgeous oranges and reds. The old driveway wound through the trees, and then all of a sudden, boom!—the whole horizon exploded with this magnificent view of the beautiful mansion off to the left. It was just like the Lord had thrown colored Klieg lights on the whole scene. Not a large man in the first place, Will Norton felt himself shrinking smaller and smaller, thinking, "This just isn't Free Church style." They went through the entire property—the lovely old mansion overlooking the little spring-fed lake; the expansive 79 beautiful, wooded acres landscaped by the well-known architect Jens Jensen; the three residences on the property; the stable; the swimming pool—the whole works. And all the time Dr. Norton was thinking about his covenant with God while trying mentally to transpose 4211 North Hermitage and 1723 West Berteau to such an environment. It all just seemed overwhelming. When the men said "goodbye" to the lady who had been showing them around, Dr. Norton posed the question, "Well, Brother Gunderson, do you think the other members of the committee ought to see this?" The president's heart skipped a beat as without a moment's hesitation and with great emphasis the affirmative reply came, "By all means, they must!"[129]

Nearly everyone who viewed the location at Bannockburn was impressed. However, not everyone favored purchasing the property and preparing to make the move. The matter of relocating the school was debated in faculty offices and pastor studies, at district conferences, and around dinner tables. There were arguments in favor of and against relocation. *The Evangelical Beacon* published an article titled "Should Trinity Relocate?" that offered two sides of the debate.[130] Those who favored the move to Sunset estate argued that it was not financially feasible to build in the city. The school faced the challenge of buying homes in the neighborhood to demolish in order to build new facilities. On the other side, it was pointed out that Bannockburn was inaccessible, whereas the Chicago campus was serviced by train and bus. Arguments for the Chicago location, such as the availability of employment and practical work assignments and library facilities, were balanced by concerns for the physical safety of the students.

Entrance to the Bannockburn campus, 1961

When the vote was taken at the EFCA conference in 1960, the purchase of the property in Bannockburn was overwhelmingly approved.[131] Under Norton's leadership, in 1961, Trinity began its move from the north side of Chicago to the Sunset estate in Bannockburn.

Chapter 3

A Gift to Evangelicalism (1963–1974)

Scott M. Manetsch

P robably no one noticed the four middle-aged men engaged in a lively conversation around the table of a restaurant in Chicago's O'Hare International Airport on May 31, 1963.[1] Contrary to all appearances, they were not businessmen waiting to catch a flight but a group of prominent evangelical leaders that included a denominational president, the president of a small seminary and college, a local pastor, and a theological professor. The meeting had been called to discuss the serious problems facing evangelical churches and Christian higher education, and to explore a daring proposal that was almost breathtaking in its scope and potential impact. The leaders sensed that God was calling them to do something new, something big and altogether unexpected—and he was. Around the table on that May afternoon, EFCA President Arnold T. Olson, Trinity President H. Wilbert Norton, Rev. Harry Evans, and Dr. Kenneth Kantzer conceived of a new theological seminary named Trinity Evangelical Divinity School that was to have a far-reaching impact on American evangelicalism and global Christianity. The story of the birth and early years of Trinity Evangelical Divinity School, and the strategic leadership of Kantzer during the school's formative early years (1963–1974), is a testimony to Christian vision, tenacity, and generosity; but even more, it is a striking example of God's faithfulness to his church.

FROM CHICAGO TO BANNOCKBURN

A new chapter in the history of Trinity began in 1957, when Norton was elected the school's thirteenth president. As noted in chapter 2, Norton had been a Free Church missionary to the Belgian Congo before coming to Trinity in 1950 as a professor of missions. By all accounts, President Norton was a man of deep Christian conviction, unbounded energy, and passionate concern for global missions and church planting. One student remembered Norton as a "ball of fire who enflamed so many of us" with Christian service.[2] Another recalled that Norton was "a man with a big heart for God and missions."[3] The school over which Norton was now president was changing in significant ways. During the mid-1950s, Trinity moved in the direction of offering a broader liberal arts curriculum; by the decade's end, the college's name was officially changed from Trinity Bible College to Trinity College to reflect these changes.[4] At the same time, the college was experiencing unprecedented growth. Between the fall of 1956 and the fall of 1959, overall student enrollment grew from 257 to 328.[5] As a result of this growth, the school was severely cramped for space. There was a desperate need for a new educational building, a new women's dormitory, and more shelf space in the library for new books. Despite President Norton's extensive fundraising efforts, the college and seminary continued to run large deficits.[6]

Unfortunately, Trinity Seminary did not enjoy the same kind of numerical growth experienced by the college. During the late 1950s, total seminary enrollment fluctuated between forty and fifty students (including full-time and part-time students).[7] In his report to the EFCA annual conference in 1959, Norton expressed alarm at declining enrollments at the seminary and asked delegates for their support: "One great concern leads us to cry out to God and plead with His people—to direct prospective seminary students to Trinity Seminary!"[8] For the fall semester of 1961, seminary enrollment had dipped down to thirty-five students.[9] Alumni who attended Trinity Seminary during these years remembered with gratitude the devout and hardworking faculty, and the practical, Bible-based education they received.[10] Even so, students recognized that the future of the seminary was in jeopardy; the school appeared to be on "life-supports."[11]

During the late 1950s, Norton and other EFCA leaders worked tirelessly to find solutions to the problems of overcrowding at the college and the faltering seminary program. The board of education, in conjunction with faculty, developed a ten-year plan that projected a student body of six hundred students, recommending the construction of several new buildings at a cost of $1.5 million. This proposal was presented to delegates of the annual conference in 1958, but with mixed results. Though the proposal was officially approved, many EFCA pastors and laypeople raised questions about the wisdom of constructing more buildings in the crowded and aging neighborhood of West Berteau Avenue. Perhaps a new site for the college and seminary should be explored? Acting on this concern, the board of education of the EFCA requested and received authorization from the "Diamond Jubilee" Conference, held in Denver in 1959, to "purchase or sell land and property adjacent to *or not adjacent to* the present location" in Chicago and to "borrow funds needed temporarily to complete or assure the acquisition of suitable property until the 1960 conference."[12] The consequences of this decision proved to be far-reaching and profound.

Over the next six months, Norton, Chairman Arley Bragg, and other members of the board of education explored potential sites for a new college and seminary campus, finally settling on a seventy-nine-acre property located in the village of Bannockburn, Illinois, twenty-five miles north of

The Sunset mansion in Bannockburn, circa 1960

downtown Chicago, adjacent to the newly constructed Tri-State Tollway. The "Sunset estate," owned by Mr. and Mrs. Richard E. Welch, boasted a twelve-room colonial-style mansion (built in 1926), a seven-room tenants' house, a three-bedroom caretaker's cottage, a three-car garage, a barn (with milking and farm equipment), and a large swimming pool. Situated on the crest of a hill, the mansion was surrounded by twenty acres of forestland and had a spring-fed lake in the backyard. In January 1960, EFCA leaders purchased thirty-five acres of the Sunset property for $146,000; the remaining forty-four acres were received as a generous gift from the Welch family.[13]

With the Bannockburn property now in hand, the board of education needed permission from the annual conference of 1960 to relocate Trinity Seminary and Trinity College to this new site. In the months leading up to the meeting, a lively debate took place within local churches and on the pages of the *Evangelical Beacon* about the costs and benefits of such a move. Some voiced concerns about the high price tag of constructing new academic buildings on the property (estimated at $3 million) and wondered how students would commute to campus, obtain part-time employment, and find practical ministry assignments in rural Bannockburn. Others saw the move as a God-given opportunity to grow the college beyond the crowded, expensive, increasingly unsafe neighborhoods of Chicago. One letter to the editor stated the prospects with words almost lyrical: "Consider the wonders of this new location! Spring ... fall ... winter snows ... the beauty and spaciousness of it all. A place to enjoy—a place in which to grow. This is the area in which our professors want to live. It is HERE that we want Trinity. Let us not lose this opportunity. One stands in awe of its possibilities."[14] In an article in the *Evangelical Beacon* at the end of May, Norton petitioned Free Church members to devote themselves to "urgent intercessory prayer for Trinity" in view of the momentous decision that was before them.[15]

On June 24, 1960, delegates to the EFCA annual conference held in Green Lake, Wisconsin, overwhelmingly approved the recommendation of the board of education to move Trinity to Bannockburn. In addition, delegates approved a second resolution that, if anything, had even greater impact in redirecting the course of Trinity thereafter: "RESOLVED, that the Evangelical Free Church of America authorize the Board of Education to maintain *and strengthen* the program of Trinity Seminary and also to operate a four year college."[16] The EFCA gave priority to seminary education, recognizing its strategic importance for the future of the Free Church movement. Two years later, the annual conference went even further, instructing the board of education "to give top priority to the seminary in their planning."[17] Most likely, this new commitment to graduate theological education was motivated not only by a concern to rescue a struggling seminary, but also by recognition of the urgent need for more pastors in a rapidly growing denomination. An official report from 1960 highlighted the problem: whereas in the past decade the number of Free Churches had multiplied from 281 to 452 congregations, during the same period Trinity Seminary had produced only ninety-five ministers. In view of the present need and new mandate, President Norton requested prayers for wisdom, financial support, and new faculty "to make Trinity the finest seminary of its kind in North America."[18]

The Sunset estate in Bannockburn was a beautiful and spacious property, but it did not yet have the infrastructure and buildings needed to support a small seminary *and* a growing college. Consequently, it was decided that the seminary should be relocated to Bannockburn immediately, whereas the college would move to the new site only after funds were secured to construct the necessary academic buildings and dormitories. Trinity Seminary classes were held for the first time at Sunset on September 13, 1961, commencing what Norton called the "year of occupation." From the start, the colonial-style mansion on the hill served as the hub of academic life. The sitting room on the main floor doubled as a spacious classroom and seminary chapel. Two second-floor bedrooms were also converted into classrooms. The basement now housed a modest seminary library, a recreation room, a coffee shop, and student mailboxes. What had once been the dining room on the main floor served as a reading room. Faculty and administrative offices were scattered throughout the building. Only six or seven single men lived on campus during the 1961–1962 school year, quartered in the caretaker's house south of the mansion. A student who lived on campus in these early years remembers enjoying the beautiful fall colors, swimming in the pool down the hill, and watching raccoons forage for food in the garbage bin behind the mansion. Academic life seemed "pretty low key" and not particularly rigorous.[19]

Arriving on campus, April 1962

Though Trinity Seminary's location had changed, most aspects of academic life remained the same during these early years. Faculty members, led by Old Testament scholar and academic dean G. Douglas Young, continued to divide their teaching labors between the seminary and the college back in Chicago. The academic schedule was supplemented by daily chapel services, student missionary meetings, choir practice, and practical ministry assignments. Many students participated in the Tract Club, distributing thousands of Christian tracts each year.[20] Once each semester, professors and students joined together for a special workday and for a day of prayer. From time to time, missionaries and prominent Christian speakers were also brought to campus, as when Carl F. H. Henry inaugurated the Dyrness Lecture Series in October 1962, addressing faculty and students on the themes of "Christ or Chaos," "The Christian View of Work," and "The Power of Truth."[21]

The move to the Bannockburn campus and the renewed commitment to theological education translated into an increase in number of students. Seminary enrollment rose from forty-two students in the 1961–1962 school year to sixty-six the following year.[22] Most of these students belonged to the EFCA and came from the Midwestern states or from California; only two or three students came from outside the United States. Thanks to the generosity of EFCA churches, student tuition and fees were well below the national average, totaling less than $150 per semester (not counting room and board).[23]

Lecture in the mansion's future Rockford Room

The decision to move Trinity Seminary and Trinity College to Bannockburn required a much greater financial commitment on the part of the mother denomination. To address this concern, a seventy-five-member Trinity Advancement Committee was created in the fall of 1961 under the chairmanship of businessman Paul Rosenquist, charged with the task of raising $3 million for the construction of eleven campus buildings: five educational units, two dormitories, an auditorium-recreation building, an administrative building, a student union, and an apartment building for married students. Despite intense effort to raise necessary funds, the committee's campaign fell far short of its ambitious goal. By October 1963, the committee had raised just over $618,000 in gifts and pledges.[24] Development of the Bannockburn campus was to move forward, but Trinity Seminary and Trinity College would face severe financial strain throughout the next decade.

KENNETH S. KANTZER AND HIS VISION

With Trinity Seminary now situated in its new home, President Norton turned his attention to carrying out the mandate to strengthen the school's

academic program. It appears that from the start, Norton had his eyes
on one specific person to provide leadership for this upgrade: Kenneth S.
Kantzer, professor of biblical and systematic theology at Wheaton College
and chairman of the department of Bible and Religious Education.[25]
Kantzer's academic training, personal character, and leadership qualities
made him particularly well-suited for directing a new theological venture.
Raised in a nominal Christian home, Kantzer experienced a dramatic
conversion to Christianity while a freshman at Ashland College in 1935.
After his undergraduate program, Kantzer studied history at Ohio State
University (MA, 1939), completed seminary training at Faith Theological
Seminary (BD and STM, 1943), and earned a PhD in philosophy and
religion at Harvard University (1950). From 1954–1955, he pursued post-
doctoral work in Europe, studying for a time with theologian Karl Barth
at the University of Basel. Appointed to the faculty of Wheaton College
in 1946, Kantzer soon emerged as an authority on the Reformer John
Calvin and as one of the leading evangelical theologians in the United
States. Colleagues and former students remember Kantzer as a gracious,
patient, and humble leader; a man of generous spirit; a voracious reader
and keen listener; a man committed to prayer; a "gentleman-scholar" who
would stand when women entered the room. Kantzer was also a devout
churchman. In the mid-1940s he had served several years in pastoral ministry in Rockport, Massachusetts. Shortly after moving to Wheaton, he
transferred his ministerial credentials to the Norwegian and Danish Free
Church Association. Thereafter he remained vitally concerned with local
church ministry and worked vigorously to promote evangelical Protestant
theology and witness in the United States and abroad.

Norton's plan to bring Kantzer to Trinity in the spring of 1963 seemed
far-fetched at best. The Kantzer family, including Kenneth's wife, Ruth,
and his teenage son, Dick, was well-established in the campus community
of Wheaton.[26] Many expected that Kantzer would be appointed graduate
dean once Merrill Tenney retired. Moreover, Kantzer had been awarded
a full-year sabbatical for the 1963–1964 school year to enable him to complete a book on Karl Barth's theology. Though Kantzer admired Trinity
Seminary's evangelical commitment, he saw the school as having "low
academic standards"—far inferior to Wheaton College. Thus, the first time
Norton approached Kantzer about the possibility of becoming Trinity's

Dr. Kenneth S. Kantzer, mid-1960s

new dean, Kantzer flatly turned down the invitation.[27] During these early encounters, however, Kantzer was given the opportunity to spell out his vision for theological education and, much to his surprise, found Norton and other EFCA leaders receptive, even enthusiastic.

What was this vision? For a number of years, Kantzer had become increasingly concerned about the near absence of high-quality evangelical education at the seminary level. Most seminaries in the United States had either abandoned their evangelical commitments or were lacking the intellectual and spiritual resources needed to respond to the challenges of the secular university and culture with a coherent and faithful presentation of biblical truth. At the same time, Kantzer believed that graduate-level seminaries were in a crucial position to shape future pastors who, in turn, would fortify the people in their churches—especially the young people—with a biblical world- and life-view that could address the reigning philosophies and social challenges of the second half of the twentieth century.[28] What kind of graduate seminary could best meet this challenge? Kantzer laid out his vision this way:

> Such a seminary must be of unquestionable orthodoxy—committed solidly, not only to Jesus Christ as the God-man, but also to

the authority of the Bible as the inerrant Word of God. ... It must also be evangelistic. What good does it do to train ministers in the things of God if they lose their hunger for lost souls while spending their years in a theological "cemetery"? A transformed life goes hand-in-hand with evangelical zeal. ... A seminary must also be Bible-centered in its curriculum, preparing men for a Biblical ministry of the preaching of the Word of God. Seminary students can learn all about the Bible and yet never really come to know the Bible. If we actually believe that the Bible is God's inspired Word, then we must be concerned to know and to preach it. Finally, a seminary should uphold high standards of Christian scholarship. Christian people rightly fear a false intellectualism which often lays hold of theological institutions and robs them of their power. ... No evangelical Christian, however, needs to fear true scholarship ... [for] true scholarship is one of God's prize gifts. ... Soldiers for Jesus Christ need the sharpest and finest weapons available.[29]

In sum, Kantzer believed that the church in the United States was in great need of an academically superior graduate seminary that was unswervingly faithful to orthodox Christianity, where biblical instruction was at the heart of the curriculum, where godly and well-trained professors formed students to be faithful biblical preachers and committed to the evangelistic mission of the church. This vision was founded on two bedrock convictions: that the holy Scripture, as the verbally inspired word of God, is without error in the original writings and entirely trustworthy in all that it affirms; and that the church must allow God's authoritative word to speak to the contemporary world and be relevant to it.[30] Kantzer rejected the idea that this was a novel or sectarian vision; rather it was a broad *ecumenical* vision, in line with the central convictions and priorities of historic Christianity, as found in the Bible, the early creeds, and the doctrinal confessions of the Protestant Reformation.[31]

THE VISION TAKES SHAPE

As Kantzer, Olson, and Norton continued to discuss Trinity Seminary during the spring of 1963, a blueprint gradually took shape to transform the small denominational school into a major academic institution serving the broader evangelical world. The leaders came under increasing conviction that God was providentially wedding Trinity's future to Kantzer's vision.[32] In late May, the Wheaton professor established four crucial preconditions for his becoming dean at Trinity that, if adopted, would significantly change the focus and direction of the seminary's academic program. These conditions were that (1) three new professors of national standing be hired immediately; (2) the seminary's dean represent the school at all meetings of the board of education of the EFCA; (3) the seminary have a budget separate from the college and administered by the seminary; and (4) the seminary faculty have freedom to solicit funds directly for the seminary.[33] These stipulations were discussed by denominational leaders in Crystal Lake, Illinois, on May 24, and approved by Olson, Norton, and chairman of the board of education Rev. Harry Evans in their meeting with Kantzer at O'Hare on May 31.

In addition, the parties agreed to a number of other provisions requested by Kantzer that would further shape the institutional DNA of the new school.[34] These commitments included to pay full professors salaries competitive with their colleagues at the best theological schools in the country, to seek accreditation in the American Association of Theological Schools,[35] to allow temporary and part-time faculty to teach at Trinity who did not agree with the school's premillennial position, to interpret the EFCA Statement of Faith so as not to exclude faculty holding a mid-tribulation or post-tribulation view of eschatology,[36] and, to change the name of the school to Trinity Evangelical Divinity School. Why was this name change desirable? In a letter to Olson in early June, Kantzer explained that the title "Trinity Seminary" was often confused with other seminaries of that name and was more suggestive of Anglican or Lutheran schools. By contrast, the proposed "Trinity Evangelical Divinity School" tied the seminary more directly to the name of the mother denomination; so too, the finest theological schools in the country were designated as "divinity schools" rather than "seminaries." Moreover, Kantzer noted, "The word evangelical is a magic word today and would have infinitely greater appeal to the interdenominational public than the name Trinity."[37] Perhaps most importantly, the change in name signaled that Trinity Seminary was to be transformed into a very different kind of school. This was to be a new day, a fresh start.

Given this strong affirmation from Norton and EFCA leadership, Kantzer formally accepted the invitation to become the new dean of Trinity Seminary in the first days of June 1963, confident that he had received "a Macedonian call from God himself for a great task to which I could give myself without reservation."[38] His name was recommended to the board of education and his candidacy endorsed at the EFCA annual conference several weeks later. The conference also approved releasing funds immediately to begin construction of married-student apartments and approved the new name for the school—Trinity Evangelical Divinity School (TEDS).[39]

The gravity of these changes, and the exciting opportunities that they presented, was not lost on Free Church members attending the conference. Kantzer's memorable statement that TEDS was to be "a love gift from the EFCA to the entire church of Jesus Christ" was reported throughout the church and became a guiding rationale for the founding of the school.[40] Norton's address to the delegates also captured the significance of the moment: "The seminary stands in a unique position to provide scholarly and spiritual training for the ministry of evangelical Christianity throughout the world and therefore can be expected to attract scores and hundreds of college and university men who love Jesus Christ."[41] As it turned out, Norton's predictions were realized sooner than anyone could have imagined.

TRINITY SEMINARY REBORN

The beginning of the new school year, and the birth of TEDS, was marked at a special convocation held on October 6, 1963, at First Presbyterian Church in Deerfield, Illinois.[42] Afterward, the several hundred guests, faculty, and students retired to the Bannockburn campus for the groundbreaking ceremony of two new married-student apartments. The convocation speaker on that hot October afternoon was the new Bible professor, Wilbur Smith, whose thirty-eight-minute address challenged students to affirm the deity and supremacy of Jesus Christ. "It would be better for Trinity Evangelical Divinity School to close today," he intoned, "rather than to send its graduates out without knowing their complete belief in the Son of God. We need to say as did the centurion, 'Surely thou art the Son of God.' " After the sermon, EFCA President Arnold T. Olson stood up and challenged faculty members to "know the Scriptures yourselves and then in turn to train the students in the use of those Scriptures." Olson then addressed the new dean: "The future of the EFCA is in a very real sense in the hands of you, Dr. Kantzer, and the members of your faculty." In his response, Kantzer pledged that, under his leadership, the divinity school would remain orthodox and Bible centered, and would endeavor to produce graduates with deep, personal knowledge of God and a commitment to the task of evangelism. Kantzer concluded his speech by assuring the audience that "I shall give every bit of mental and physical energy I have to give our young men the Word of God and to serve the EFCA and the entire evangelical world."

The 1963–1964 academic year brought with it dramatic changes. During the summer, the new dean worked quickly to secure three new full-time faculty members: Smith, considered by many to be the finest Bible teacher in the United States, was hired to teach English Bible; Walter Liefeld, who was finishing his PhD at Columbia University, was appointed to teach Greek New Testament; and Lloyd Perry, previously at Gordon Seminary, was hired as professor of practical theology.[43] Three other professors were hired on a part-time basis: Lacy Hall (pastoral counseling), Arthur Holmes (philosophy of religions), and Richard Longenecker (New Testament).[44]

Dr. Kantzer responds to the charge given at the divinity school convocation, October 6, 1963

These men were outstanding scholars and wholeheartedly committed to the EFCA statement of faith; they were also fine Christian men. As Kantzer explained to Free Church leaders: "These are giants of spiritual power and Christian scholarship. They are unequivocally committed to the standards of the Evangelical Free Church. They are uniquely equipped to prepare our young men for a great service to God, in our church and on the mission field."[45]

Announcement of the founding of TEDS in late summer 1963,
placed in *Christianity Today, Eternity,* and *Moody Monthly*

Although overall enrollment at the seminary during this first year remained somewhat modest, at seventy-three full-time students, the uptick in applications for the following school year was most encouraging—even dramatic. When classes began in October 1964, the student body had more than doubled. By that time, two new married-student apartments had been constructed (today known as North and South

Apartments), and bulldozers were preparing the ground for the seminary's first classroom and office unit, named the Peterson Academic Building. Students who witnessed the transition from the "old" seminary to the "new" divinity school recognized that Trinity was changing in significant ways. Rev. Howard Matson recalls that the new school year brought "an excitement to Trinity and theological education that we'd never seen." Dean Kantzer fostered "a new understanding of what it meant to be a godly conservative minister of Jesus Christ."[46] Rev. Clayton Lindgren remembers that Kantzer and the new faculty emphasized the importance of studying the word *and* the contemporary world, and of being current in the application of theology. All these changes constituted "a big upgrade—a step forward."[47]

MORE FACULTY—AND A NEW PRESIDENT

But this was only the beginning. Over the next several years, as the student population burgeoned on the Bannockburn campus, Kantzer attracted to TEDS some of the most notable evangelical scholars in the country. In the fall of 1964, the school welcomed to the faculty Robert Culver (systematic theology), John Warwick Montgomery (librarian; church history), Walter Kaiser (Old Testament), Richard Troup (Christian education),

TEDS Faculty, 1965. Second row, left to right: Richard Longenecker (New Testament), Paul Little (evangelism), Walter Liefeld (New Testament), Gleason Archer (Old Testament), Douglas Culver (Old Testament), J. Oliver Buswell (New Testament), John W. Montgomery (church history, director of library). First row, left to right: Kenneth Kantzer (dean), Lacy Hall (pastoral counseling), Lloyd Perry (practical theology), Robert Culver (systematic theology), Roy Thompson (reference librarian), Jerome Ficek (church history), Harry Evans (president).

Paul Little (visiting professor in evangelism), and J. Oliver Buswell (visiting professor in New Testament). The following year, Gleason Archer (Old Testament) and David Hesselgrave (missions) arrived. By the end of the decade, Trinity's academic arsenal had been further fortified by such faculty additions as Clark Pinnock (systematic theology), Herbert Kane (missions), Thomas McComiskey (Old Testament), Gary Collins (pastoral psychology), David Wells (church history), and John Gerstner (visiting professor in church history). In addition, Carl F. H. Henry, theologian and editor of *Christianity Today*, became a regular visitor to campus to deliver special lectures. In fall 1965, for example, he presented a lecture series titled "Current Trends in European Theology"; in the spring, his topic was "The Biblical Doctrine of God."[48]

Carl F. H. Henry

Carl Ferdinand Howard Henry (1913–2003) was one of the leading evangelical theologians and Christian leaders in twentieth-century America, and a regular visiting professor at Trinity Evangelical Divinity School.[49] Born on Long Island, New York, into an unbelieving family, Henry experienced a dramatic conversion to Christ at age twenty while he was working as a journalist for *The Smithtown Times*. Thereafter, he attended Wheaton College (where he met his wife, Helga), earned his ThD from Northern Baptist Theological Seminary (1942), and received his PhD in philosophy from Boston University in 1949. During his long and productive career, Henry applied his journalistic skills and his razor-sharp theological judgments to address the most urgent questions of contemporary culture and evangelical Christian faith. His most notable writings were *The Uneasy Conscience of Modern Fundamentalism* (1947), in which Henry calls conservative Christians to leave behind their intellectual isolation and develop a comprehensive worldview to address political issues and social problems from a biblical perspective; and his six-volume *God, Revelation and Authority* (1976–1983). Henry took part in the founding of the National Association of Evangelicals in 1942, was the first dean of the original faculty of Fuller Theological Seminary from 1946–1956, and helped launch the evangelical periodical *Christianity Today* in 1956, where he served as chief editor for twelve years. In the final decades of his life, Henry visited TEDS frequently to teach classes, speak in chapel, and interact with students and faculty. In 1985, he donated his twenty-thousand-volume library to Trinity's Rolfing Library. In that same year, Trinity named the major addition to the Rolfing Library after Henry, in recognition of his strategic place in American evangelicalism and global Christianity. Speaking at the dedication of this addition, Henry noted: "If we are to make a turning-impact, young evangelicals must become lovers of books: and of the truth; we need more tough-minded scholars to do battle with the intellectual Philistines of our day as Augustine and Luther and Calvin did

Carl F. H. Henry
in the 1990s

in theirs."[50] Today, the papers of Henry are housed in the library's archives.

What attracted men of such caliber to come to Bannockburn in the mid-1960s? Although many reasons might be given, certainly chief among them was Kantzer's personal influence as well as his theological vision and its potential impact on American Christianity. Liefeld, who had first encountered Kantzer at InterVarsity conferences in New York City in the early 1960s, was impressed with his handling of tough theological issues and the way he treated students. "I wanted to be where he was," Liefeld remembered.[51] Archer, who left Fuller Theological Seminary and came to Trinity in 1965, did so in large part because of Kantzer's vision for theological education: "Ken Kantzer indicated to me in the early 1960s that he had a deep concern for the trend away from the inspired view of Scripture in many seminaries. He had a vision of building a seminary, keeping the evangelical stance, while opening it to all denominations. He felt the basics for this lay in an ideal curriculum (where Greek and Hebrew are essential) and a good nucleus of evangelical scholars on the faculty. These are not unlike the ideals coming out of the Reformation."[52] This vision of a solid evangelical

Gleason Archer,
mid-1960s

school that was confessional (adhering closely to the Statement of Faith of the EFCA), ecumenical (drawing students and faculty from many different faith traditions), culturally engaged, and committed to first-rate Christian scholarship was what attracted Archer and other evangelical scholars to Trinity.

In many ways, the emergence of TEDS as an academic heavyweight in the second half of the 1960s signaled the growing confidence and intellectual prominence of evangelicals in America in general. For conservative Christians who had long been caricatured as boorish and backwoods, the

Clark Pinnock with student James Akinola, early 1970s

revitalized seminary, with its excellent faculty, seemed the perfect antidote for a long-standing intellectual inferiority complex. Moreover, some conservative evangelicals now looked at Trinity as a kind of replacement for Fuller Theological Seminary, which had abandoned its commitment to the doctrine of biblical inerrancy in 1962.[53] Consequently, leaders of the EFCA and Trinity regularly noted and celebrated the fine academic pedigree of the new faculty as well as their scholarly achievements. In describing the school to Free Church constituents in 1965, Kantzer noted that TEDS "maintains high scholastic standards," with a faculty "possessing fifteen earned doctorates from Harvard University, Columbia University, University of Chicago, University of Edinburgh, University of Strasburg, Northwestern University, and others."[54] In a similar vein, presidential reports to the EFCA described the several hundred books authored by faculty members and expressed gratitude to God for bringing "so many excellent minds and influential and dedicated 'teachers of preachers' to the divinity school."[55]

Although proud of his faculty and their accomplishments, Kantzer made it clear that academic achievement, scholarly reputation, and teaching proficiency were not enough. All full-time faculty members were required to affirm the EFCA twelve-point Statement of Faith *without reservation*— including provisions regarding the inerrancy of Scripture and the premillennial return of Jesus Christ. Those who could not do this were expected to resign. From Kantzer's perspective, the future orthodoxy of TEDS depended on strict subscription to the school's doctrinal position. Theological integrity was always more important than academic respectability.[56]

The growth of TEDS in the mid-1960s was not without its casualties, including Norton himself. With exploding enrollments and mounting deficits, EFCA officials became increasingly frustrated by aspects of Norton's leadership style. On February 1, 1964, the EFCA board of education passed a secret resolution stating that "the expanded program of Trinity will require a stronger leadership" and that "change is now required."[57] Later that month, the board requested Norton to resign from his post effective in August, which he agreed to do—though he later expressed deep hurt by the "cold" and "hard-hearted" manner in which he was dismissed without due consultation.[58] The following summer, Rev. Harry Evans, pastor of the Arlington Heights Free Church and chairman of the board of education, was appointed by the annual conference as the fourteenth president of Trinity College and TEDS.

The Trinity Board of Directors, 1976. Back back row, from left to right: Rev. Harry Evans (future president of Trinity College), Rev. Bernie Fosmark, Rev. Wes Engstrom, Rev. Larue Lindquist, Rev. Wes Carlson (partially seated), unknown, Rev. Paul Thompson, Rev. LaRue Thorwall, Rev. Ken Meyer (future president of TEDS and Trinity College), unknown, Dr. Robert Hanson, Mr. Loo, Rev. Thomas McDill, unknown, unknown, Mr. Joseph Horness. Seated front row, from left to right: Dr. Gordon Johnson, Mr. Arnold Peterson, Mr. Ray Carlson, Rev. Arley Bragg, Rev. Robert Fallt, Rev. A. T. Olson (executive president of the EFCA), unknown. Photograph and information provided by Mrs. Rogene Nelson.

STUDENTS AND PROFESSORS

A headline in the *Evangelical Beacon* from the summer of 1967 proclaimed Trinity as the "fastest growing seminary in America"—and it was.[59] During the first eight years of its existence, TEDS increased in size nearly eight-fold, from a total enrollment of 73 students in 1963–1964 to 534 students in 1970–1971.[60] Enrollment increases would have been even higher had there been more space for new students. In the fall of 1967, only 125 students were admitted, out of 300 applicants.[61] What kinds of students came to TEDS during the 1960s? A closer look at the student body in 1966–1967 provides some answers. Around three-quarters of the students who enrolled at the divinity school in that academic year received their undergraduate training at a Bible college or Christian liberal arts college. The student body was overwhelmingly male, with no women in the BD (MDiv) program and only nine in the MA programs. Though Trinity was attracting a larger number of international students, in 1966–1967 the number was still relatively small, at twenty-seven students from nine different countries. In terms of denominational affiliation, students came from many different Protestant traditions, including Evangelical Free, Baptist, independent churches, various Presbyterian and Reformed churches, Assembly of God, Methodist, Evangelical Covenant, Lutheran, and Mennonite.[62]

Although the reasons that students came to Trinity in the 1960s were varied, clearly a primary motivation was the high-powered professors whom Kantzer had assembled on the Bannockburn campus. Faculty members such as Wilbur Smith, John Warwick Montgomery, Clark Pinnock, Walter Kaiser, Lloyd Perry, and John Gerstner were men of large personality whose books and public ministries were admired throughout the evangelical world. In particular, Montgomery was the "ultimate star in the evangelical orbit in the 1960s" as he brilliantly defended orthodox Christian faith in public and radio debates against all comers, whether Muslim imams, "Death of God" theology advocate Thomas J. J. Altizer, liberal theologians, or atheist Madalyn Murray O'Hair.[63]

In the early 1970s Montgomery was joined by Norman Geisler and Paul Feinberg, who helped make Trinity into a major center for training a new generation of Christian philosophers and apologists, including William Lane Craig, John Ankerberg, and Paul Copan. Word about the new divinity school also spread as Trinity professors such as Kantzer, Richard Longenecker, Lacy Hall, and David Hesselgrave traveled widely, speaking to campus ministry groups, at Christian camps, and at missionary conferences. Evangelism professor Paul Little played an especially important role in attracting students to Trinity. As staff evangelist for

John Warwick Montgomery (left) and David Wells (right), 1971

InterVarsity Christian Fellowship, Little was passionately convinced of the transformative power of the gospel, and he proclaimed this message

Paul Little, early 1970s

on university campuses and at student conferences on almost a weekly basis. His book *Know Why You Believe* (1967) became essential reading for many Christian college students. Little served as the director of the Urbana Missionary Convention at the University of Illinois in December 1970, an event attended by more than 12,000 students.[64]

But if famous apologists such as Montgomery and popular campus speakers such as Little attracted students to Trinity, it was frequently other members of the faculty who played the most important role in shaping their minds, nurturing their souls, and preparing them for Christian ministry. Former students and colleagues during these early years remember with appreciation the intellectual richness and spiritual depth of many of the courses taught by Trinity professors. They speak of Smith's spellbinding expositions of biblical texts; Kaiser's persuasiveness and sparkling humor in the classroom; Longenecker's well-organized and "beautiful" lectures on the New Testament; Archer's formal erudition and remarkable command of (more than twenty-five) foreign languages; Liefeld's deep piety and concern for students; McComiskey's statesman-like lectures, precise elocution, and warm humanity; Kantzer's rich and insightful prayers that seemed to part the heavens.[65] Statements made in class were often remembered long afterward, shaping how students understood Christian life and ministry. One early student remembered Carl Henry challenging his students to spend more time "over the books and on their knees."[66] Other maxims and memorable statements were treasured as well. Lloyd Perry: "This is not the only way to preach, but it is the only way I know how to preach." Walter Kaiser: "Keep your finger on the text." John Gerstner: "Life gets harder and harder. But He gets better and better."

Dr. Kantzer in the Classroom— A Tribute by Duane Elmer (1969 Graduate)

Kenneth Kantzer teaching

As a scholar and classroom instructor, Kenneth Kantzer modeled Christian intellectual virtues that he hoped would characterize all Trinity faculty members. Duane Elmer remembers taking a theology course from Kantzer in the late 1960s in which the professor spent several class periods articulating the view of revelation defended by liberal theologian John Baillie. So compelling was Kantzer's presentation of Baillie's position that Elmer began to assume that Kantzer shared Baillie's view. Elmer recalls, "Just as I was getting concerned about Dr. Kantzer's own orthodoxy, he started class in a very different tone. 'We have been looking at Dr. Baillie's view of revelation these past weeks. You need to know that he is a fine gentleman and that I pray for him regularly. I do not know his standing before God'—and at this point Kantzer's eyes watered noticeably and his voice turned more tender, more personal, more pastoral as he continued—'but he is close to a real faith and a biblical view of revelation. Now, we will begin to build a view of revelation on the Scripture itself.'" According to Elmer, this incident significantly shaped his view of Christian scholarship thereafter: "That day I realized I was sitting under an extraordinary person: a scholar and a gentleman. I had found the gold standard for the nurturing of the intellect, the pursuit of truth while embracing the person."[67]

BUILDINGS, BUDGETS, BOOKS

In fall 1965, Trinity College joined Trinity Evangelical Divinity School on the Bannockburn campus. By that time, the dirt road through the forest had been replaced by a paved two-lane road that divided the seminary complex from the new college buildings.[68] The divinity school campus on the east side of the road consisted of five primary buildings: the mansion, North and South Apartments, the Gundersen Apartments, and the Peterson Academic Building. The next year, a "temporary" block building was constructed on the east side of the pond to house single students while the quad dormitories were under construction. The first wing of the quad was finally completed in December 1966, after long construction delays.[69]

President Norton and Dr. Kantzer
view the progress of construction, 1963

Along with the mansion, the Peterson building now served as the academic heart of the seminary campus, equipped with five offices for faculty, a secretary office, restrooms, five classrooms, and one seminar room. The classrooms were separated by partitions so they could be converted into the seminary chapel each day.[70] As welcome as these physical improvements were, they did not keep pace with skyrocketing enrollments during the 1960s and early 1970s. "We are still terribly crowded for space," President Evans complained in a report to EFCA leaders during this period.[71] In the fall of 1968, 150 married students were on a waiting list for on-campus apartments.[72] Chapel services were frequently crowded, and students had to sit on the floor. Faculty offices were shuttled to various corners of the campus, in the Peterson building, in the basement of the mansion, and even in married-student apartments.

Despite the excitement created by exploding enrollments, the financial situation at the divinity school and college was always precarious, a hair's breadth away from insolvency. Through the tireless efforts of Kantzer, Evans, and Trinity's administrative team, and the remarkable generosity of supporting churches and donors, the school operated in the black from 1965 through 1969—an achievement the *Evangelical Beacon* described as "The Miracle at Bannockburn."[73] During these years, as many as 136 Free Church congregations supported Trinity by joining the "$10 per member per year program."[74] Unrestricted giving to Trinity increased year by year, from around $310,000 in 1964–1965 to around $575,000 five years later. Writing to constituents in 1967, Evans expressed his amazement and gratitude for their generosity and God's rich provision. "This is the Lord's doing and it is marvelous in our eyes!"[75]

At the same time, Kantzer regularly reminded Free Church leaders and laypeople that TEDS was *their* school and needed their continued financial support. In an article in the *Evangelical Beacon*, Kantzer spelled out this relationship with exceptional candor: "In a very real sense, the future of Trinity Evangelical Divinity School rests in the hands of the Evangelical Free Church. In the providence of God the reverse is probably true also: the future of the Evangelical Free Church of America rests in the hands of Trinity Evangelical Divinity School. The Evangelical Free Church and Trinity Seminary stand or fall together."[76]

The urgent need to build new buildings on campus caused additional financial strain and demanded new revenue sources. Thus, in 1966, the Free Church launched an ambitious three-year capital fundraising program called the United Development Crusade to raise money for capital expenditures at the denomination's national headquarters and three schools.[77] Based on projected income, Trinity moved forward with the construction of several new buildings, including a gymnasium-auditorium and a much-needed college women's dormitory. The Mel Larson Gymnasium was completed in the fall of 1966 and became home to athletic events as well as special college and divinity school convocations.[78]

These building projects strained Trinity's relationship with the small village of Bannockburn, whose residents were understandably concerned that the school's meteoric growth would increase traffic congestion and require village expenditures in education and for police and fire protection. A seemingly endless number of public hearings and zoning disputes as well as bureaucratic red tape led to significant construction delays and cost overruns. A case in point was the seminary library. In summer 1967, the James E. Rolfing family gave the divinity school the first installment of what would become a $400,000 gift toward a new library.[79] Soon, architectural plans for a two-story library (with eleven faculty offices and a two-hundred-seat auditorium) were drawn up, and a groundbreaking ceremony was held on April 27, 1969.[80] After several years of false starts, delays, and financial setbacks, a redesigned (and much smaller) Rolfing Library was finally completed and dedicated in November 1973.[81]

Of course, there was a library at TEDS before the construction of Rolfing Library. In the earliest years, a small library of several hundred books was located in the basement of the mansion. In fall of 1964, the library—now numbering around seven thousand volumes—was moved to the basements of the North and South Apartments. The next year, it was moved yet again to the Peterson Academic Building. In January 1967, two hundred students and faculty participated in a "book moving day," transporting the fourteen-thousand-volume library to the newly renovated block building (now named the Gundersen Building) on the east side of the pond—the volunteers were "paid" a cup of coffee for their labors.[82] Three years later, the library was moved a fourth time, to a newly constructed receiving center called the Aldeen Building on the north side of campus.

Regardless of its location, the seminary library offered little space and few books. Trinity's first part-time librarian, John Warwick Montgomery, stated the problem bluntly in 1965:

> Our seminary hopes to become a Harvard of evangelical seminaries. Yet, the Harvard Divinity School has over 200,000 volumes. Union Seminary in New York has 350,000 books. Can we hope to do our job of training evangelical Christians to proclaim Christ's pure word in a darkling age of unbelief and rationalism if

we, in contrast, offer a pitiful fare of learning to our students? Do the potential leaders of conservative Christianity in the next half century deserve less than the best?[83]

The problem of the library became all the more pressing during the next decade as Trinity pursued accreditation through the American Association of Theological Schools. Officials made it clear that final accreditation was in large part dependent on Trinity having a permanent library facility and more books.[84] Thanks to the timely purchase of two theological libraries containing twenty-seven thousand volumes in 1970 (at a cost of $38,750) and the donation of books from Carl F. H. Henry's large personal library, Trinity's library exceeded fifty thousand volumes by 1973.[85] In that same year, as construction on Rolfing Library neared completion, TEDS received final accreditation with the American Association of Theological Schools.

Walter Kaiser with students
in Rolfing Library

COMMUNITY LIFE

The Trinity seminary community during the 1960s and early 1970s was a vibrant and active one. The snack bar in the basement of the mansion was usually bustling with students who came to read their mail, engage in conversations with friends, or meet with professors. In addition to daily chapel services, students participated in such extracurricular activities as faculty-advisee groups, prayer partners, student council, student missionary fellowship, and choir. Many students participated in a variety of intramural sports. For several years an "official" seminary basketball team competed in the Seminary Chicago League, even achieving an undefeated season in the winter of 1972.[86] Likewise, broomball and hockey games were played at the municipal ice skating rink (the "Dome") that was located on school property beginning in 1970. Single male seminary students who lived on campus often gravitated toward the women's college dormitory, hoping to interact with some of the young women enrolled at the college. One former student fondly remembers the college-seminary hymn sings that took place in the lounge of Johnson Hall on Sunday evenings in the early 1970s—the hymn "Great Is Thy Faithfulness" was a favorite at the gatherings.[87]

The academic calendar was punctuated by other special events, such as the annual Christmas party, the faculty-student talent show every February, and the spring banquet, but also by more spontaneous activities. Single students in the quad who announced their engagements were sometimes carried by their dorm-mates and "baptized" in the pond behind the mansion.[88] The pond was the venue for other pranks and exploits. In fall 1971, for example, divinity students and faculty organized the Great Sculling Contest, where a faculty canoe captained by Professor O. J. Brown challenged a student crew to four laps around the pond. After

A sign on campus

taking a commanding lead, the faculty vessel was attacked and swamped by three students swimming from shore. The dramatic race ended with the two canoes locked together at the finish line, showered by water balloons from the cheering crowd.[89]

The wives of Trinity's professors played an important role in building community spirit on campus. In the mid-1960s, Mrs. Wilbur Smith, along with Ruth Kantzer, Olive Liefeld, and Marge Kaiser, was instrumental in starting the Clothes Horse ministry, providing used clothing and household goods to needy student families. The original home of the Clothes Horse was in a large safe in the basement of the mansion; later it was moved to the basement of the North Apartments. Over the years, Ruth Kantzer, Olive Liefeld, and a host of other faculty wives sponsored and lent their support to a student wives' group, known as the "Seminettes" (later called Trinity Wives' Fellowship), which met regularly for guest speakers, fellowship, and mutual encouragement. In addition to their weekly activities, during the early 1970s, the Seminettes hosted a number of weekend retreats for student wives and their spouses, featuring such well-known speakers as Gladys Hunt, Elisabeth Eliot, and Paul Meier.[90] Faculty wives also served the Trinity community in other important, though often forgotten, ways: by gathering to pray, by opening their homes to students and their families (Ruth Kantzer's lemon meringue pie was famous), by mentoring female students, and by encouraging and supporting their husbands. Ruth Kantzer's statement, "Trinity has just been our life," was true for many other faculty couples as well.[91]

In addition to their studies, it was expected that all students would be involved each week in Christian ministry off-campus.[92] These assignments provided students an opportunity to sharpen their ministry skills, explore ministry callings, and serve area churches. One article in the *Evangelical Beacon* from this period reported that one hundred divinity school students taught Sunday school in local churches each week, sixty-eight students served as youth workers, a dozen students were active as Boys' Brigade leaders, fifteen students were full-time ministers, thirteen students

TEDS chapel service in the Gundersen Building, early 1970s. Professors in center foreground (left to right): Arthur Johnston, John Stott, Kenneth Kantzer.

were assistant pastors, and other students served on staff with Young Life, Youth for Christ, InterVarsity Christian Fellowship, and Awana.[93] A less traditional ministry was started by John Ankerberg, who in 1969 created a half-dozen coffeehouses in the Chicago area where young people could meet, hear music, and learn more about Christianity.[94] Additionally, during the 1960s and 1970s, two church congregations were planted near campus in large part through the leadership and participation of Trinity professors, administrators, and students.[95]

STUDENT ACTIVISM

The late 1960s and early 1970s was a period of violent demonstrations on many university campuses around the United States, as students protested the military draft, the Vietnam War, the assassination of Martin Luther King Jr., and the Kent State massacres. TEDS was in no way immune from such student agitation and political activism—"Virtually all of us were activists of one sort or another," remembers Mark Senter.[96] Students regularly congregated in the coffee shop in the basement of the mansion for loud and animated conversations about urban ministry, war and peace, racial justice, and Black theology.[97] Many students attended class barefoot, wearing ratty T-shirts, sporting long hair and bushy beards—prompting professor Gilbert Peterson once to quip: "I've never taught so much hair in my life."[98] Students frequently had strong opinions on issues ranging from politics to ethics to theology and enjoyed vigorous classroom debates. Perry Downs remembers: "If someone said, 'Good morning,' three students would want to debate it!"[99]

In spring 1968, a group of seminary students mobilized to provide material and physical assistance to victims of the riots in the wake of Martin Luther King Jr.'s assassination.[100] Some divinity school students probably also attended the memorial service in honor of the "Kent State Four" held at Trinity College in May 1970.[101] Nevertheless, the Bannockburn campus remained largely isolated from the explosive student demonstrations of the period—until Jim Wallis and several members of the People's Christian Coalition enrolled as students at TEDS in fall 1971. A former radical student leader at Michigan State University, Wallis, along with his coalition, was mobilizing young people "to create radical Christian consciousness, commitment, and action" in protest against an

American church that, they believed, had been co-opted by the values and lifestyle of secular culture. The group's magazine, titled *The Post-American*, promoted this agenda; the cover of the first issue of the magazine depicted Jesus with a crown of thorns on his head, draped in an American flag. The headline read, "... and they crucified Him."[102]

TEDS students, early 1970s

During the 1971–1972 school year, Wallis and his People's Christian Coalition staged a number of protests on the seminary campus. On one occasion, they paraded bare-chested through campus carrying a casket with the name TRINITY emblazoned on the side of it, and then they buried the casket in a "grave" dug in front of the mansion. Another time, using scissors, they excised from a Bible all the passages referring to God's concern for the poor; they then waved the tattered Bible in a chapel service, crying out, "Trinity, this is your Bible!" Student agitation reached a high point when members of the coalition organized a sit-in protest in the mansion. As demonstrators mounted the staircase to occupy the administrative offices on the second floor, they met Dean Kantzer coming down the stairs, who said, "I have only one request. Please don't harm my violets."[103]

Occasional outbursts of student activism—and Jim Wallis's presence at TEDS—raised concerns among some conservative Christians that the school was becoming "liberal" in its political commitments. Already in 1969, President Evans attempted to correct this misperception in an *Evangelical Beacon* article titled "Is Trinity Going Liberal?"[104] Two years later, Kantzer found it necessary to reassure friends of the school who feared that TEDS endorsed the views of the People's Christian Coalition and its controversial magazine. Writing to one such constituent in October 1971, Kantzer assured him that the protesters were in no way representative of the student body as a whole, nor was their provocative message shared by Trinity's faculty or administration. The protesters were allowed to remain on campus, he reported, because they avowed personal faith in Christ, were committed to the authority of Scripture, and wished to win university students—even leftists—to a saving faith in Christ. To have dismissed them from Trinity would have meant thrusting them to more liberal schools.

Kantzer explained further that, though Trinity did not usually take a formal position on political questions, most faculty were grateful for the freedoms they enjoyed as Americans, even as they recognized that "our country, in many ways, is not a Christian country and that there is rampant materialism throughout the U.S. that has even infiltrated the nominal Christian Church." Ultimately, Trinity's priority rested with gospel proclamation rather than patriotism or campaigns for social betterment. "We would like our students to find their supreme concern in the preaching of the Biblical message as a witness to Christ, rather than to the social benefits that in some cases may even be good in themselves."[105]

FINANCIAL CRISIS—AND
THE PARTING OF WAYS

After five years of relative financial stability, in August 1971, a mild economic recession, mounting inflation, rising educational costs, and (perhaps) donor fatigue spelled an end to balanced budgets at Trinity. The overall operational deficit for the fiscal year was over $400,000. Around the same time, President Evans was informed that income projected from the United Development Crusade would be $350,000 below expectation.[106] Compounding the problem, the Trinity Opportunity Program—a campaign that attempted to raise $1.5 million by selling ten-year certificates at 6 percent—had never gained traction with investors. By September,

Trinity's cumulative deficit was $1.5 million; cash flow required that the school pay creditors $700,000 by the end of January 1972 or declare bankruptcy and close its doors.

Evans immediately ordered that a quarter-million dollars be cut from the current 1971–1972 budget and imposed a hiring freeze. In a desperate appeal to supporters, the president begged for support for the Trinity Opportunity Program and issued a dire warning: "Let there be no mistake, my friends, your schools are hanging in the balance."[107] In the meantime, EFCA officials, watching the crisis unfold, decided to step in. On October 2, 1971, the denomination's executive committee appointed a three-member board of regents that was given authority to take over the administration of the school. In response, on October 13, President Evans and all of Trinity's administrative leaders—with the exception of Kenneth Kantzer—submitted their resignations (effective August 1972) to protest this action and to dramatize the gravity of the situation.[108]

The announced resignation of Evans in mid-October 1971 signaled the beginning of one of the most dramatic chapters in Trinity's history. At an emergency meeting convened by EFCA president Arnold T. Olson on October 24, seventy-eight laymen and laywomen from all over the country met in Bannockburn to discuss the crisis and offer their assistance. By the end of the meeting, the group had requested that Evans reconsider his resignation, had pledged cash gifts of $136,000, and had promised to raise more than $220,000 in loans for the Trinity Opportunity Program.[109] Two weeks later, the board of education met and refused to accept Evans's resignation. The president gave three conditions for withdrawing his announced resignation: outside consultants must be called in to assess the present financial crisis; EFCA churches, pastors, and laypeople must henceforth show support for Trinity; and the executive boards of the EFCA and Trinity must examine the structural relationship between the schools and the denomination and make a recommendation to the upcoming annual conference.

During the next three months, the *Evangelical Beacon* orchestrated a massive campaign of prayer and financial support for Trinity. More than 180 EFCA churches and many, many private individuals pledged their support or sent checks big and small. Seminary students took up an emergency collection to assist their cash-strapped school. A TEDS alumnus, serving as a missionary in Colombia, sent a contribution along with a telegram that read: "Dear Trinity: Here is my gift to help Trinity meet the current expenses. I am thankful for the training I received there and know it is helping me to be a better missionary here in Colombia, South America. *Yo tengo solamente una palabra por Trinity: ADELANTE!* (I have only one word for Trinity: Forward!)."[110] When the fateful deadline of January 31 arrived, contributions to the Trinity Opportunity Program along with unrestricted gifts of more than $400,000 enabled Trinity to pay its creditors and avoid insolvency. This flood of support continued through the remainder of the fiscal year, with unrestricted giving exceeding $950,000 and 120 churches committing to Trinity's "$15 per member per year program."[111] God, through the generous gifts of his people, had saved Trinity College and TEDS.

In retrospect the financial crisis of 1971–1972 was crucial in shaping Trinity's future in a number of ways. The crisis laid bare deep personal and philosophical differences between EFCA president Arnold T. Olson and Trinity president Evans. So too, Kantzer's refusal to resign along with Evans and his administrative team in October caused a "breach of confidence" between the two men; in the months that followed, Evans attempted, and nearly succeeded, to have Kantzer dismissed from the dean's office.[112]

Most importantly, the crisis revived questions about whether or not the EFCA had the resources to sponsor a premier theological school *and* a Christian college. In fall 1973, a group of educational consultants was hired to study the structural and financial relationship between Trinity and its sponsoring denomination. In its report issued in April 1974, the commission noted that despite the school's fiscal frugality, the lack of endowment, limited denominational resources, and a suffocating debt service threatened Trinity's mission and future existence. The best solution, the report stated, was that "Trinity College be made an autonomous, independently governed, but Free Church-affiliated institution—while the Divinity School maintains its current relationship to and governance by the Free Church."[113] It was hoped that by making Trinity College a non-denominational Christian college, it would receive greater financial support and attract more students from the broader evangelical community.

Accordingly, on April 6, 1974, President Evans and Trinity's executive board recommended that the college should be divested from the divinity school and the denomination.[114] Later that summer, after a vigorous floor debate, delegates to the EFCA annual conference voted overwhelmingly to approve this recommendation. Hence, when classes commenced in the fall quarter of 1974, Trinity was no longer a single institution but two different schools with different presidents and separate budgets. The main road on campus dividing the college from the divinity school had never seemed wider.

Chapter 4

A Christian Liberal Arts College (1957–1996)

Bradley J. Gundlach

I n the nearly forty years from 1957 to 1996, the college experienced tre-
mendous growth and change. It was of course a generation of change in
America and the world, as even a fleeting mental picture of the difference
between the Eisenhower and Clinton years will attest. Youth protests, the
Civil Rights Movement, failure in Vietnam, a presidential resignation,
Supreme Court decisions limiting school prayer and legalizing abortion,

Trinity's sign in 1967—cover of the annual Trinity
issue of the *Evangelical Beacon*

the rise of the Christian Right and the Moral Majority, the end of the Cold War and the rise of terrorism—these developments and others made the last decades of the twentieth century both a tumultuous and an invigorating time to train Christian students to take on the world.

Among the unstable things about those years was the relationship between the college and the Free Church. Trinity's institutions blossomed, but the cost of growth outran the commitment of the EFCA churches to support them both, especially during the economic "stagflation" of the second Nixon term. The stresses of the larger culture added to the EFCA's ambivalence about its college, and the combination of financial, ideological, and lifestyle concerns led the church, which had earlier explicitly decided to prioritize the seminary over the college, to cut the college free for nearly a decade. During those independent years, Trinity College gained a reputation as one of the most progressive Christian schools in the nation—attractive and exciting to many young evangelicals, but worrisome to others. Renewed financial woes brought the church to the rescue, and under the leadership of Kenneth Kantzer the college was set on a path the conservative EFCA constituency could believe in. There followed a period of rebuilding and diversification that culminated in a new joint entity, Trinity International University.

Choir President, Quartet, Basketball, Digest Staff

BERNARD LUNDSTROM, B.A., Bible
Loves Park, Illinois
"Let no man deceive himself. If any man among you seemeth to be wise in this world, let him become a fool, that he may be wise."
I Corinthians 3:18

ALBERT E. PEPPERS, B.A., Bible
"For, brethren, ye have been called unto liberty; only use not liberty for an occasion to the flesh, but by love serve one another." Galatians 5:13

JEAN POTTER, B.A., Elementary Education
Regina, Kentucky
"All the paths of the Lord are mercy and truth unto such as keep his covenant and his testimonies." Psalms 25:10

EDWARD M. UNDERWOOD, B.A., Bible
Big Rock, Illinois
"And truly, if they had been mindful of that country from whence they came out, they might have had opportunity to have returned." Hebrews 11:15

Graduating seniors, 1958

These were dramatic years for the college—soul-searching years, identity-morphing years—challenging years, with earnest believers disagreeing sometimes deeply as to how the college ought to serve the church and the world.

FROM BIBLE COLLEGE TO LIBERAL ARTS COLLEGE: "AN EDUCATION FOR LIFE"

POISED FOR GROWTH

The *Evangelical Beacon* announced the election of H. Wilburt Norton as president of Trinity Seminary and Bible College (TSBC) in January 1957. His presidency marked a new era, enhancing the seminary program, developing the college "into a full-fledged liberal arts curriculum," and moving the campus "from the run-down inner city location to the spacious site at suburban Bannockburn," wrote Trinity historian and insider Calvin Hanson.[1] A few years earlier Norton, as dean, with Acting President Madsen, had launched the college's first liberal arts majors: French, Spanish, humanities, and music, in conjunction with the new and

H. Wilbert Norton, president

timely major in elementary education. These programs attracted more students than the traditional Bible course did. The 1957 TSBC yearbook, *The Trinitarian*, shows fifteen graduating college seniors: three majors in Christian education, two in missions—and *ten* in elementary education. Soon the college would graduate its first liberal arts majors as well.

The times were auspicious for this liberal arts vision of a Christian college. The EFCA membership by the 1950s was joining other ethnic churches in entering the American middle-class mainstream, moving beyond working-class unconcern for higher cultural attainments. Some in the pews, eager to keep Trinity a Bible college, questioned the value of liberal arts education and worried about its potentially

secularizing tendency. But many EFCA
leaders cordially believed in the value of
liberal education to fit the Christian for
responsible participation in the public
square, and dearly treasured the opportunity to carry the gospel to all areas of
life. The Free Church's core commitment to evangelism dovetailed with the
Cold War sense of competition against
communism for the hearts and minds of
the future. Roy Thompson, editor of the
Evangelical Beacon and Evangelist, cited
an East German official who urged his
fellow communists to capture "the citadel

Violet Youngberg,
dean of women

of learning ... at any price." In view of such dedication by the secularistic,
atheistic Eastern bloc, shame on evangelicals for their comparative indifference to the crucial importance of training Christian young people!

Visiting missionary and TSBC instructor in anthropology Monroe
Sholund urged, "With present figures of population 'explosion' before
us, ... the need for accredited, thoroughly evangelical colleges will not
come tomorrow—it is on top of us NOW." Indeed, the swelling numbers
of elementary school children presented a wonderful opportunity and
challenge, argued education professor Warren Franzen. He described the
public school as "a mission field worthy of highly skilled Christians who
have dedicated their lives to God's service. And what a mission field it is!
Forty million children eager to learn from and follow the example set by
their teachers."[2] When the Roman Catholic Church opened its African
mission schools to Protestant teachers, this straightforward tie to foreign
missions, always a core Free Church commitment, furthered the appeal
of an education program at the college.

Soon Trinity added a program to train high school teachers, and with
it new majors in English and social science. President Norton announced,
"There has been a concerted effort to make the Lord Jesus Christ relevant
and meaningful in all courses offered—an 'Education for Life.' " By 1960
the school changed its name: it was now Trinity College, dropping the
word "Bible." The change meant not loss of commitment to Scripture, but

a broadening of the mission of the college to address the intersection of
faith and learning across the disciplines. And the change, together with
baby boomers entering their college years, brought growth: 270 students
in 1959, 403 by 1966.

Graduation, 1960

Beginning in 1957 the college had its own dean: the young and energetic Gunnar Urang, "with a passion for integrating Bible truth and the
liberal arts."[3] Under his leadership and that of his successor, Ed Neteland,
the college faculty grew in numbers and in the attainment of higher-level
degrees. Of the nine college faculty in 1957, none held a doctorate, five
held a master's degree, and four a bachelor's. In 1966 there were twelve
faculty just in the humanities, four of whom held a PhD.[4]

The Trinity Bible College of 1957 was a cozy, largely homogeneous
community of unabashedly Christian students drawn very largely from
the EFCA. The sense of belonging, and the sense of church ownership,
was very strong. Though the graduating class numbered only fifteen, the
other classes totaled 177, a clear sign of an upward enrollment trend. One
of the most conspicuous activities was the Student Missions Fellowship
(SMF), a staple at the college for decades. That year its members included

five foreign students from Portugal, Jordan, Mexico, and Norway, the fruit of EFCA missionary presence in those places. Their presence contributed to the missions and evangelism emphasis that was a hallmark of the Free Church and its schools. Every student was considered a member of the Student Missions Fellowship. A world map with the locations of EFCA missionaries was a constant reminder. Student-led prayer groups, organized by continent, met weekly to uphold the work. Each year a Foreign Missions Institute replaced classes for at least part of a week, as missionaries spoke in augmented chapel programs, dined with students, and urged them to consider whether God was calling them into missionary service.[5] Missions was of course one of the longstanding majors offered by Trinity since its beginnings as a Bible institute.

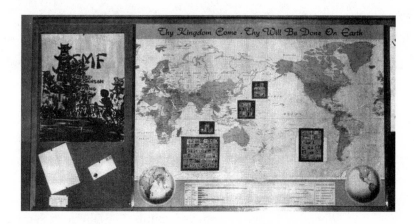

The Student Missions Fellowship bulletin board

Music also figured very largely in the TSBC student experience. In 1957 there was a forty-member Women's Choir, a Male Quartet, and a Trumpet Trio in addition to the Christian Service music groups that performed and gave testimonies at churches near and far: Girls' Sextet, Girls' Trio, and Men's Quartet (plus a Faculty Trio).[6] These gospel teams were an important link to Free Church congregations, encouraging the church's young people to follow the example of these college students in serious commitment to the Lord—and perhaps in coming to Trinity. As the student body grew, so did the number and range of musical opportunities. In 1958–1959 music director James Monson organized a selective twenty-five-voice

Chapel Choir. The group sang J. S. Bach's "Jesus, Priceless Treasure" at the National Church Music Festival and other venues. Monson also organized a Festival Choir for "all students interested in singing" and a pep band to enliven the already lively Trinity men's basketball games.[7] By 1961 the college choir was traveling farther afield, with a tour that year to Texas.[8]

A humorous heading from the *Trinitarian 1960*

These musical groups numbered among the many Christian service activities. Others included teaching Sunday school, hospital visitation, Boys and Girls Clubs, summer daily Vacation Bible Schools, summer camps, and Bible study classes supplemented by shirts-and-skins basketball at the Allendale Home for troubled youth.[9] The Christian Service Program grew as the college did in the coming years, adding a course required of all incoming freshmen to train and inspire them for witness and the ministry of helps. Long before the secular university trend toward "service learning," Christian service was a basic component of a Trinity college education.

Rounding out the religious program at TSBC were daily chapel services, the annual Hilding Ahlstrom Memorial guest lectureship, and Deeper Life Meetings. These remained staples of the Trinity experience in the coming years. A notable marker of the increased liberal arts emphasis in a Christian context was the 1960–1961 lecture series "Christ and Aesthetics" by Clyde Kilby of Wheaton College, published that year as an influential book. Kilby followed neo-evangelical leader Harold

John Ockenga's exhortation that, in a student's paraphrase, "evangelical Christians have failed within the last thirty years by abdicating responsibility on the cultural scene." The student commented, "Dr. Kilby's lectures delved into areas of thought that were new to many of us."[10] This sense of entering territory heretofore unexplored by EFCA folks conveyed both the excitement and the potential for unease among the constituency, as some people worried that such topics distracted students from evangelism and missions. At the college itself, however, a sense of anticipation was building, anticipation of the broadening and deepening that a program of "education for life" could accomplish.

For sports at the TSBC of 1957, there was a football club (no helmets or uniforms) and a girls' basketball club—but the big Trinity sport was men's basketball (A and B squads), complete with cheerleaders in modest midi-length dresses.[11] The college team competed against the seminary and other Christian schools.[12] Students also enjoyed activities such as a Camera Club, the Inter-Dorm Council, Student Council, and work on the *Trinitarian* yearbook and the bimonthly student newspaper, the *Trinity Digest*. Social life highlights included the junior banquet and the Christmas Concert and Smorgasbord.

The 1959 Christmas Smorgasbord and the very
first Santa Lucia Queen, Sandra Geier

THINKING BIG WITH GOD

Living, learning, and fellowship at this little seminary and college took place in a cluster of buildings near the corner of Berteau and Hermitage

Avenues on the near north side of Chicago. As the seminary and especially the college grew—by 1959–1960, college students outnumbered seminarians four to one—it was clear that larger and more modern facilities were needed. EFCA president Arnold T. Olson had launched an ambitious and successful capital campaign, the Jubilee Program, in 1955, earmarking a large portion for development of TSBC. As described in chapter 2, the original plan to expand and modernize the Chicago campus was scrapped in favor of relocating to a lovely suburban property on Half Day Road in Bannockburn, the Sunset estate. The same EFCA Conference (1960) voted to purchase another property, the Seal Kap Dairy Farm in British Columbia, to start a Free Church junior college in Canada.[13] Suddenly the EFCA was committed to enlarging two institutions of higher learning and launching a third, emboldened by the providential opportunities that these two properties afforded.

Dorm houses on the Chicago campus. The largest is Historic 4211.

These were heady years of stepping out in faith that God would enable the Free Church and the evangelical movement to accomplish great things in missions, evangelism, and influence on the larger culture. In his EFCA president's report to the annual conference, "Decade of Destiny," Olson declared, "We need members in our churches who are free from small-ness, who can think big with God. We need people who are more keenly aware of the greatness of God than the difficulties ahead."[14] That same year Olson chaired the National Association of Evangelicals' campaign to "Return the Bible to the Heart of the Nation." Well in advance of the reawakened public presence of evangelicals in the 1970s and '80s, Trinity and the EFCA, with the National Association of Evangelicals, were work-ing to bring gospel Christianity back into a place of cultural influence.[15]

This "thinking big with God" was not without its opposition and prob-lems. To allay fears that the college, with its broader program, might drift away from its biblical moorings, Olson proposed to the EFCA conference the creation of a "Commission on Safeguarding Our Spiritual Heritage." Only after that motion had passed was it moved to establish separate cor-porations with the new names Trinity College and Trinity Theological Seminary.[16] The outlay of funds required for the move and the develop-ment of the schools prompted the decision in 1962 "that the conference instruct the Board of Education and Trinity Advancement Committee to give top priority to the seminary in their planning." This move, wrote Calvin Hanson, was chiefly motivated by the church's desire for more EFCA-trained pastors, since so many EFCA young men were opting for other seminaries.[17] But it boded ill for the college. The two institutions, now separate corporations under the parent corporation of the EFCA, inevitably competed for donor dollars and EFCA allocations, and the church had made it clear which institution would suffer should finances get tight. Compounding the issue was the visionary and energetic lead-ership of the seminary by its new dean, Kenneth Kantzer. According to Hanson, concern repeatedly arose among Free Church people that the EFCA "was so swept off its feet by the coming of Dr. Kantzer that he had in effect been written a blank check to build whatever kind of seminary *he* desired."[18]

For the next few years, though, the excitement over the new opportu-nities for TEDS and the college was well rewarded. Dean Urang started the college on the path to accreditation, assured, after an encouraging meeting with officials from the North Central Accrediting Association, that the college could take this step toward secular recognition "without losing its soul."[19] The state of Illinois accepted Trinity College graduates

Gunnar Urang,
dean

Edward Neteland,
dean

Nellie Choi,
mathematics

to teach high school social studies, English, music, and history.[20] Urang's successor as college dean, Edward Neteland, consulted with key leaders in higher education, including the chairman of the North Central accrediting body, to reconfigure the college curriculum, enhance the library, and develop a five-year plan that wowed the candidacy examining team.[21] Meanwhile EFCA people were eager to help. By 1963 the Trinity Women's Auxiliary had established twenty chapters nationwide, holding group prayer for Trinity each month. Individuals, too, were encouraged to use "a prayer calendar which covers the activities and personalities involved in the great program of educating and training our seminary and college students." The sense of shared zeal for the work of Trinity, and shared trust in God for success, was truly heartwarming. Norton wrote, "As the consistent and persistent prayers of God's people mount to the Throne of God and the Spirit of God works in the hearts of all who are concerned in the actual teaching and administrating of the school as well as in the hearts of the supporters, we can expect the work of God at Trinity to go forward."[22]

As the seminary moved to Bannockburn in September 1961, the college remained behind in Chicago, itching with anticipation of more space and modernized facilities. College yearbooks carried pictures of cramped quarters, noting especially the long waits to get into the dining room at Historic 4211. In the meantime, though, important traditions were being established. The student Social Committee added a Santa Lucia contest to the annual Christmas Smorgasbord in 1959, which went over so well that it has continued ever since. Other new traditions included Sadie Hawkins Day, the Junior-Senior banquet, a fall weekend retreat called Senior Sneak, and the Big-Li'l Sis program to help freshman girls feel oriented and included in campus life. *Logoi*, the campus literary magazine, was launched. The student newspaper, the *Trinity Digest*, went from a bimonthly mimeographed product to a weekly, professionally printed paper. By 1961 a corps of forty-four students labored on the *Digest*, bragging that it had "the same system of production, the same type of management ... and the same headaches as a large community newspaper."[23]

Some of the men of dorm house 1726, eager for more space

CRISIS AND PROVISION

But while curriculum, administration, and student experience were moving forward, the ambitious efforts to grow three schools simultaneously (college, seminary, and Canadian junior college) hit a financial wall. The year 1964 went down in Trinity history as one "of unparalleled crisis"[24]—though arguably there would be worse crises yet. From the interplay of high hopes, spiritual commitment, and financial realities would come periodic crises and moments of evident divine intervention, so that the Trinity story has come to have a leitmotif of God's intervening and rescuing—an identity grounded in the humility of constant dependence.

Norton's heartwarming words about the Trinity Women's Auxiliary were one small part of a glowing presidential report to the EFCA conference in 1963. He touted the deep spiritual commitment of new faculty, some of whom brought the beautiful testimony of a convert. He dramatized the need for Christian higher education "to prepare the hearts and minds of our youth to face the terrors of the missile age and the opportunities for witnessing to a living, loving Savior." And he lauded the service Trinity would render to the children of the postwar baby boom about to enter college. "Thousands of growing Free Church boys and girls today in the grades and high school will find the answer of Christ tomorrow to the basic questions of space-age thinking as they discover for themselves the significance of the Christian world and life view and dynamic in their biblically integrated Trinity College courses."[25]

But the financial picture was not nearly so rosy. The 1963 conference heard a very different report from EFCA president Olson—different not only from Norton's report that year, but also from Olson's own "Decade of Destiny" address two years previously. Now Olson argued that the EFCA had been trying to do too much at once. "We have not faced realistically the question of how large a school a small denomination of less than 40,000 members can afford to maintain," Olson warned. He then posed a series of startling questions, including whether to sell the Bannockburn property and revert back to Chicago, and whether to "consider going back to a junior college or even eliminate the college altogether and concentrate on a graduate school or seminary located at Bannockburn."[26] He ended, however, with a call to faith and action, for this was an opportunity to see God's hand. "It has been true historically that at the spot where the resources of human wit have come to an end, there the multitudes have found God. The entrance into the riches of God has been through the bankruptcy of the court of human devices."[27]

The Trinity Sunday issue of the *Evangelical Beacon* in January 1964 carried pleas from Harry Evans, pastor of the Arlington Heights Evangelical Free Church and chairman of the board of Trinity College–TEDS, and from Ed Neteland, then assistant dean of the college. Evans, convinced that part of the giving problem was that EFCA people saw the growth of

TEDS as diverting dollars away from missions, argued that the training of pastors when "evangelicalism in America is crying for a school such as we are trying to develop" was actually a great missionary opportunity. Neteland, meanwhile, pointed out that TEDS depended on the college, since for the past several years the larger college enrollment and increasing college tuition had "underwritten most of the overhead for the divinity school." The next month a special joint meeting of the EFCA boards launched the SOS Campaign: "Save Our Schools," raising one hundred thousand dollars by July. Still, the poor condition of the Chicago campus attracted fewer students to the college, and word was that the EFCA board of education was leaning toward closing the college in 1965. The college faculty, hearing this, voted unanimously to resign. Here was a crisis indeed.[28]

A student having devotions

And at this critical juncture the Lord provided, as Olson had urged the church to believe he would. Despite the ominous situation, Neteland, who by this point was college dean, looked for a way through. He later recalled,

> The key in my mind for the future of the college was to eliminate the word "if" from the board's thinking and move to the word "how." The word "if" is looking to people, things or circumstances

to make the decision for the board. When it is "how," it becomes a partnership between man and God—faith with works. That is when the Lord led me to Bill Tandy of Tandy Enterprises and the C.I.T. Financial Corporation of Tulsa, Oklahoma.

Neteland flew to Tulsa and returned with a lending offer to *build rather than cut*—a three-hundred-student residence hall and a student union with dining facilities—"without any cash," by amortizing the property against the income from future enrollment. As 1965 came, instead of closing the college, construction began on the two new buildings. That fall the college moved to Bannockburn.[29]

A GROWING COLLEGE IN A CHANGING CULTURE

NEW BEGINNINGS

President Norton resigned graciously in April 1964. Ever the optimistic booster for Trinity, his report to the EFCA in June stressed the bright future ahead for the seminary and college.[30] His friend and former pastor, Harry Evans, took the reins in his place. Though not an academic, the energetic and charismatic Evans was every bit the booster for Trinity College that Norton had been, full of excitement for the role a Christian liberal arts college could play in a changing world. Students loved him. Paul Satre ('72 grad) recalled Evans's transparency and frankness, whether speaking in chapel or chatting informally with students in the dining hall.

The college academic building under construction (*Trinitarian 1966*)

His disarming manner made him "a great father or grandfather figure." Lee Eclov ('73 grad) expressed a similar appreciation: "Harry Evans taught me about being authentic as a Christian."[31]

Neteland now served the college as its able and forward-thinking dean. The following year's catalog announced a new curriculum. As hoped in the lending agreement Neteland had brokered, enrollment boomed when the college relocated to the suburban campus. From 229 college students in spring 1964, numbers climbed to 403 in 1967, 691 in 1969, and 772 in 1972. This spectacular growth coincided with the baby boom generation's coming of college age. In God's providence, Trinity had moved at just the right time. When Neteland became dean, he asked EFCA people to pray "that God may direct us to the faculty we need and the students who can benefit from a Trinity education.[32] It seems these prayers were answered in abundance.

L. Shafer, R. Foote, L. Sabourin, M. Herlein, P. Clinton, Coach VanDixhorn, G. Jeffs, R. Carlson, P. Swan, B. Smith, J. Foote

It is hard to express the feeling of Trinity's student body when basketball season approaches. There is a charged quality to the air. An undercurrent of enthusiasm ripples through the school. Pride in the practice—accomplishments of the boys on the floor is shared by everyone.

Trojans 1966

The class of 1966 produced an unusually handsome and informative *Trinitarian* yearbook documenting the energy and excitement at the college as the boom years began. This was the last year that would see a small graduating class: 42 seniors, whereas the freshman class alone numbered 154! The majors these graduates chose show the trend toward teaching and liberal arts, with eighteen in elementary education, ten in history, eight in either French, Spanish, English, or social science, and one in music education. In contrast, just four graduates that year majored in Christian education, and one in Bible.[33]

French professor Ruby Lindblad, a "veteran member of the 'Iron Brigade,' a select group of professors known for their exacting standards"

The student Publications Board reported "a radically different newspaper" in 1966. The *Digest* now had multiple departments, including the "Student Forum" for grievances and compliments, "Kyle's Korner" weighing fact and opinions, a regular missions column and occasional devotional essays, "Good-night David" on current world events and crucial issues, and "The Bureau of Useless Information" with humor and satire.[34] Other student activities included the Fine Arts Committee, showing films and presenting each year a major choral-work concert; the Social Committee, hosting a fall game night, the Christmas festival with the Santa Lucia crowning, a talent night, Sadie Hawkins Day, the spring banquet, and spring picnic; and a Devotional Committee, sponsoring a tract rack, special speakers, and chapel music. Christian service remained a mainstay, with several gospel teams sharing music, testimonies, and the benefits of a Trinity College education. And of course sports continued in importance at Trinity, with men's basketball, tennis, track, and cross-country competing intercollegiately, plus intramural football and table tennis.

```
advisor:   don't get hysterical, it's only a history test.
student:   only a history test! my gosh, don't you know who my teacher is?
advisor:   no, but I'm sure he's both a scholar and a gentleman.
student:   yeah, but he's also dr. vos!
advisor:   hmmm. well, then, you know what i'd do if i were you?
student:   what?
advisor:   i'd start getting hysterical.
```

Don't get hysterical, it's only a history test.

STUDENT EXPERIENCE
Lee Eclov (1973 Graduate), the Gospel Teams, and a Thinking Faith

Lee Eclov came to Trinity College from rural South Dakota in fall 1969. He was the only high schooler from his little church to come to Trinity. What drew him was a visit by two of the college's gospel teams—one to his Christian camp, another to his church. "I wanted to come to Trinity College to sing in one of those teams," he recalled with a chuckle, reflecting on his rather naive

The gospel team "Heirborn." Front row (left to right): Bryan
Johnson, Trudy Stewart, and Richard Ahlberg. Back row:
David Benson, Susan Foote, Ilene Foote, and Lee Eclov

and nonacademic priorities as he considered college. Sure enough, as a student he and some friends put together a group and went on tour to promote the college and encourage fellow believers in the faith. Later Eclov served as coordinator of Trinity's gospel teams. Christian colleges from the 1950s to the 1970s all had such gospel teams. Churches in those days could call a service any night of the week and people would come, attracted by the opportunity to hear special music and testimonies. Lee's team would sing, staff a presentation booth with information about the college, and go to the church's youth group. Sometimes the president or other advancement staff would travel with them.

Gospel teams traveled extensively during the summers. Lee's group visited more Free Churches than the college president, traveling in a college van with fifty dollars of petty cash and no oversight. Their group—four men and three women—comprised a men's quartet, brass ensemble, and various combinations. They stayed in the homes of church families and were paid $100 per week. In the summer of 1970 his group had the privilege of singing for the EFCA Annual Conference.

When they sang "Children of the Heavenly Father" in Swedish, some conferees were so moved that they wept.

Eclov found Trinity College a place that expanded his horizons and opened his mind to the depth and riches of learning in a Christian context. Entering the college as freshmen, "our faith was cultural to a certain extent," he explained. "Most of us came from small EFCA churches" that functioned as ethnoreligious enclaves. His college experience at Trinity "was a very formative time for me. This is a place where I learned to think." Analyzing *The Red Badge of Courage* in English class, Doris Rothlisberger asked, "Who is the Christ figure?" Eclov at first rolled his eyes. "It never crossed my mind that artists are up for more than one thing at a time." Walter Liefeld, teaching a class on the Synoptic Gospels, showed how Bible passages and themes work *together*, asking students simply but profoundly, "You *see*?" History professor William Nix asked on a final exam why a certain trend happened, leading Lee to realize that he was supposed to go beyond facts and discern trends and meaning. "An electric moment for me," he recalled. "To learn literature or history from Christians who are able to make you *see*—that's a great preparation for the pastorate."[35]

SOCIAL UNREST AND THE GENERATION GAP

Besides the student activities noted above, the 1966 yearbook reported the creation of a Judicial Board, the "proper outlet for airing student grievances," which

> made headlines with its review of the administration-produced *Student Handbook*. Feeling that parts of the book were impracticable, yet realizing the job required discretion and diplomacy, the board managed to come forward with recommendations that bridged the gap between the conservative Handbook and the more liberal desires of the student body, while maintaining the traditions and convictions that have made Trinity a testimony throughout the years.[36]

Here was an indication of the changing culture of America in the mid-'60s. Along those lines, Trinity's Student Association in 1965–1966 established a Contemporary Affairs Committee to provide lectures, films, literature, and discussion groups on current events. It published the cleverly named *Digestive Tract*, distributed in the dining hall, to brief students on current events each day. In 1968–1969 the committee brought two lecturers to campus: Peter Landon, who spoke and fielded questions on Southeast Asia, and a Dr. Yuen of San Francisco State University, who "discussed the riots that tore his school." The unrest at San Francisco State went down in history as its Black Student Union pressed for the establishment of programs in ethnic studies, starting a trend of curricular diversification that would sweep the nation.[37]

The 1968–1969 Contemporary Affairs Committee (left to right):
Brent Thorwall, Dawn McNeal, Vernon Mitchell, Henry F.
Brown, Chairman Steve Phillips, Sharon Short

With the wider youth culture beginning to criticize openly their parents' generation for failing to live up to its ideals—and even questioning the ideals themselves—how would Trinity students respond? Student Association president Paul Johnson wrote, "I hope that Trinity will never be known for the rebellious contracultural behavior found on so many U.S. campuses today." There was such a thing as "valid individual indictment of the existing social order," yet Johnson hoped the Trinity student would be known not as an unthinking conservative, but as a "prudential realist," someone who "can get quite excited and totally involved in a *reasonable* program of change."[38]

The EFCA, too, was awakening to the social issues that concerned the younger generation, and doing so initially in a perhaps surprisingly positive way. Evangelicals had long worried about secularization and moral decay. Now the denomination urged as well a sympathetic concern for social justice and a willingness to get involved to help. The new EFCA Committee on Social Concern in 1967 called for "a renewed sense of responsibility for the social problems of our time, such as race relations, war, peace, poverty, divorce, delinquency, and mental illness." It also called for "the formulation of a Biblical philosophy of social action." [39]

The 1968 EFCA conference met on the Bannockburn campus in mid-June, two months after the assassination of Martin Luther King Jr. and less than two weeks after the assassination of Robert F. Kennedy. The conference theme that fateful year was "A Word for a Broken World." Riots in Chicago following King's death had devastated Black business districts on the west side. Trinity president Evans reported that TEDS students had formed "the largest delegation to help with assuaging the physical and material needs of those who were the innocent victims of the riots." Two months later Chicago would again erupt in violence outside the Democratic National Convention. In the midst of those developments the EFCA Committee on Social Concern quoted ancient Athenian statesman Solon that justice could be achieved "if those people who are not directly affected by a wrong are just as indignant about it as those who are personally hurt," and stated, "This is the time that every evangelical should do some soul-searching." EFCA president Olson had just assumed the presidency of the National Association of Evangelicals. In his acceptance speech he stressed the importance of coupling social action with the presentation of the gospel of salvation of the individual.[40] Now in Bannockburn as president of the EFCA, he asked the denomination to appoint a special committee to study "methods for approaching the problems of the inner city and race." He also appealed to EFCA people "to exercise prayer and patience in these difficult days. One senses division not only in America but among our own people. In relating the Gospel message to the social scene we find a sincere search for the right answers among some, a refusal to face the real problems on the part of others."[41]

The EFCA and the National Association of Evangelicals under Olson's leadership engaged in more consistent action on the issues of personal morality that would become core concerns of the rising "New Christian Right" in the next decades than on the social issues, such as poverty and racial inequality, that energized some of the younger generation. Meanwhile students at Trinity College, identifying both with their parents and with their peers in the larger culture, made strides toward social engagement. In 1968–1969 some seventeen college students founded a tutoring program in an African American neighborhood. As one of them reported, "On Tuesday nights the college students pack themselves into vans and go to Chicago, to the ghetto on the north side, and tutor the black junior high students in whatever area they need help," yielding "a new dimension of new experiences, new learning (for both groups), and hopefully of new friendships."[42] Other Trinity students joined a coffee house outreach of InterVarsity Christian Fellowship called the Chicago Evangelism Project. "Discussions may start on any topic, as viewpoints are expounded and traditions challenged. Talking with students, derelicts, runaways, and addicts, workers are constantly challenged to know and apply their faith in a practical way."[43]

Students were taking seriously the liberal arts ideal as a preparation for both reflection on and action in their contemporary world. In so doing they wanted to take part in the direction of their education. Trinity College philosophy professor Norman Geisler celebrated this attitude of responsibility and engagement. He wrote, "Monologue is out and dialogue is in—and rightfully so. Education involves the interaction of student and teacher, and the former brings at least as much to the process as the latter."[44] Accordingly, the annual Trinity issue of the *Evangelical Beacon* proclaimed, "Trinity means interaction." Dean of Students Larry Zentz explained that as a small Christian college Trinity had a real advantage over the faceless "multiversity" to provide meaningful interaction among students, faculty, and administration, not only because of size, but especially by cultivating relationships in an atmosphere of trust. While acknowledging that "we have not yet 'arrived,' " Zentz noted student-initiated efforts such as Faculty Home Nights, "where students are invited to the homes of the faculty of their choice for an evening of social involvement," and an open forum for students and administration to "exchange reactions and attitudes."[45]

The editor of the college paper, the *Digest*, reported in 1970 a distinct change at Trinity in his three and a half years there: "Students are more in line with their generation—criticizing, analyzing, evaluating everything they are confronted with in higher education." He credited college faculty for encouraging students "to weigh their beliefs and opinions,"

On the cover of the 1969 Trinity issue of the *Beacon*

and applauded the change from "constant chapels emphasizing how the 'Christian life' should be lived" to "chapels that present contemporary problems and manners in which they can be attacked by a Christian." Indeed, "Trinity is undoubtedly one of the most open Christian colleges in the nation. Students are encouraged to express themselves, the ideas they really hold and believe."[46]

By 1970 the college offered four foreign languages: French, Spanish, German, and Greek. Here professors Mark Noll and Norm Ericson sport culture-specific headwear. (*Trinitarian 1971*)

President Evans found himself increasingly needing to address the charge that Trinity students (college and seminary) were imbibing too much of the spirit of the age. At the 1968 EFCA conference he met the rumors head-on, answering "the criticism of our schools." Not every student on a combined campus of over a thousand students would behave in an entirely Christian way. Trinity students were certainly straight and upstanding compared to their peers elsewhere. Customs and fashions change with time, he urged. "The Free Church has changed from the days that women neither cut nor bobbed their hair and pastors were not allowed to wear handkerchiefs in the breast pockets of their suits." What matters is whether such external things "affect the depth of the spiritual life of the individuals involved."[47] As these remarks suggest, concern centered on behavioral standards more than on politics or doctrine. However, in 1969 Evans asked outright, "Is Trinity Going Liberal?" and answered with a resounding "No!" citing the Christian witness of students to a businessman in Deerfield who testified, " 'There is a difference in those kids at Trinity ... in the light in their eyes ... and now I realize that this is the light of the Holy Spirit.' " Evans asked EFCA people "not to confuse our attempts to struggle with contemporary issues ... with a tendency toward theological liberalism."[48]

Meanwhile the college continued to grow and to encourage Christian contemporary engagement. The official statement of educational philosophy ran as follows:

> Believing that the Christian message is relevant today, the college encourages students to accept the challenge of the personal and social implications of the Gospel. Therefore, it seeks to create an educational climate which promotes commitment to Jesus Christ as Lord and Savior and acceptance of the responsible role in society required by such a commitment.[49]

Two brothers at Trinity College, Tony and Joel Ahlstrom, made a widely reported run from California to New York to raise awareness about the problem of pollution. Along the way they spoke to connect their Christian faith to their environmental concern and testify to the power of Jesus in their lives.[50] Meanwhile Trinity's traditions of Christian service through gospel teams and community outreach continued. The college band toured the Midwest in 1970, presenting "instrumental music with a gospel message," coupled with the reading of Scripture and hymn texts, at EFCA churches.[51] Three years later professor Morris Faugerstrom took a group of college musicians on Trinity's first European Music Ministries Tour.[52] The Student Missions Fellowship reported having sent more than thirty students overseas as summer missionaries in the past several years. A group of ten Trinity College students biked across Europe while witnessing, ministering in churches, and serving in youth camps.[53] The *Evangelical Beacon* carried these and many other stories in its annual Trinity issue, encouraging EFCA people to send students and support to their schools.

Joel and Tony Ahlstrom on their
"Save America: Solution to Pollution" run

FEATURED FACULTY
Morris Faugerstrom and Jackie Bell—
A Tribute by Paul Satre (1972 Graduate)

Any recollection of my time at Trinity goes quickly to remembrances of Dr. Morris Faugerstrom (or "Doc," our affectionate nickname for him) and Professor Jacquelyn Bell ("Please call me Jackie"). As a student at the college, I was fortunate to have been taught my subject and my art with excellence from these two professors—and others—and I owe much of my career direction to their insightful and helpful guidance. I always felt that my best was required in the classroom, the rehearsal room, and in the music studio from them, but although

Morris Faugerstrom shares
the joy of music in 1976

the demands of the music major were significant, there was always time for after-class or mid-lesson chats about many topics. Personal and spiritual advice was readily available, and if extra time from them was required, it was freely given. I never felt an intruder into their already overloaded schedules.

In the late '90s, when I joined the music department faculty, I saw them from a different vantage point. There was still their quick availability to students for advice and counsel outside the classroom, but there was also the willingness to help their new colleague navigate a new environment. I was made aware of many of the behind-the-scenes tasks that these teachers had performed through the years, usually without much notice. Doc spent countless hours planning tours for each spring break trip. My freshman year, the Concert Choir flew to California for an extended three-week concert tour of EFCA churches, a monumental planning effort. He was also frequently called on to teach an overload course, often without overload compensation. Jackie tutored me one-on-one to make up a course I needed for graduate school. I was well prepared for graduate work by my education at Trinity.

The large touring ensembles provided a hugely impactful and positive experience for so many Trinity students through the years, music majors and nonmajors alike. Doc conducted the Concert Choir, and Jackie first directed the Women's Chorale and later took over the Concert Choir. I then succeeded her when I joined the Trinity faculty in 1996. Working together for a wonderful musical result in the concerts, staying overnight in church members' homes, the pressures and enjoyment of the tours—often including personal time with the directors not possible during the busy semester on campus—all of this added up to some unforgettable experiences. With the benefit of social media, I have read of the many positive influences that the large ensembles and tours with Doc and Jackie had on undergrads through the years, experiences never

Jackie Bell

to be forgotten and ones that affected future daily lives and relationships. There are really no other experiences quite like these, and adding the spiritual component made them transformative. Their legacies cannot be overstated. As J. S. Bach often wrote on his compositions, *Soli Deo Gloria*—to God alone be the glory![54]

A SECOND FINANCIAL CRISIS

Unfortunately all this growth came at a financial cost that exceeded the Free Church's ability or willingness to pay. For the next several years Evans encouraged, chided, and pleaded with the Free Churches to support their schools. Time and again the annual conferences would urge all congregations to give to Trinity, and time and again some would give much while many gave nothing. Evans lamented, "Under our congregational polity, the action of the General Conference, as strongly as it is worded, does not insure any thought of complying" in any particular congregation. A modest $10 per member per year would make a great difference, but that goal proved ever elusive. It was not all the church's fault; higher education across the US faced mounting costs. Trinity operated with amazing frugality; tuition and room and board charges covered the entire cost of a Trinity College education, not counting mortgage payments. There was no endowment. Students came in increasing numbers, but the institution could not afford to build enough dorm space to house them. Both Trinity College and TEDS were in financial trouble even as they were growing. The problem became acute in 1971, in what Evans called "the crisis to end all crises."[55]

Rolfing Library, today an admirable research resource for so small an institution, stood—or rather did not yet stand—at the center of the crisis. Mr. and Mrs. R. C. Rolfing donated $400,000 for the erection of a library in memory of their son James, tragically killed in a plane crash. As noted in chapter 3, a proper library would meet a very important criterion for the seminary to achieve accreditation. In April 1969 an enthusiastic groundbreaking ceremony took place—but then, as Olson later recalled, "the dream of a building continued as nothing more than a small hole in the ground for close to four years." As Trinity's debt mounted, that specially designated gift money was diverted to cover operating expenses. Even so, the institution remained over a million dollars in the hole—that small groundbreaking hole, we might say—by 1971. Mr. Rolfing, wondering whether the library would ever be built, sent word that he might transfer the gift (money that, unbeknownst to him, was no longer there) to another institution. Olson was in the unenviable position of having to meet with him. "What should I tell him?" he recalled. "Should I admit the gift had been temporarily applied to operations?" All he could do was ask for more time.[56]

Meanwhile Trinity committed itself to a ten-year plan, devised by a consulting firm, that would take the institutions further into debt before turning the corner. In September 1971 a Chicago bank demanded payment of a large loan and informed the EFCA that as guarantor it would be responsible to come up with the money if Trinity could not. Now the crisis went public. The EFCA executive board stepped in, sending an investigative committee and then appointing a board of regents, which Evans feared would take over the administration of the schools. Evans and all the other top administrators, except Kantzer, tendered their resignations.

Students drew up a petition, signed by almost 90 percent of the student body, in support of Evans. A sharp disagreement developed between the president of the Free Church and the president of Trinity. The boards of Trinity and the EFCA, meeting on the Trinity campus, instructed Olson and Evans to settle their differences or else both resign—and this ultimatum came on the morning of a crucial donor meeting, giving the two presidents just a few hours. After "give and take—and tears—mixed with mutual confession of faults," Olson and Evans agreed to "walk and work together." Convinced now that God would help them despite their faults and missteps, they met with a group of nearly eighty laymen who pledged $136,000 on the spot and another quarter of a million in the next thirty days. It was a beautiful lesson in the power of Christian reconciliation.[57]

Groundbreaking for Rolfing Library, 1969

Olson and two other EFCA officials frankly reported the financial crisis in the November 16, 1971, issue of the *Beacon*, alerting the church to the alarming fact that the schools still needed $700,000 in the next three months, a new bond program of more than a million dollars, and a program of regular congregational support for Trinity. They called on "all of our people to join with us in humbling ourselves before the God of grace, wisdom, and power in confessing our failure where we may have ignored his guidance, in seeking His wisdom for the months ahead and in imploring His help in meeting the needs of the hour." Beyond the immediate crisis was the need for "a long-range program for higher education in the EFCA" that the people could actually accomplish.[58] Reactions to the call were mixed: some urged closing both Trinity College and Trinity Western College (the former Trinity Junior College, in Canada) in order to save the divinity school, regarding them as luxuries that came at ever-increasing cost. The very fact of their impressive growth was viewed as a financial threat to the seminary. Others joined the call to confession and humbling before God, trusting that he would respond in mercy and provide through his people.[59]

A burst of support in 1971–1972, together with drastic budget cuts, kept Trinity Bannockburn open. But Evans reported that giving fell back by 40 percent after the immediate crisis had passed, and concerns about student behavioral standards continued to plague the college. E. Lee McLean, a well-regarded college development consultant, recommended in spring 1974 that the colleges (plural—Trinity Western as well, despite its excellent financial record, and to the great consternation of its people) be separated from the EFCA. President Calvin Hanson was successful in keeping Trinity Western in the EFCA fold. Trinity College in Bannockburn, on the other hand, embraced the McLean report and voluntarily separated. Its board of directors "voted unanimously to recommend to the Evangelical Free Church of America that they relinquish control of the institution to an interdenominational, self-perpetuating board with minority Free Church representation."[60]

AN INDEPENDENT EVANGELICAL
LIBERAL ARTS COLLEGE

Trinity College now embarked on a new and exciting adventure. The college would retain the EFCA Statement of Faith while the denomination pledged to encourage its people to continue to send students and support. But the great hope was for Trinity College to attract students and faculty from a broader swath of the evangelical world and, in Evans's words, "simply to become the best Christian liberal arts college around."[61]

Now president of the college alone, Evans devoted his energies to the Christian liberal arts ideal with gusto. He continued to report to the EFCA annual conferences, speaking in glowing and inspiring terms about the school's mission. "I feel more keenly than ever that the centers of Christian learning with a liberal arts emphasis are more needed than ever in the Christian church."[62] As a negative example he quoted Hitler's architect, Albert Speer: " 'It was the lop-sided education that made it so easy for so many of us to fall under the spell of Nazism. We were technical barbarians who did a fine job, but never inquired about the purpose or ultimate results of the job.' " Evans continued,

> Such subjects as history and philosophy are the only subjects that ask fundamental questions—"What is the nature of man? What are the proper ends of civilization?" and so on. ... How desperately important it is for us to preserve the option in American higher education of distinctive evangelical centers which are "rock-ribbed" in truly Biblical faith and morality yet unthreatened in the cultivation of the minds of our young people.[63]

That last sentence is particularly important for what the college became in these independent years. Evans sympathized with the strong desire among that generation of students for open, critical examination of society and of the church. He trusted that an education grounded in a Christian worldview and fidelity to Scripture had nothing to fear from the most searching inquiry. He also believed that a small Christian college such as Trinity offered an ideal environment for the give-and-take of ideas and experiences between faculty and students and across disciplines.[64] Through the years the college faculty have continued to cherish the opportunity

President Harry Evans

Dean Edward Hakes

for fertile interdisciplinary dialogue within a common Christian worldview, something impossible at larger, secular schools.

INITIAL SUCCESSES

To realize this vision of evangelical openness grounded in the Bible and framed by the liberal arts, Evans worked to build connections to the evangelical world beyond the EFCA, build an ever more impressive faculty, and build *buildings* to make it all possible. First on the agenda was to gather a board of directors, enlarging it slowly over several years. At the end of the first year he proudly reported a board of ten members: besides himself, Thomas McDill (EFCA president), and Kenneth Meyer (TEDS president), the list included US Congressman John B. Anderson (who in 1980 ran against Jimmy Carter and Ronald Reagan—the famous trio of three evangelical candidates—for the US presidency); Robert Andringa (staff director of the Education and Labor Committee of the US House of Representatives), James N. Lew of Beech Aircraft (after whom the future Lew Library was named), and George Beverly Shea,

John B. Anderson
delivers the
commencement
address in 1967

whose resonant bass voice was heard for decades at the Billy Graham Crusades. A new Ministers' Advisory Board included Chuck Swindoll, a rising star in the EFCA soon to be heard nationwide on his "Insight for Living" radio program. Swindoll gave the first commencement address in Trinity College's independent era.[65] Shea became a great friend of the college. He quickly took leadership of an individual giving program called the Presidential Gold Chain, a centerpiece of which were his dinner concerts, which proved highly successful advancement events. Evans announced in 1981 that the next new building on the college campus would be named in honor of this widely loved singer and Trinity promoter: the George Beverly Shea Chapel.[66]

Alongside this vision casting and networking, Evans succeeded in attracting impressive new professors, many of them young and energetic. Viewing himself as a promoter and entrusting the academic direction of the college to its faculty—a policy followed as well by dean of the college J. Edward Hakes—Evans brought in new

George Beverly Shea sings at
a Billy Graham Crusade

blood with top-tier credentials, enlarging on a trend that had begun around 1970. By the end of the '70s the college boasted PhDs from Northwestern, Chicago, Princeton, Yale, Michigan, Wisconsin-Madison, Berkeley, St. Andrews, Vanderbilt, Johns Hopkins, Case Western, and more.[67] Bible professor Bill Moulder recalled the stimulation of heated discussion among brilliant colleagues in the faculty lounge.[68] Three of the most respected historians of American evangelicalism, John Woodbridge (later of TEDS), Mark Noll (later of Wheaton and Notre Dame), and Joel Carpenter (later provost of Calvin College) started their careers at Trinity College in these heady years of independence.

Indeed, Trinity College was becoming one of the leaders in Christian college education, invited to join the exclusive Christian College Consortium (alongside Wheaton, Messiah, Westmont, Calvin, and others) in 1976. Evans reported the excitement this association brought:

> Direct benefits to the institution will include marketing studies and strategy, consideration of Christian standards of behavior, special seminars in the integration of Christian faith and the liberal arts (four of our faculty are attending such a 10-day seminar this summer), financial and accounting procedures, joint legal strategy regarding governmental impingements on private higher education, faculty and student exchange programs, the expansion of financial

and educational resources and the study of the feasibility of a university system of Christian colleges.[69]

1974–1975 wrestling team

Cross-country team, including a cousin of star Olympic runner
Kip Keino, Daniel Song'on, who later taught business at the college.
The team took second place in the NCCAA in 1976 and third place in 1977.

FEATURED FACULTY

Bill Graddy, Professor of English— A Tribute by Joshua Held (2009 Graduate)

William E. Graddy earned his PhD and earlier degrees from Southern Illinois University at Carbondale. Committed to remain in Illinois through his work with the Navigators, a parachurch ministry, he began teaching in the English department at Trinity College in 1973 and retired in 2011. During his tenure, he taught American literature, British literature (especially Renaissance and Romantic literatures), literary theory, and many sections of general education courses in writing and literature.

Bill Graddy shares a laugh while teaching in 1975

The authors he knew best were A. E. Housman and Nathaniel Hawthorne; the two he most loved, John Milton and George Herbert. From 1970 to the present he has contributed essays and one poem to magazines and journals. He is an avid lover of music and met his wife while she was on Trinity's adjunct faculty in music.

His class lectures were intense, stimulating, and carefully prepared, often accompanied by handouts. His self-effacing demeanor made his humorous stories the more entertaining. He remains in touch with many of his students, and a scholarship in the English department—for a disadvantaged student—is named after him.

On a more personal note, I recall with gratefulness Graddy's dedication to helping me with my senior thesis: he walked with me to Rolfing Library after classes one afternoon and showed me around the various reference sources in print and online (in 2008). He made time to talk over coffee during my time as a student at Trinity and later, after I entered graduate school, a path he helped to open with his recommendation letters. In the classroom, his lecture on the literary structure of the Gospels—parallel: Herod's feast, featuring the slaughter of

John the Baptist, followed by Christ's art of interpretation. He taught and feeding the thousands—brought new modeled this art gracefully to his own vividness to scriptural texts and to the thousands at Trinity.[70]

Trinity College hosted the Faith/Learning/Living Institute in 1977 and again in 1979. Upwards of sixty faculty attended from the fourteen consortium schools. Christian College Consortium presidents met together regularly, as did academic deans and personnel officers. When the consortium founded a university press, among its first publications was Trinity history professor Mark Noll's book *Christians in the American Revolution*.[71] Noll also served as social science editor for the *Christian Scholar's Review*, and in 1977 Dean Hakes was elected its publisher.

Students flocked to the newly vibrant college, undaunted by its woeful lack of space. Bill Moulder recalled teaching 110 students in each section of Biblical Interpretation, meeting in the room used for band rehearsals, with instruments along the walls and students sitting on the piano. With fifty students in first-year Greek, some sat in the hall listening through the doorway. Enrollment climbed to 878 in 1976 and 914 in 1978. That year Carl D. Johnson, head of a major land-planning firm and now a member of the college board of trustees, presented an ambitious building plan for the campus of the future.[72] Sports boomed as the college grew, so that by 1980 Trinity students competed in men's basketball (varsity and junior

Hockey and softball were among the many
sports offerings in 1980

varsity), soccer, track, tennis, baseball, and hockey; and women's tennis, volleyball, basketball, and softball.

INNOVATING, EXCITING—AND GOING LIBERAL?

The 1975 student yearbook opened with the mixed statement, "Trinity College ... nestled in the monotonous flatlands of Illinois is a place where students become thinkers in their own right." The physical environment might not have been stimulating, but the intellectual and spiritual one was. Pictures showed a relaxed atmosphere of camaraderie between students, faculty, and administration. On the faculty pages, the formal portraits of just a few years before had given way to candid shots and nicknames. English professor Bill Graddy was shown laughing; philosophy professor David Schlafer posed with a miniature of Rodin's *The Thinker*. On another of the opening pages, a student wrote, "When Christianity surrounds our every action and attitude, exciting friendships are created."[73]

David Schlafer, philosophy

An innovative expression of this spirit of community exploration was the creation of the Oregon Extension, brainchild of history professors Doug Frank and Kevin Cragg. On the site of an old logging camp in the Cascade Mountains, twenty juniors and seniors spent the fall semester living in community with five faculty members and their families. The program emphasized "cross-disciplinary studies and the relation of learning to everyday life," studying "Modern Visions of Man, Religion and

Modern Man, Modern Visions of Society, and Science and the Modern
World" as they were "related to each other and to Christian truth." There
were no exams, just reading, discussions, and a major paper—with "a
wider latitude for student initiative."[74]

Another new venture was the Christian College Consortium affiliate
San Francisco Externship, a nine-week summer program where "you are
able to put textbook theories in both psychology and sociology into practice" by working in a community institution, coupled with weekly seminars with faculty. "You will be learning much more than your field of study,"
the catalog explained. "You will be essentially on your own and will have
many domestic responsibilities such as finding housing, planning meals,
and learning how to budget your money." Other such opportunities by
the late '70s included the European Seminar, an eight-week summer pro-

gram combining tours "conducted by
experienced historians from a number
of colleges, and individual study and
exploration"; and the Urban Life Center:
Chicago, where Trinity students lived
with students from other colleges "in an
integrated community." While "working in an agency of your choice (Day
Care Center, Theatre Group, Crisis
Intervention, Drug Treatment Centers,
Schools, Churches) you will come into

Oregon Extension
students enjoy the
great outdoors

contact with a variety of interesting people with insight into the urban culture." Like the others, "This program places an emphasis on self-directed learning."[75]

Such initiatives followed trends in education in the '70s, deliberately giving students freedom and responsibility to a degree that might worry many today. It worried many at that time, too, though some students reveled in it. Bible professor Bill Moulder explained, "There's always a danger when opening a world of new ideas that a student will run with it, reject an upbringing they now regard as repressive, and adopt a superior and cynical attitude." That did happen, especially at the Oregon Extension. The 1978 student yearbook seems to have been heavily influenced by that kind of experience. It opens with a montage of photos overlaid with lyrics by Seals & Crofts ("We will never pass this way again") and the musical *Alfie* ("What's it all about?"), and is peppered throughout with quotations about mystery from Einstein, Merton, Yeats, and Kettering. The Oregon Extension montage quotes Kahlil Gibran, Thoreau, and Whitehead. Student Tom Johnson reports on Christian Life Week: "Chapel as an institution has been characterized as everything from 'forced spirituality' to castor oil." Why go? Well, Bruce Lockerbie (September 1977) at least was worth it.

> "The Christian and the Arts" was his topic, and his account of Christian involvement in and response to art was sometimes scathing, embarrassing, and explosive. ... At this time in the history of the Christian Church, young evangelicals are a very penitent lot, mourning over the "sins of the fathers" as it were. We are ashamed of the naive, shabby, racist, sexist, anti-intellectual presentation Christianity has been afforded in times past. We feel scrutinized (and are) by the rest of the world, realizing now that it's not so much the goods but the packaging that's been all wrong. And so, it is almost with relish that we listen to Lockerbie's indictment, confident that we are enlightened and on the right track.

Echoing sentiments increasingly common on the evangelical left, this obviously talented Trinity student also managed to sound cynical even about his cynicism. Valuable though many of these explorations and correctives might be, the outcome in attitude and behavior alarmed quite a few parents. College and church were on diverging paths. While the college was encouraging students to spread their wings, the EFCA was calling its members to renewed holiness of lifestyle, choosing as its annual theme in 1979 Ephesians 4:1, "Walk worthy of your calling." EFCA president Thomas McDill explained, "This theme emphasizes personal holiness of life style that characterized one emphasis of the early Free Church. ... Our founding fathers deplored ungodliness and worldly lusts and urged the Christian 'to live godly and righteously in this present world.' "[76] The EFCA Social Concerns Committee, originally interested in issues of poverty and racism, had by this time shifted its focus mainly to the issues of personal morality and family values that were driving a political reawakening among evangelicals and fundamentalists, the "New Christian Right." It was now in the process of issuing "a series of booklets on critical social issues": *Affirming the Family*; *Abortion*; and *Homosexuality*.[77] The neo-evangelical vision of faith-learning integration combined with social relevance was in the process of bifurcating—some turning to the political right, others to the political left.[78] While it is too simplistic to picture the EFCA on one side and the college on the other, that perception was certainly present and growing.

History professors Doug Frank and Kevin Cragg,
founders of Trinity's Oregon Extension

In 1979 Evans again strove to assure the church that the college remained spiritually faithful and active. In his annual report he pointed out, "We still have required chapel. We still have required Christian Service assignments. We still have explicit behavioral guidelines. And, we have seen exciting spiritual growth and vigorous witness in many of our students." Rumors of spiritual decline were nothing new, he said, and "those who really know us best, love and trust us the most!" In particular Evans was proud of the faculty for doing "a more serious job of wedding Biblical truth and their course subject matter than ever in the history of the college."[79]

A THIRD CRISIS

In that same year—1979—Evans, now recently widowed, became engaged to a twice-divorced woman. That proved to be the last straw. The church constituency was no longer willing to trust his assurances about the spiritual health of the college.[80] Trinity College still relied heavily on Free Church students and giving, refusing state or federal aid. The number of EFCA churches sending financial support began to fall drastically, as did enrollment—from 807 students in 1979 to 511 in 1983.[81] At the end of 1982 the college was in dire financial straits, nearly $3 million in operational and capital debt. David Martin wrote, "Notes held by EFCA church members fell into default, and trusts and annuities held by Free Church people were jeopardized. School and denominational officials discussed the implications of filing a Chapter 11 bankruptcy." Evans tendered his resignation.[82] The college had endured two previous crises, in 1964 and 1973. Would it survive this one?

"In the late winter and spring of 1983, the outlook for Trinity College was indeed bleak," reported Kenneth Kantzer to the EFCA a year later. "The banks were threatening to foreclose their loans, students were making plans to transfer elsewhere, the faculty was in despair, the Free Churches had stopped giving, and evangelicals outside the Free Church would not support the school." But this third crisis, like the ones before, became an opportunity to see the Lord provide a way through. With a full heart Kantzer continued, "We give thanks to God for the marvelous things he has done for Trinity College. ... The agony and fear we have undergone and the joy that has come to us as we observe how God worked things out for good are utterly beyond me to communicate."[83]

That fateful winter of 1982–1983, a week before submitting his resignation as president, Evans asked Kantzer to consider assuming leadership of the college. After prayer and consultation with family and close friends, Kantzer agreed, on certain definite conditions, including "the movement of Trinity College back into the Free Church orbit," changes in the board, "full cooperation and assurance and support" from EFCA leadership, a free hand to release some faculty and final approval of any subsequent faculty hires, full authority to control spending that year and set the budget for next, and "the public announcement of a renewed emphasis on lifestyle among students, faculty, and staff, which would be consonant with the highest standards and ideals of the Evangelical Free Church." To Kantzer's great surprise, the college board agreed to his terms. Now, if the concerns of the bank could be met, Kantzer would accept the position of chancellor of Trinity College in February and assume the presidency on July 1.[84]

The bank concerns were considerable indeed: the college was in default of more than $2 million. TEDS, now under president Ken Meyer, had loaned the college $200,000 to meet payroll. Since the divinity school was a creditor, the president of the Deerfield State Bank called Meyer to notify him the bank was planning to shut down the college and assume control of its land and buildings. Meyer managed to get the bank to give him sixty days to come up with the full amount owed the bank. He recalled, "Immediately, with the counsel of the TEDS executive board, I set out to save the college." He undertook a sixty-day emergency fundraising campaign.

> With three days to go, I was still $150,000 short with no contacts. I was scheduled to preach at a new Free Church in Oklahoma. It was a weekend prophecy conference ending on Sunday morning. The pastor, without any knowledge of the crisis, asked me to share any burden before I preached. I shared the fact that we needed $150,000 in gifts or loans by Tuesday morning, less than 48 hours away.
>
> I preached, and before I could leave the platform, a farmer clasped my hand and put a piece of paper in it. I couldn't wait to see it—went into the washroom, and here was a check for $50,000.

I walked to the lobby and another man handed me a check for $50,000 and said to send him a note for the check. How thrilling! I nearly ran to the car to drive to the airport. A man in a cowboy hat was leaning against my Hertz rental car and said, "Preacher, this your car?" I responded affirmatively. He went on to say he was a Methodist and had come for the prophecy series. He said, "My seminaries are not faithful to the Bible. I want to help." I asked him how much. He said he would wire transfer $50,000 on Monday morning.

I could hardly drive to the airport. Never would I doubt that God wanted to have Trinity College continue.[85]

RETURN AND REBUILDING

The crisis brought both the EFCA and TEDS to the realization that they needed a strong liberal arts college. The annual conference of 1983 voted enthusiastically to bring the college back into the EFCA and to support it. An "outpouring of gifts from across our Free Churches" totaled more than $630,000 in fiscal year 1983—a record high.[86]

Ken Meyer accepted the presidency of the college (while remaining president of TEDS), succeeding Kantzer's interim term. He credited Kantzer as "the man of the hour in 1963 and 1983," for successfully restoring confidence in the evangelical tone of the college. It is easy to forget that many conservative evangelicals found the early '80s more dislocating than the '60s and '70s had been, as it became clear that the moral

Kenneth M. Meyer,
president

climate was declining not just in one segment of the population but in the culture as a whole. In 1985 *Newsweek* reported more moral change in the past five years than in the previous fifty.[87] Kantzer assured parents that Trinity College would recommit itself to the EFCA's tradition of evangelical lifestyle and doctrine for both students and faculty. Kantzer himself would teach a course on doctrine at the college each semester. To the 1983

Kenneth S. Kantzer,
chancellor

annual conference he asked, "Can Trinity College be kept on the right track doctrinally and spiritually? Under this new arrangement, that depends on you. The Evangelical Free Church will have absolute authority because it will completely control the Trinity College Board and own all its assets. It can choose to make Trinity College what it wants."[88] Indeed, in order to convince the bank that the college would henceforth prove a better risk, the entire board resigned and the church was given full control in determining the structure and means of choosing the new board.[89] Kantzer concluded, "We invite you to once again be partners with us in an institution which can, and will, be distinctively Christian—to the glory of Christ ... and for the good of His Church."[90]

The 1984–1985 college catalog touted Trinity's atmosphere as "A World of Personal Integrity," where students enjoyed "a protected environment" without being isolated from the contemporary world. "Students learn to meet modern problems with the same integrity with which Christians of the first century met the problems of their time. Personal integrity and a sense of discipline can make the difference between a world that challenges and one that overwhelms." Prospective students and their parents were assured that "Trinity students are committed to a lifestyle without drugs, alcohol, cigarettes or social dancing." Dorm rules were tightened "to bring these into conformity with the standards of evangelical Christian colleges." This new emphasis paid off, according to Meyer, as he reported that the freshman class "has brought not only large numbers, but a new spirit to campus." And beyond lifestyle rules, the new atmosphere owed to a positive spiritual discipleship program. Margaret Detzler, a student at TEDS, working with chaplain Keith Davy, created a program matching each incoming college student with an older Christian friend, from the divinity school or the college, trained in discipleship. The program grew under chaplain Mel Svendsen, so that by 1990 there were eighty-three individual disciplers plus group activities for spiritual growth and for Christian action. Students reported that the program was helping to bring the college and seminary together.[91]

These efforts succeeded beautifully in reconnecting the college to the EFCA. By 1989 Meyer could report, "Our Free Church students have come home to Trinity College," now comprising some 40 percent of the student body. In 1991 the student body of 903 included a record number of pastors' and missionaries' kids. With growth and reconnection to the church came an increased political conservatism as well. Professor of English communications Lois Fleming recalled widespread dismay among the students when Democrat Bill Clinton won the presidency in 1992.[92] Trinity had successfully realigned with the conservative identity of 1980s evangelicalism.

BUILDING ANEW

"Trinity College today is an evangelical college miracle," President Meyer reported to the EFCA annual conference in summer 1990. Enrollment had quadrupled in the past four years, and the growth rate in 1989–1990 led all Christian colleges.[93] Science and sociology, cut in 1984 because of severe budgetary distress, were relaunched in 1985–1986 and immediately grew, in part because of successful promotion. Newly hired biology professor Angelo Rentas was featured in the inaugural issue of the reborn college magazine, *Direction*. Chemistry students graced the cover of the annual Trinity issue of the *Beacon*. Science students were prominent in the new honors program, launched by Kantzer in 1985.[94] Meanwhile the business program attracted attention for its excellent internship arrangements, forming "heads for business and hearts for the Lord."[95] And one of the greatest growth programs of the late '80s was youth ministry, under the innovative leadership of professor Rick Dunn and Sonlife ministries, with its emphasis on relationship building for the current generation.[96]

To clear the college debt and set the institution on this path for growth, the college arranged to sell sixty acres of property along the Tri-State Tollway for some $5 million. The sale took three years to complete and almost fell through due to a threatened court challenge, but "God intervened," a grateful Meyer reported in 1987.[97]

Donna Peterson, dean

Chemistry students featured
on the cover of the *Beacon*

Chicago Bears head coach Mike Ditka welcomes an enthusiastic
crowd to Trinity's first football season in fall 1989. With him
are Trinity coach Leslie Frazier and President Meyer.

Much credit for the college's academic flourishing belonged to the
new dean of the college, Donna Peterson, a dynamo of energy and dedication. A former French teacher at New Trier High School on the North
Shore, holding an EdD from TEDS, she succeeded Bob Baptista in 1987.

Under her leadership the number of majors grew to twenty-eight, with programs added in pre-nursing, pre-med, and pre–physical therapy, greatly boosting the departments of biology and chemistry. Also added was a pre-law program, enhanced by a debate team that competed intercollegiately and in 1989 earned an octa-finalist trophy in Washington, DC, at the George Mason University National Debate Tournament.[98]

The year 1989 also brought a momentous first in Trinity sports: intercollegiate football. The program was launched in April 1988 with a "Chicago's Genuine Heroes" Sports Night Benefit honoring two Christian sports stars from Chicago, Mike Singletary of the Bears and four-time Olympic speed skater Nancy

Freshman player Herb Coleman, fall 1989 (*Trinitarian 1990*)

Swider-Peltz. The event raised money for bleachers and for a football scholarship fund.[99] As Meyer reported to the EFCA,

> God led us to invite Mr. Les Frazier as our first football coach. He is a former star with the Chicago Bears and is known for a positive, dynamic Christian testimony. He will be aided by volunteers from the Bears this summer [1988]. Christian athletes like Mike Singletary, Jim Covert and Wilbur Marshall have volunteered to aid in a number of ways. We anticipate 60–70 additional students from this program in the fall of 1989.[100]

Frazier was an All-Pro defensive back for the Chicago Bears who led the team with six interceptions in its 1984–1985 Super Bowl championship season. Eager to use football as a means of helping players become disciples of Christ, he brought a spiritual and evangelistic commitment to football at Trinity that has remained a chief focus of the program.[101]

DIVERSIFYING

Football brought a larger number of African American students to the college, enhancing a trend that had begun in a small way in the late 1960s with

IMPACT—Trinity College's first gospel choir

a handful of minority students—Black and Asian, mostly from Chicago—in each entering class. At that time the white majority began to take an interest in racial issues with the Contemporary Affairs Committee and in student fine arts activities. The 1968–1969 drama club took as its theme "Black and White in Literature," airing the movie *A Raisin in the Sun* and staging the play *In White America*. The latter, a documentary history of Black America, "shook that satisfied self that wanted to believe equality is, was, and ever will be."[102] Concern for race relations grew in the 1970s alongside the left-leaning tendencies among some faculty and students, but greater change began, interestingly enough, in the conservative, more tightly church-connected 1980s. It seems two trends were occurring simultaneously: a more deliberate cultivation of conservative evangelical identity and lifestyle, and a more deliberate diversification of the church and college population ethnically and racially.

The EFCA and its partnership with the National Association of Evangelicals played an important role. In 1985 the association reported to the EFCA that it had added a new Hispanic emphasis to its work, providing translation and workshops for Spanish-speaking delegates to its national convention and organizing an ongoing Hispanic commission.[103] In 1989 the EFCA passed a resolution for its Social Concerns Committee calling for gospel proclamation to minority populations "in their language and cultural settings," a mission area every bit as important as the foreign field. It urged "churches and church members to consistently pray and creatively plan for outreach to the various ethnic groups and by-passed peoples of our land," by recruiting and training ethnic leaders with a goal of having six hundred minority churches in the EFCA by the year 2000. "We recognize that such effort and inclusion will bring change. We view this as valued change."[104] In 1992 the EFCA passed a stronger resolution, titled "The 'New' Racism," calling for repentance and action against what today is called systemic racism.

> As Christians, we deplore racism as sin against fellow human beings who are created in the image of God. Racism has undergone a recent resurgence, with an increase in violence evidenced by racial confrontations on college campuses, numerous racially biased crimes, the increased visibility and boldness of hate groups. ... Racism is also present in more subtle and passive forms in institutional settings where systems of discrimination prevent the upward mobility of gifted and qualified individuals.

The resolution went on to describe patterns of racial discrimination in housing, "in the neglect and avoidance of people who are racially different, in the use of racially offensive language and humor, and at the level of individual prejudices and biases." It called on Free Church people "to search our own hearts and repent of any racist attitudes we may have, no matter how subtle," and "to work toward eliminating racism in our local churches, educational institutions, and throughout the EFCA family as a whole." One of the specific steps it recommended was to develop "relationships of mutual education and submission (Ephesians 5:21) with people of different races," both individually and institutionally.[105]

Just at this time Trinity College was beginning its relationship with what would become its South Florida campus. Miami Christian College, founded in 1946, was an accredited but struggling Bible college with a powerful radio station, WCMU-FM. Its attorneys had approached Ken Meyer in 1988 with an offer to hand the school over to TEDS or the EFCA or some other board. After some negotiation, Trinity assumed responsibility for Miami Christian College and its assets. David Martin writes, "Trinity now found itself with a new multiethnic partnership, a large new pool of potential students, and a new base for EFCA mission expansion in Latin America." Miami Christian College officially took the name of Trinity College at Miami in 1993. By the mid-1990s the radio station was generating annual income of half a million dollars "and introducing hundreds of young people to the college."[106]

From the cover of the student handbook, TIU South Florida Campus

What attracted many students initially to Trinity at Miami was the EXCEL program, adapted from Trinity College's adult degree-completion program, REACH. Begun in 1983, REACH stood for Relevant Education for the Adult Christian. It was a highly innovative, flexible program designed for the working adult learner. Adults with any number of prior college credits could join a cohort and proceed one course at a time toward completing a fully accredited bachelor's degree in interpersonal and group communication, within the framework of Christian liberal arts. When it was first launched, the program had no real competition in the Chicago and Milwaukee area. Before its transfer to Trinity, Miami Christian College paid the college a $125,000 franchise fee to use the REACH model with a new name, EXCEL, in Florida.[107] These programs were truly missional. They performed a wonderful service, bringing a Christian college education to many capable working adults, mostly Black and Latino students, whom a traditional daytime residential program could not serve. At college commencements, the whole Trinity community felt a special joy to see these midlife students receive a Trinity College degree.

Promotional material for the REACH program

With its two campuses in Illinois and Florida, Trinity College enrollment reached a head count of 1,233 in 1994 and was fast becoming one of the most racially diverse institutions in the Coalition for Christian Colleges (now the Coalition for Christian Colleges and Universities). The Miami campus was so full that it was looking for new facilities for 1995–1996. Aiding this process was the decision to accept federal funding—not directly to the institution, but to individual students—through the new government GAP loan program launched in 1991–1992.[108]

RETROSPECTIVE: FROM TSBC TO TIU

The Trinity College of 1995 had changed significantly from the Trinity Bible College of 1957. A larger, more diverse, more complex institution, located in the suburbs rather than in the city, it had weathered three major financial crises and seen the Lord provide just when hope seemed lost. Never the top priority of the Free Church, which always and not without reason favored the seminary as more essential to the denomination, the college managed to thrive (at times) and innovate both within and outside official church ownership. Through all the ups and downs, two constants may be observed: Trinity College's dedication to integrate Christian faith with a liberal arts and preprofessional education, and its atmosphere of close-knit Christian fellowship.

Even during the years of separation from the EFCA, Trinity College shared some personnel and facilities with TEDS. At times the college supported the seminary financially, as when college enrollments were booming in the early 1960s and again in the early 1990s. At times the divinity school helped to float the college.[109]

Greg Waybright, the first president of TIU,
watches a college sporting event

As early as 1971 Kantzer drafted a white paper for the boards of both schools, outlining how they might be combined into a university. By the early 1990s the college had achieved growth and reputation sufficient to consider a merger with the internationally known divinity school. Ken Meyer began restructuring the administration and moving toward the goal of shared services. With encouragement from the accreditors at North Central and a helpful report by Milo Lundell, the boards of the two schools agreed to merge. Meanwhile, Meyer decided to step down as president of both schools, and, in the tradition of Harry Evans's appointment, another pastor of the Arlington Heights Evangelical Free Church was elected president: the young and winsome Gregory Waybright. The EFCA annual conference approved the schools' decisions to merge, and on July 1, 1996, Trinity International University was officially formed.[110]

Chapter 5

Decades of Consolidation
(1975–1996)

Scott M. Manetsch

T he decision to make Trinity College an independent liberal arts college in 1974 produced a variety of consequences—some intended, others unintended—that culminated in the crisis of 1983, when the school returned to EFCA oversight. During this decade, the college and divinity school existed as two separate institutions with unique religious cultures and (seemingly) very different future prospects. Over these years, TEDS's ministry continued to grow even as its influence expanded well beyond the Bannockburn campus. Several crucial events mark this period: the presidency of Kenneth Meyer (1974–1995), the retirement of Kenneth Kantzer in 1978, and the appointment of academic dean Walter Kaiser in 1980. After the return of Trinity College to the EFCA fold in 1983, a new trajectory was set as the two schools worked to consolidate services and governance, and as President Meyer and Free Church officials began to envision the formal merger of the two schools and the creation of Trinity International University. Amid these significant changes in organization and leadership, however, two things remained constant: TEDS continued each year to equip hundreds of gifted and godly men and women for ministry to the global church, and God remained faithful in providing financial resources and talented faculty for the cash-strapped school on Half Day Road.

RECOVERY AND ADVANCE

The 1974–1975 school year brought with it new enthusiasm and brighter prospects for the future. The decision of the EFCA to divest itself of Trinity College seemed to signal a renewed commitment to support TEDS and its central mission to train young people for Christian ministry. The appointment of Rev. Kenneth Meyer as interim president of the divinity school in September 1974 was further evidence of the continued close relationship between the seminary and its mother denomination. A graduate of the old Trinity Seminary, Meyer had served as pastor of the flagship

First Evangelical Free Church of Rockford, Illinois, since 1969 and was a member of the executive board of Trinity.[1] Meyer was widely recognized as a strong and dedicated Christian leader, a man of "evident sincerity, common sense, tender spirit, and tremendous drive."[2] After an initial year as interim president (while he continued his pastoral duties in Rockford), Meyer was elected to a three-year term as president of TEDS. At his inauguration in November 1975, the

Ken Meyer, 1970s

new president pledged that, under his oversight, the seminary would "continue to be an institution of academic excellence, committed to the inspired Word of God and the principles of the EFCA."[3]

Under Meyer's leadership, the financial situation of the divinity school stabilized and noticeably improved. The school balanced its budget each of the next ten years, despite an unfavorable economic climate of rapid inflation and high unemployment. During this period, the seminary was able to retire the $700,000 debt it had assumed from the divestiture of 1974.[4] This financial turnaround was partly due to the steady support of EFCA churches and individuals. In 1980, for example, slightly more than five hundred of the EFCA's seven hundred congregations provided some form of financial support to TEDS, comprising 13 percent of the school's institutional income.[5] TEDS's more positive budgetary position was also made possible by significant hikes in student tuition. For the 1974–1975 school year, tuition at TEDS was set at $1,200 (not including fees). Four years later, tuition had risen to $2,175—more than a 75 percent increase.[6] By 1983, tuition was $3,200 per year. TEDS had become one of the largest—but also one of the most expensive—seminaries in the United States.[7]

From a broader perspective, however, not only were budgets balanced through tuition dollars and generous donors—they were also balanced through God's gracious provision as he answered the prayers of his people on behalf of the seminary. One of these faithful prayer warriors was a teenage girl from Dolton, Illinois, who wrote the following message to President Meyer: "Dear Rev. Meyer: I would love to give a contribution to your school, but since I'm only 15 years old, I really don't have any money to give you. ... I will ask God to send you the money that you need."[8]

With American Association of Theological Schools, accreditation in hand and the financial storms behind it, the divinity school was poised for rapid growth. Over the next decade, the seminary's enrollment climbed steadily from 600 full and part-time students in 1975, to 942 students in 1979, to more than 1,100 students in 1984.[9] High student enrollments justified (and were fueled by) new academic programs. The blueprint for these programs was first laid out by Kantzer in a white paper he presented to Trinity's executive board in 1970. In that document, titled "Ten Year Projection," Kantzer reaffirmed TEDS's priority to "prepare effective pastoral ministers for the EFCA and other evangelical groups," while at the same time recommending the gradual rollout of doctoral programs in education, missions, biblical and Near Eastern studies, history and philosophy of religion, and practical theology.[10] Kantzer also proposed the creation of a doctor of ministry program, and expansion of curriculum in such areas as Christianity and contemporary society, Christianity and Black studies, church planting, and the rural church.[11]

The Ten Year Projection reflected Kantzer's emerging vision for a Christian research university in which the seminary, together with the college, would attract the best Christian faculty and the brightest students to address the most pressing questions of church and culture from a Christian worldview.[12] Kantzer insisted that this expansive vision would require hiring more faculty members, including African American scholars: "It is imperative," he noted, "that Blacks be represented in more than token amounts on the teaching faculty, and preferably Blacks should be teaching in areas other than sociology of religion and Black Studies."[13]

Kantzer's vision for new academic programs, including doctoral education, began to be implemented over the following decade. In 1977, the DMin program was launched. Two years later, Trinity began to offer the doctor of missiology degree. Through the efforts of missionary faculty David Hesselgrave, Herbert Kane, Arthur Johnston, and Paul Little, Trinity's School of World Missions was expanded into a major center for training future and furloughed missionaries, equipping international leaders, and formulating global missionary strategies. The School of World Missions, which was situated in the refurbished Gundersen Building, attracted a growing number of international church leaders to Trinity's campus. During the 1976–1977 school year, sixty-two international students from seventeen different countries came to TEDS for ministry training.[14] Many of these foreign students were prominent church leaders in their home countries. Howard Matson recalls feeling deeply humbled when he learned that the international student who cleaned his office each day was the dean of a seminary back in Nigeria.[15] Within two years, more than one hundred students had matriculated in these two doctoral programs, including President Meyer himself, who was awarded the DMin degree in May 1978.[16] By 1985, these programs had tripled in size, with two hundred students enrolled in Trinity's DMin program and more than one hundred students in the doctor of missiology program.[17]

Faculty in TEDS School of World Mission. Seated in front row left to right: Kenneth Kantzer, Herbert Kane, Paul Krishna, Paul Little, and David Hesselgrave.

Herbert Kane with students

Notwithstanding these advances, several goals in Kenneth Kantzer's Ten Year Projection were not accomplished during his tenure as dean. The divestiture of Trinity College from the EFCA in 1974 made the idea of a Christian university impracticable, at least for the time being. So too, the launch of academic doctoral programs in education, biblical studies, and history and philosophy of religion had to be put on hold until the mid-1980s due to inadequate funding. Finally, Kantzer's vision to hire Black professors in the core theological disciplines was never achieved. Trinity's regular faculty continued to be entirely Caucasian, with the exception of two Black scholars, William Bentley and William Parnell, who served as part-time visiting professors at TEDS during the 1970s. It was only with the hiring of theologian Bruce Fields in the early 1990s that the seminary had its first full-time Black faculty member.

One faculty member from this period remembers that Kantzer was "innovative to his toenails."[18] Indeed, innovation was very much in vogue in the 1970s and early 1980s as TEDS promoted a variety of nontraditional programs to serve the broader church. These programs included a summer extension school at Camp-of-the-Woods in upstate New York, an alumni Institute for area pastors and friends of the school, and an annual conference called "Week in the Word" for Free Church pastors following the EFCA's national meetings each year.

Kantzer's innovative spirit, however, did not override what he saw as the foundational blocks of quality theological education. The curriculum that was put in place in 1963–1964, with its emphasis on training in biblical Hebrew and Greek, and its extensive exposure to the classical theological disciplines of biblical studies, systematic theology, and church history, was not significantly altered during the following decades. In the early years, students were expected to participate in practical ministry experiences on the weekends, but did not receive academic credit for these assignments. This changed in 1973, when the faculty revised the MDiv curriculum to require students to enroll in three two-credit pastoral internship classes in their senior year.[19] Rev. Ted Olson was subsequently hired to serve as the director of the new internship program.[20] Nevertheless, feedback from TEDS's alumni serving local churches indicated that the MDiv program was still weak in preparing students for the practical demands of pastoral work.[21] Hence, in 1977, the faculty approved a second revision requiring all full-time MDiv students to be involved in practical field experiences during the first two years of their seminary program as a prerequisite for the senior internship.

These efforts to make the seminary curriculum more practical were admittedly modest, indicating the faculty's unwavering commitment to a traditional model of theological education. As one professor averred, "When you have it right, why change?"[22] This conservative approach was not shared by President Meyer, however, whose pragmatic temperament, extensive pastoral experience, and regular interaction with EFCA leaders caused him to value curricular revisions focused on spiritual formation and practical leadership development. Consequently, one of Meyer's four stated goals for TEDS in 1984 was to "produce a balanced curriculum between academic strength and practical experience."[23] Six years later, Meyer created a special task force charged to make a sweeping assessment of Trinity's programs and curriculum in light of the changing needs of local churches. In announcing this long-range study, titled TEDS 2000, the president stipulated that the only limitation was that "the status quo is not self-justified."[24] In effect, TEDS 2000 represented Meyer's effort to circumvent what he saw as the faculty's intransigence in establishing significant revisions to the traditional curriculum.

FACULTY SNAPSHOTS

By the time that Kenneth Meyer began his presidency in 1974, Trinity's faculty roster had changed significantly from the previous decade. Wilbur Smith had long since retired. Notable educators and scholars such as Elmer Towns, John Warwick Montgomery, Clark Pinnock, Richard Longenecker, and Robert Culver had come and gone. Their places were now taken by a highly talented group of younger scholars, many of whom were to become leaders in American evangelicalism in the decades to come, including John Woodbridge (church history, 1970), Murray Harris (New Testament, 1971), Charles "Chick" Sell (Christian education, 1971), Norman Geisler (philosophy of religion, 1971), Victor Walter (pastoral theology, 1973), Gilbert Peterson (Christian education, 1974), Paul Feinberg (systematic theology, 1974), and Arthur Johnston (missions, 1974). By the end of the decade, such familiar names as Barry Beitzel (Old Testament), Warren Benson (Christian education), Harold O. J. Brown (systematic theology), D. A. Carson (New Testament), William Lane Craig (philosophy of religion), Perry Downs (Christian education), Doug Moo (New Testament), Grant Osborne (New Testament), and William Secor (pastoral counseling) had also joined Trinity's faculty.

John Woodbridge,
early 1970s

These professors came to Bannockburn for a variety of reasons, but many of them were undoubtedly drawn to the school by the prospect of training for ministry the outstanding Christian young men and women that God consistently brought to Trinity. So too, scholars found especially inviting Trinity's creative intellectual culture. Perry Downs remembers that, when he joined the faculty in 1976, Trinity was a dream place for Christian scholars because it was "where creative, cutting-edge biblical and theological work was being done" within the boundaries of evangelical orthodoxy.[25]

During the 1970s and early 1980s, most faculty families lived close to Trinity's campus, and many enjoyed rich and meaningful relationships with one other. "Back then, faculty had fun!" Olive Liefeld remembers. The Trinity faculty was "more like a family."[26] Many faculty members attended the same churches on Sundays. They were frequently in one another's homes for meals and fellowship; they watched one another's children grow up. Each year, a number of social events were planned to bring faculty families together: a hymn sing at a local church,

Grant Osborne,
early 1970s

a barbeque at Norman Geisler's home (he had a swimming pool in his backyard), a volleyball or softball game in a local park. These faculty gatherings were invariably rich in conversation, laughter, and meaningful fellowship. Memories of these events continue to sparkle. One old-timer remembers a dinner party where Gleason Archer became more and more amorous toward his beloved wife, Sandy, in full view of other colleagues. Finally, exasperated, Sandy said: "Gleason, would you stop it! Go learn another foreign language!"[27] Olive Liefeld recalls yet another event that has become part of Trinity lore: during a faculty-spouse softball game, held the day before commencement, Olive hit a pop fly into the infield. Robert Culver, yelling "Get her out! Get her out!" hustled to catch the ball—and ran squarely into a visiting professor named H. Dermot McDonald, breaking his nose and giving him a black eye. At the graduation service the next day, McDonald wore sunglasses to hide his battle scars.[28]

The faculty laughed together—but they also grieved together. The seminary community experienced deep sorrow when Paul Little was killed in an automobile accident during a ministry trip to Canada in summer 1975. The biblical text read at his memorial service was a most appropriate epitaph for his fruitful life: "He served his own generation according to the will of God" (Acts 13:36).[29]

Though Trinity's seminary faculty was close-knit in the 1970s and early 1980s, it was also combustible. Many professors whom Kantzer attracted to Bannockburn were men of international reputation, possessing brilliant, creative minds and strong opinions. Leading this talented group proved to be one of Kantzer's greatest challenges. As he later commented, "First-rate scholars and great pedagogues are seldom milquetoasts. At times, I felt I was holding the reins of a team of wild horses, each tearing off in a different direction."[30] Faculty meetings often became "wild and raucous" as faculty members aired their views, debated their differences, and criticized administrative policies. Several professors were sharply critical of Kantzer for closing the school on the day of the funeral of Martin Luther King Jr. in 1968 as well as his decision to cancel classes in observance of Good Friday. Decisions related to departmental hiring were especially contentious, as strong personalities and minor theological differences made unity elusive.

The most monumental clash occurred in the mid-1970s, when a faculty member, livid with rage, accused Kantzer in public of lying and stormed out of a meeting. Kantzer quietly responded: "I'm sorry that you think that, but I'm not lying."[31] By this time, faculty meetings had become so conflict ridden that President Meyer began chairing the sessions. Colleagues who participated in faculty meetings like these have for the most part forgotten the specific issues that triggered such explosive interchanges. What they do remember is Kantzer's gentle, gracious response to his critics. All the same, faculty members remember this period in the 1970s and early 1980s as a dynamic and exciting time at Trinity. There was "over all a good spirit" on campus: faculty families enjoyed warm relationships with one another; the school was growing in size; scores of graduates were leaving Trinity each year to serve evangelical churches all over the world.[32]

PASSING THE BATON:
FROM KANTZER TO KAISER

The final years of Kenneth Kantzer's tenure in the dean's office at TEDS provided many reasons for optimism and gratitude. The budget was balanced year to year; talented new faculty members arrived on campus; student enrollments continued to rise. Money was raised and new buildings were constructed, including the Arnold T. Olson Chapel and the campus bookstore (both completed in 1979). TEDS's reputation among evangelicals worldwide had never been stronger, garnishing the praise and strong endorsement of Christian leaders such as Carl F. H. Henry, Francis Schaeffer of L'Abri Fellowship, and Bill Bright, president of Campus Crusade for Christ.[33] Rev. John Stott of All Souls Church in London called Trinity "his seminary in the United States."[34] A *Time* Magazine article highlighted TEDS as a conservative theological seminary of high academic standards that was growing in student enrollment, in contrast to the declining influence of liberal seminaries.[35] Much had changed over the years since Trinity was a small, struggling seminary on West Berteau Avenue.

In late summer 1977, Kantzer was chosen to be the successor of Harold Lindsell as the senior editor of the evangelical periodical *Christianity Today*.[36] Initially, Kantzer had hoped to combine his dean work with these new editorial responsibilities, but this arrangement soon proved to be unmanageable. Consequently, by the first months of 1979, a search committee for a new dean was constituted and Kantzer's tenure as dean of TEDS had effectively come to an end. To honor Kantzer's enormous contribution, the Trinity community organized a Kantzer Appreciation Day, which was held in the beautiful, newly constructed Arnold T. Olson Chapel on April 27, 1979. Accolades and well-wishes came from colleagues and friends from throughout the evangelical world. Rev. Billy Graham described Kantzer as "one of the three or four leading theologians in the mid-twentieth century" and as "one of the finest Christian gentlemen I know. To me, he has always been the personification of what a

Ruth and Kenneth Kantzer in retirement

Christian ought to be."[37] President Meyer praised Kantzer's "vision, balance, theological acumen and deep spiritual commitment." Indeed, the divinity school owed "a great debt of gratitude for God's man for the hour."[38] One of the most colorful testimonials came from Kantzer's secretary of eleven years, Lois Armstrong: "He has extreme patience. For years he has brought in four or five plants to have in the office, which I consistently get 'sick' in a few months. He cheerfully encourages me, takes them home to his 'hospital', and brings back gorgeous blooming plants."[39] These qualities of patience, encouragement, and nurture described well Dean Kenneth Kantzer.

On February 8, 1980, Dr. Walter C. Kaiser was installed as the new academic dean of TEDS. For many, Kaiser seemed the obvious choice to succeed his colleague and friend Kantzer. Having earned his MA and PhD in Mediterranean studies at Brandeis University, Kaiser had taught alongside Kantzer at Wheaton College for several years before coming to TEDS as an Old Testament professor in 1964. Kaiser was a man of commanding personality and exceptional leadership, known throughout the evangelical world as a brilliant scholar and popular public speaker. Though not yet fifty years old, Kaiser had already served as the president of the Evangelical Theological Society in 1977, and authored several highly regarded monographs on Old Testament theology and interpretation. Colleagues who served under Kaiser remember him as a popular classroom teacher, a gifted preacher, and a committed churchman, with a sparkling sense of humor and abundant energy.

Dean Walter Kaiser,
early 1980s

Walter and Marge Kaiser were especially generous in their hospitality shared with faculty members, their families, and students alike. As time would tell, however, Dean Kaiser could also be heavy-handed and harsh toward colleagues who disagreed with him.[40] Kaiser's vision for TEDS mirrored closely the priorities articulated by Kantzer before him. Writing in the *Evangelical Beacon* in 1983, Kaiser noted that "a seminary exists for the sake of the Church and for the special office of the ministry both at home and abroad." As a community of learners, the central task of a seminary "is the work of entrusting the Gospel to men and women who have been privileged to be 'called' of God to be his 'captives' in equipping the saints to do the work of ministry." As a result, the seminary was responsible to nurture both heart and mind, with the goal of producing lives characterized by obedience and faithful service. "Learning must always be a verb and it must always have an object," Kaiser insisted. "When it ceases to be such, learning becomes an end in itself, and that is sheer idolatry."[41]

CHALLENGES AND NEW OPPORTUNITIES

The first years of Dean Kaiser's tenure were shaped significantly by fallout from the unfolding crisis at Trinity College. The college's decision to separate from the EFCA in 1974 had proven to be a disastrous one. Between 1978 and 1983, student enrollment dropped by over 40 percent, a decline caused in part by the widespread perception that the college was straying from its evangelical commitments and lifestyle standards.[42] This precipitous decline in enrollment, combined with a soaring debt of nearly $3 million, forced President Evans to announce his resignation in January 1983. In the tense months that followed, the college's board of trustees appointed Kantzer (who had recently retired from *Christianity Today*) as interim president and requested the Free Church to receive the school back into its fellowship.

Trinity College was officially welcomed back into the Free Church at the EFCA national conference in summer 1984; by that time, Kantzer was the school's chancellor and Kenneth Meyer had been appointed its president.[43] This same church conference directed the boards of the two schools to consolidate services and "develop a working model for the cooperation and consolidation of these institutions."[44] These important decisions had sizable implications for TEDS going forward. Kenneth Meyer's executive leadership and Free Church resources would hereafter be shared between the two institutions. More importantly, TEDS and Trinity College would now begin taking administrative steps toward uniting the two schools under a single board with a common academic mission.

Kantzer's dream of shaping Trinity into a major Christian research university had been reborn.

Over the course of the 1980s, Trinity continued to build its academic programs. In 1985, the seminary launched the doctor of education degree program, with Ted Ward as its first director. Ward, who had taught at Michigan State University for thirty years before coming to TEDS, was a world-recognized authority on nontraditional education in the Majority World.[45] He was also known as an iconoclast in his approach to church-based education, famously stating that traditional "Christian Education is neither Christian nor education." His presence on the education faculty, along with Warren Benson, Perry Downs, Mark Senter III, and (slightly later) Linda Cannell, added prestige to Trinity as a major center for Christian education and international theological education.

Two years later, after extensive study and planning, TEDS also began its long-awaited PhD program in theological studies under the direction of Kantzer. The implementation of this doctoral program, covering the four disciplines of Old Testament, New Testament, systematic theology, and historical theology, did not come without extensive discussions and some disagreements. Many faculty members expressed concerns as to the financial viability of this program and the increased workload it would require of them. They also debated whether the program should primarily serve international scholars or American students. Some Free Church leaders voiced additional concerns that TEDS was losing its focus on congregational ministry and missions. Kantzer addressed these misgivings in an article published in the *Evangelical Beacon* in June 1987. He heartily agreed that "the highest educational priority of the church is the training of evangelists and pastors who, under God, will become future leaders and servants of the church." TEDS remained fully committed to this priority. Nevertheless, at this particular cultural moment, the creation of a high-caliber, evangelical doctoral program in biblical and theological studies that was committed to the doctrine of biblical inerrancy was especially strategic and necessary. "Such a program will prove to be a great boon to our Evangelical Free Churches," Kantzer insisted. "It will add a significant boost to our overseas mission program. It will provide a broad and very necessary ministry for the worldwide church of Christ. ... In our time, this represents one of the truly great needs in the worldwide church." Kantzer believed that TEDS was "uniquely qualified" to fill this crucial need in theological education.[46] Even so, it was expected that the rollout of the PhD program would be gradual. Only eight students matriculated in the first cohort of doctoral students in 1987.[47] Over the next decade, however, the PhD in theological studies mushroomed in size, enrolling 127 active students by 1995.[48] During this same period, enrollment in the doctor in education program remained more modest, fluctuating between twenty and thirty-two students.[49]

Ugandan students James and Grace Ndyabahika and children

In addition to doctoral programs, TEDS also created new extension programs during this time. Under the leadership of Larry McCullough (and later Mark Senter III), TEDS's Office of Extension and Continuing Education was launched in 1985 to provide quality theological education for laymen and laywomen beyond the reach of the Bannockburn campus.[50] By 1994, more than a thousand students were enrolled in this program at ten extension sites spread around the United States.[51] Among the students enrolled in this program were Susan Vergeront, a fifth-term legislator in the Wisconsin State Assembly, and Mose Fuller, a Black church planter and full-time member of the Milwaukee Fire Department. Fuller reported, "I could never go to seminary if it weren't for Trinity's extension program."[52]

TRINITY STUDENTS IN PROFILE

By the early 1990s, the makeup of TEDS's student body had changed in significant ways from the earlier years. The percentage of students coming from secular colleges and universities (as opposed to Christian colleges and Bible schools) had grown slightly, making up around 40 percent of the student body.[53] The student population was also older and more diverse; a sizable number of students now came to Trinity to pursue ministry as a second career.[54] One big change was the burgeoning number of foreign students attending TEDS. By the fall of 1994, there were 220 international students on campus from forty-four countries, comprising roughly 15 percent of the student population. A sizable number of these foreign students came from a select group of countries: Canada, Hong Kong, Taiwan, India, and South Korea. One such student was Yong Park, who earned his PhD in historical theology in 1991 before becoming a professor at Chongshin University and one of the most celebrated church historians in South Korea. Maureen Yeung was another notable graduate who, after earning her ThM degree in 1991, returned to Hong Kong to become president of Evangel Seminary.[55] One additional foreign student was Dr. John Senyonyi, a professor of mathematical statistics, who came to Trinity in the early 1990s to study theology, after which he returned to Uganda and became vice chancellor of Uganda Christian University.

International students such as these, along with their families, made incalculable contributions to the campus community with their vibrant Christian testimonies and rich cultural traditions. Their children who attended Bannockburn elementary school made that district one of the most ethnically diverse in the state of Illinois. Mark Senter remembers spending a wonderful evening with a Korean student and his family and being surprised to learn that the student's son had recently attended a birthday party at Chuck E. Cheese for a classmate named Jeffrey Jordan, the son of basketball legend Michael Jordan, who also attended the Bannockburn school.[56]

Students who attended TEDS in the 1980s and 1990s continued to come from a large variety of denominational traditions. In 1989, for example, there were no fewer than sixty-eight denominations represented on campus, with the largest representation coming from the EFCA (235 students; 17 percent of total), nondenominational churches

(183 students; 13 percent of total), and various Baptist groups (175 students; 13 percent of total). That EFCA students comprised a smaller percentage of the overall student population at matriculation raised eyebrows among some in the Free Church, though President Meyer attempted to put the matter in a positive light. The total number of Free Church students on campus was far higher than it had been in the 1970s. Moreover, as the president often reminded Free Church constituents, TEDS effectively recruited dozens of non-EFCA students into the Free Church each year.[57] In fact, as Meyer reported proudly, nearly 60 percent of Free Churches were now being served by Trinity graduates.[58] Clearly, the EFCA as a religious movement was being significantly shaped by her divinity school in Bannockburn. Kantzer's maxim had never seemed truer: "As the seminary goes, so goes the church."

Unfortunately, the racial makeup of TEDS's student body did not reflect this same pattern of diversity. During the 1960s and 1970s, nearly all American students who attended the divinity school were Caucasian, and the vast majority of them were male. In 1980, four African American students began meeting regularly in the White Horse Inn (in the basement of the chapel) to discuss issues of race and its impact on life at TEDS. This group included Bruce Fields, who was the group's unofficial theologian, and a retired lieutenant colonel from the US Army named Raleigh Washington, who was the visionary and driving force behind the group. Over time, these four men created a student organization named ABBA— Association of Brothers for Black America—which met on a monthly basis for the purpose of mutual support and to challenge the school to be more proactive in its ministry to minority students.[59] Fields went on to pursue his doctorate in New Testament at Marquette University; Washington, after his graduation in 1983, became the first Black ordained minister in the EFCA. In that same year, Washington, along with six Trinity students, planted a multiethnic and multicultural congregation in the Austin neighborhood of Chicago named the Rock of Our Salvation Evangelical Free Church. The Rock teamed up with the Circle Community Center to form a holistic ministry addressing the physical, social, and spiritual needs of residents in the community.[60]

In his ministry vision, Washington was pushing back against the homogenous unit principle of church growth, proposed by prominent missiologists

Rev. Raleigh Washington

such as C. Peter Wagner, which stated that gospel proclamation is more effective (and the church grows more rapidly) when people are not expected to cross ethnic, cultural, or class barriers. To this, Washington retorted: "When we get to heaven, it's not going to be homogeneous. Where better for us to start than right here?"[61] Washington, along with TEDS professor James Westgate, was also instrumental in the creation of TEDS's MAR / Urban Ministries program, launched in 1986 to provide ministry training for minority students in urban church contexts. Around sixty students graduated from this program over the next two decades.[62] In these early years, the urban ministry program was offered at two church sites in south Chicago; in 2005 the program was relocated to its own campus in Dalton, Illinois, where it trained men and women for Black and multiethnic church ministry under the leadership of Dr. Michael Reynolds.

The number of women students on TEDS's campus was also relatively small during this period. In 1964, there were only sixteen female seminary students on campus (out of 135 students total), none of whom were enrolled in the three-year MDiv program.[63] A decade later, there were seventy-two women attending classes at the divinity school, but only a handful of them taking the MDiv curriculum.[64] During the 1980s and early 1990s, the number of female students at TEDS continued to increase, though it appears that the percentage of female students as part of the overall student population remained relatively static, at around 10–15 percent. Women pursued their theological studies at Trinity in preparation for missionary service, campus ministry, Christian counseling, social work, Christian secondary education, and doctoral studies.[65] Many received training alongside their husbands and then became ministry partners with them in local congregations.

Women who studied at the divinity school during these years faced a unique set of challenges and obstacles. Many evangelicals in that period—and most of Trinity's professors and students—believed that Scripture disallowed women from exercising spiritual leadership over men in local churches. This was the EFCA's official position as well; it did not permit women to be ordained to church offices. Although TEDS welcomed women to enroll in the MDiv program, some male students wondered whether they belonged there.[66] The climate for women on campus was made all the more difficult by the fact that there were few female professors at Trinity to serve as role models or provide encouragement. During the 1970s and early 1980s, a handful of female visiting scholars and part-time instructors taught courses in missions, Christian education, and Christian counseling.[67] The first full-time female faculty member at the divinity school was education professor Linda Cannell, who arrived in 1988.

While remaining respectful of the EFCA position on women's ordination, several faculty members, including Kenneth Kantzer, Walter Liefeld, and Walter Kaiser, believed that Scripture allowed greater latitude for women to exercise teaching and leadership gifts in local churches. Kantzer clarified his viewpoint in a letter to EFCA president Thomas McDill in 1987: "the Bible does not flatly rule out under all circumstances that a woman may speak in a public meeting or teach men or hold an office ('rule') in a Christian church."[68] Because of this understanding, Kantzer and his wife, Ruth, were particularly sensitive to the needs of female students and worked hard to make the Trinity community one that was hospitable to women students preparing for church ministry. This sensitivity was reflected in Kantzer's classroom teaching, as this anonymous letter attests: "Dear Dr. Kantzer: A number of times in class last quarter you made a point of saying, 'men *and women*' & 'male *and female*.' This always made me feel like my name was being called! Sometimes it's lonely at this place. When you said, 'male and female' it reminded me that I'm important to God, too. Thank you, Sir. God bless you." Signed: "A female student."[69]

Student life at the divinity school during the 1980s and early 1990s was intense and busy. In addition to their studies and local church ministries, many students had to work to pay rent and tuition. A sizable number of them worked the graveyard shift at UPS, served as security guards for local businesses, provided childcare for local families, or washed office windows to pay the bills.

TEDS Students from the quads, early 1980s

On campus, students were encouraged to attend chapel services four days a week, Tuesday through Friday, featuring many of the best-known pastors and scholars in the evangelical world. The chapel schedule for the 1983–1984 school year included such luminaries as Herbert Kane, John Stott, Francis Schaeffer, Anthony Campolo, Joe Aldrich, Richard Halverson, and Leon Morris.[70] One especially impactful week of chapel services occurred in early April 1995, when a student revival that began at Wheaton College spread to Trinity's campus. Over a four-day period, as many as four hundred seminary and college students, staff, and professors gathered in the chapel each day for impromptu prayer services of confession, repentance, and worship that stretched beyond the chapel hour and into the early hours of the morning.[71]

In addition to chapel services, Trinity Missions Fellowship sponsored a weekly prayer meeting that promoted global awareness and missionary service. Trinity Missions Fellowship recruited seventy seminary students and their spouses to go overseas to serve as short-term missionaries during the summer of 1985.[72] Likewise, each year Professor John Nyquist and the Trinity Evangelistic Team organized One Great Day of Sharing, where several hundred faculty, staff, and students spent the day sharing the gospel on street corners of downtown Chicago.[73] Gospel initiatives such as these gave some justification to President Meyer's frequent claim that TEDS's core ministry remained "to train pastors and missionaries" in the service of the Great Commission.[74]

Other organizations that were active on campus during these years were student government, ABBA, Trinity Wives Fellowship, and the Clothes Horse. Many students also participated in intramural sports (football and basketball), attended the annual faculty-student talent show, and enjoyed Christian concerts sponsored by Trinity's Artists Series. Single students who lived in the quad found less formal ways to entertain themselves, whether through hymn sings, snowball fights, pick-up soccer matches, or stealth raids on the Sara Lee factory in neighboring Deerfield to forage in dumpsters for discarded cakes and cookies.[75] Likewise, once a year TEDS students celebrated Dallas Daze, wearing formal attire and sporting dispensational charts and Scofield Bibles, in recognition of Dallas Theological Seminary's more straight-laced ethos.

Dallas Daze, 1984

FACULTY ARRIVALS

Thanks to Dean Kaiser's leadership, TEDS continued to attract leading evangelical scholars to its faculty. A Trinity advertisement that appeared in *Christianity Today* in the late 1980s depicted several prominent Trinity professors—Coleman, Collins, Kaiser, Sell, Ward, Woodbridge—each leaning on a stack of books written by members of the faculty. The caption emblazoned across the top read: "Study with the ones who write the books!" Trinity's much-published professors continued to be perceived as the crown jewel of the seminary. During the 1980s and early 1990s, the seminary's biblical studies departments were especially strong, fortified by newcomers Dennis Magary, John Sailhamer, Ray Ortlund Jr., Willem VanGemeren, and Richard Averbeck in Old Testament, and Wayne Grudem, Scot McKnight, and Bob Yarbrough in New Testament. The missions and evangelism faculty also continued to attract attention. Following the retirements of David Hesselgrave and Herbert Kane, the missions department was now chaired by world-recognized anthropologist Paul Hiebert, who was joined by missiologists Robert Coleman, Bill Taylor, and Edward Rommen, and evangelism professor John Nyquist. Through their prominent influence, TEDS continued to serve as a global leader in missiology and Christian outreach.[76] This period also witnessed the arrival of Nigel M. de S. Cameron in 1992, to replace Kantzer as

Some TEDS faculty, 1990s. Left to right: Nigel Cameron, Lois McKinney, Perry Downs, Paul Feinberg, Milo Lundell.

the director of TEDS's PhD programs, and John Kilner in 1993, who became the first director of the Bannockburn Institute for Christianity and Contemporary Culture. Under Kilner's direction, this nonprofit institute quickly emerged as a major center for the study of contemporary issues related to bioethics and human dignity.[77]

Other important additions to the seminary faculty during the 1980s and early 1990s included David Dunbar, John Feinberg, Bruce Fields, Bruce Ware, Kevin Vanhoozer, and Harold Netland in theology; David Larsen, James Speer, Howard Matson, and Michael Bullmore in practical theology; Mark Senter III in Christian education; Thomas Nettles in church history; and Stephen Greggo in counseling and psychology. Significantly, TEDS faculty also became more gender-inclusive during this period, with the arrival of three full-time female professors: Linda Cannell in education (1988), Lois McKinney in missions (1990), and Miriam Stark (later Miriam Stark Parent) in counseling (1993), who navigated their roles as female educators with courage, tact, and grace. Stark Parent has especially fond memories of faculty prayer meetings and animated lunch conversations in the faculty lounge—although her presence as a woman created awkward moments at first. As she remembers: "Part of the ongoing issue was getting Dr. Kantzer to stop standing every time I walked into the lunchroom, even for coffee; of course, when he stood all the faculty followed suit. After a week he and I came to a quiet agreement that allowed me to settle in somewhat less obtrusively."[78]

Like any academic community, TEDS had its own unique culture, with professors filling specific niches or roles.[79] New Testament professor D. A. Carson served as the informal theological leader of the faculty with his formidable knowledge of Scripture, his grasp of critical issues, and his persuasive logical reasoning. The faculty's jocks included former college athletes McKnight, Nyquist, and Fields. Gleason Archer and Robert Coleman

Miriam Stark (parent),
mid-1990s

Paul Hiebert and Lois McKinney, mid-1990s

were the faculty's prayer warriors—their fervent prayers ignited faculty prayer gatherings with deep concern and evangelical piety. Perry Downs was invariably the faculty clown, as his self-deprecating humor and memorable stunts brought levity to faculty life. Walter Liefeld was one of the faculty's pastors, remembered for his care and encouragement of female faculty colleagues and students.

Walter Liefeld,
late 1990s

Paul Feinberg and John Woodbridge were the faculty's storytellers. One of Paul's favorite stories (which he told many times) came from his college days at UCLA, when he and a group of his fraternity brothers decided to sabotage Tommy the Trojan, the statue-mascot of their archrival USC, a few days before a big football game. Feinberg and his friends loaded up a helicopter with horse manure, flew over Tommy the Trojan, and dropped the payload—only to miss the intended target and, instead, scatter manure all over a California freeway. Finally, every faculty has its absentminded professor, and this role was ably filled at Trinity by the eccentric and brilliant Harold O. J. Brown, who defied all conventions in his wardrobe (he often wore Swiss pantaloons and suspenders) and classroom behavior. On one occasion, having forgotten his classroom notes, he began a brilliant but rather dull lecture. In the middle of the class session, Harold's wife, Grace, arrived, bearing a stack of lecture notes. Plopping them on the lectern, she turned to the class and said "It's only going to get worse now!"[80]

Harold O. J. Brown,
early 1990s

FEATURED FACULTY

D. A. Carson

Donald Arthur Carson was born to devout Christian parents, Thomas and Elizabeth Carson, in Montreal, Canada, on December 21, 1946. As the son of a Baptist minister, Donald was frequently the target of ridicule from Catholic classmates, who mocked him as a *maudite* (cursed) *Protestant*. After earning his bachelor's degree in chemistry and mathematics from McGill University (Montreal) in 1967, Carson's calling to formal Christian ministry crystallized as he responded to a sermon preached on Ezekiel 22:30: "It was if God by his Spirit was compelling me

D. A. Carson,
early 1980s

to say, 'Here, please send me!' " Thereafter, he earned his MDiv at Central Baptist Seminary in Toronto, served as the pastor of Richmond Baptist Church in British Columbia for three years, and then pursued doctoral studies at Cambridge University under New Testament professor Barnabas Lindars from 1972–1975. While in England, Carson met and fell in love with a British schoolteacher named Joy Wheildon, whom he married in August 1975.

While serving as an assistant professor at Northwest Baptist Theological College in Vancouver, Carson presented a paper at a theological conference in 1977 that caught Dean Kantzer's attention, who invited the promising young scholar to join Trinity's faculty in fall 1978. For the next forty years, Carson served as a professor (and then research professor) of New Testament at TEDS, while at the same time maintaining an expansive global ministry of teaching and speaking, as well as writing or editing more than sixty books and numerous essays. Carson's unflagging commitment to the Christian gospel, his stature as a conservative biblical scholar, and his penetrating analysis of the contemporary culture are on full display in the vast repertoire of topics covered in his published writings, including *Scripture and Truth* (1983; editor, with John Woodbridge), commentaries on the Gospel of John (1991) and Matthew (1994), *The Gagging of God* (1996), *The Inclusive Language Debate* (1998), *Justification and Variegated Nomism* (2001, 2004; editor, with Peter O'Brien and Mark Seifrid), *Christ and Culture Revisited* (2008), and *The Enduring Authority of the Christian Scriptures* (2016; editor).

Equally significant, Carson was a cofounder with Timothy Keller of The Gospel Coalition in 2005 and served as the general editor of the NIV Study Bible, first published in 2015. But perhaps Carson's greatest contribution is reflected in the lives of thousands of former students who have been shaped for faithful Christian ministry by his burning passion for the gospel of Jesus Christ, his God-honoring humility and courage, his unflagging labor on behalf of Christ's church, his deep pastoral concern, and, together with Joy, his gracious hospitality extended toward students and their families. As Carson frequently reminded his students and colleagues: "Long after people have forgotten what we taught them, they will remember what impassioned us."[81]

FACULTY CONTROVERSIES

TEDS's faculty weathered a number of minor squabbles—and one major squall—during the years that Kaiser was in the dean's office. Prominent faculty members sometimes locked horns with Kaiser over departmental appointments and the fitness of junior faculty members to receive tenure. Several veteran professors feared that the dean was so pro-missions and pro-practical that he was devaluing the importance of quality scholarship.[82] Kaiser's unexpected decision to shut down the philosophy of religion department and dismiss philosopher William Lane Craig in 1986 compounded these concerns and further multiplied mistrust. Another point of contention swirled around professor John Sailhamer's controversial method for interpreting the Old Testament. In his scholarship, Sailhamer employed a text-oriented approach that disallowed the use of all historical events or artifacts outside the Hebrew text itself in the interpretation of Scripture.[83] Kaiser threw his support behind Sailhamer (though he didn't endorse his extreme biblicism) and came down hard on several respected faculty members who raised objections to it. An additional matter of controversy related to Kaiser's decision to hire and support Ted Ward as the dean of international studies and director of the doctor of education program in 1985. While Ward's presence added prestige to Trinity, some of his faculty colleagues were concerned that his scholarship was too wedded to social-scientific methods and not adequately informed by theology. These concerns were exacerbated when Ward was tapped to be the chair of the TEDS 2000 task force, whose Preliminary Report in 1993 expressed sharp criticisms of the traditional MDiv curriculum, the intellectual fragmentation caused by departmental structures, the lack of unity among faculty, the tepid

Murray Harris,
early 1990s

spiritual climate on campus, the underrepresentation of minority professors and students, and the insensitive treatment of female students.[84] An ad hoc faculty committee wrote a formal "Response" to the final report of TEDS 2000 that challenged several of its findings and rejected its overall critical assessment.

But the biggest controversy of Kaiser's tenure was triggered from outside the seminary's walls by former TEDS faculty member Norman Geisler, who accused New Testament professor Murray Harris of denying the historic doctrine of Christ's bodily resurrection. In 1983, Harris (who was then the warden of Tyndale House, Cambridge) published a book titled *Raised Immortal: Resurrection and Immortality in the New Testament,* in which he defended the unusual view that, in his essential state, Jesus's resurrected body was characterized by invisibility and immateriality, though Jesus could materialize and enter sensory human experience whenever he desired.[85] This was the position that Harris articulated when he interviewed to return to the TEDS faculty in 1986; at the same time, he affirmed without equivocation the bodily resurrection of Jesus Christ and subscribed wholeheartedly to the EFCA's Statement of Faith on this point.[86] Dean Kaiser, Kenneth Kantzer and the rest of Trinity's faculty found Harris's doctrine of the resurrection well within the parameters of historic Christianity and evangelical orthodoxy—but Geisler did not.

Over the next two years, Geisler and a group of his supporters launched an aggressive campaign against Harris, accusing him of denying the bodily resurrection of Jesus Christ and demanding that he be dismissed from TEDS for his heretical position. This campaign proved to be a public relations nightmare for Trinity and the EFCA, as Geisler and his supporters raised the alarm through books, magazine articles, mailings, radio programs, and phone calls, charging both the school and denomination with countenancing false teaching. The controversy was finally quieted—at least momentarily—in the summer of 1988 when, after extensive meetings and deliberations, delegates at the EFCA national conference voted five hundred to ten to drop charges against Harris and moved to initiate disciplinary action against Geisler for contentious behavior unbefitting a minister of the gospel.

Two years later, in 1990, Harris expanded on his views in his book *From Grave to Glory,* and once again Geisler was quick to attack. Eliciting the support of a group of anti-cult leaders, Geisler and his supporters sensationalized the controversy by likening Harris's doctrine to that of the Jehovah's Witnesses; in the fall of 1992, they even distributed a press release that stated "Cultic Doctrine Endorsed by Leaders of the Evangelical Free Church of America."[87] The following spring, *Christianity Today* headlined the controversy in an article titled "The Mother of all Muddles."[88] In an effort to silence this quarrel once and for all, President Meyer asked Dr. Millard Erickson, a respected theologian from Southwestern Baptist Theological Seminary, to organize a commission of his choosing to investigate Harris and evaluate his positions related to the resurrection of Jesus Christ and the resurrection of the body in light of the EFCA Statement of Faith and the boundaries of evangelical orthodoxy.[89] President Meyer promised to dismiss Harris from TEDS should the commission judge his theology heretical. For several months, Erickson, along with well-known theologians Bruce Demarest and Roger Nicole, pored over Harris's published statements and spent several hours interviewing the New Testament professor. At the conclusion of their investigation, they fully exonerated Harris: "It is the unanimous opinion of the committee that his views in these two doctrinal matters are compatible with the doctrinal position of Trinity Evangelical Divinity School, the Evangelical Free Church of America and the wider evangelical movement."[90] This judgment was formally ratified by the board of directors of the EFCA in June 1993, and, despite continued agitation by Geisler, the controversy was for the most part pacified.

THE BIRTH OF TRINITY
INTERNATIONAL UNIVERSITY

In fall 1992 something happened at TEDS that had not occurred since its inception in 1963: the school experienced a slight reduction in student enrollment.[91] For several years prior to this, President Meyer had been warning constituents that a downturn was inevitable due to stagnant financial support from donors, a shrinking pool of male college graduates, and decreasing interest in seminary education within the EFCA.[92] No doubt, an additional factor was the changing landscape of evangelical higher education, as the number of conservative seminaries multiplied around the country, many of which offered less expensive

Dedication of the Carl F. H.
Henry Resource Center

alternatives to Trinity's prized education. Equally significant was the conservative "takeover" of the seminaries
in the Southern Baptist Convention in
1988, which now made those schools
more attractive to evangelical Baptist
students who might otherwise have
been drawn to Bannockburn.[93]

In the face of these challenges,
leaders at TEDS reaffirmed and
slightly modified their presentation of
the school's distinctive qualities and
priorities. Trinity's commitment to
the doctrine of biblical inerrancy, its
reputation for excellence in evangelical scholarship, its affiliation with the
EFCA, and its service to the broader evangelical church—these strengths
and priorities had not changed. What was new, however, was the recognition of the strategic role that TEDS's academic doctoral programs
were now playing in the training of future leaders in the global church. So
too, Trinity's leaders emphasized the school's centrist position within the
broader scope of evangelicalism. As Kenneth Meyer noted shortly before
he stepped down from the president's office in October 1995: "Trinity
Evangelical Divinity School has been almost given the place of being
the middle of the pendulum in evangelicalism. That's a tenuous but very
important spot because we're able to be used of God to keep that mid-
stream evangelicalism there."[94] In a theological climate that was increasingly polarized and sectarian, Trinity was providing crucial balance for
the evangelical movement in the United States and abroad.

A second change that took place in 1992 was even more significant:
President Meyer dismissed Kaiser from the dean's office and reassigned
him as vice president of distance learning. The following year, Kaiser left
TEDS to become the president of Gordon Conwell Theological Seminary
in Hamilton, Massachusetts. Though the reasons for Kaiser's dismissal
from the dean's office are still disputed, a number of factors were probably
in play. By the early 1990s, Dean Kaiser had become increasingly critical

of Meyer's leadership of the school, opposed to the president's expansionist vision for Trinity that included the takeover of Miami Christian College in 1989[95] and plans to transform the seminary and college into a major Christian research university. He feared that resources earmarked for the divinity school were being diverted to support the college and its programs. In addition, Kaiser's leadership style and controversial decisions had created widespread discontent and mistrust among the faculty. Even so, the unexpected departure of such a prominent evangelical leader and scholar from Bannockburn proved to be a significant loss for Trinity.

Later that same year, W. Bingham Hunter, the former academic dean of Talbot School of Theology at Biola University, was installed as Kaiser's replacement in the dean's office. Hunter was an able administrator and faithful Christian leader with a deep concern for spiritual formation and personal holiness. As the author of a well-known book on prayer, *The God Who Hears* (1986), Hunter was a strong advocate for an integrated theological education that pursued academic rigor and practical ministry training within a religious community shaped by deep pastoral concern.[96] Faculty and administrators alike were responsible to model "prayer, humble obedience to Scripture, integrity, godliness, and a heart for evangelism" in an environment that valued "the fruits of the Spirit" and the "uniqueness

Dean W. Bingham
Hunter, early 1990s

and importance of each individual."[97] No doubt, Dean Hunter was also hired with the mandate to employ his spiritual leadership experience to foster greater harmony among TEDS's strongly opinionated faculty and to address many of the institutional weaknesses that were being identified by the TEDS 2000 taskforce.

As we have seen, as early as 1970, Kantzer had proposed creating a major Christian university on the Bannockburn campus, joining together the liberal arts college and the divinity school into a single institution where students' hearts and minds would be shaped by top-flight evangelical scholars and educators and where the pressing cultural issues of the day would be addressed from a Christian perspective.[98] President Meyer was also attracted to this idea, which by the early 1990s seemed more feasible given the stabilization of the college's enrollment and academic program. Early in 1993, Meyer invited Kantzer to come and explain his expansive vision to his cabinet.[99] Later that year, Meyer announced to the delegates at the EFCA national conference that, within eighteen months, a single administration would govern both the college and divinity school. "We will function as a University without the parallel academic structure," he promised.[100] Initially, Meyer had intended to name this new institution Trinity University—until a school in Texas by that same name threatened legal action. Thereafter, Meyer settled on the name Trinity International University, which, he believed, captured well the international makeup of the student body as well as the global vision of the school. The new name would also create space for other (foreign) institutions to affiliate with the school.[101]

The official merger of college and seminary was completed on July 1, 1996, when the EFCA national conference granted final approval to the university structure. With the merger, TIU became a school with over three thousand students, around five hundred employees, and a budget in excess of twenty-five million dollars.[102] By that time, the university's leadership team had been significantly modified: Gregory Waybright, the former senior pastor of Arlington Heights Evangelical Free Church, was installed as the thirteenth president of Trinity in October 1995. Meyer, Trinity's "entrepreneurial president," had assumed the role of chancellor of the school. The following year, in 1997, the indefatigable Kantzer was named the first dean of TIU's graduate school. A dream, in gestation for more than twenty-five years, was now coming into reality.

Chapter 6

Trinity Blossoms as a Christian University (1996–2019)

David M. Gustafson

In 1996, Trinity began to flourish as a Christian university. The board of regents christened the school Trinity International University (TIU). A number of reasons prompted the board to append the word "International" to Trinity's name. One stood out above the others: Trinity's renewed commitment to reach the world with the marvelous gospel of Jesus Christ.

Trinity soon added new campuses and schools. The university made advances in computer technology and the internet. It enhanced new educational modes of delivery. The establishment of academic centers generated scholarly collaboration and new sources of funding. Other kinds of exciting opportunities for Christian witness emerged. They ranged from Trinity's athletes winning championships on the soccer field to interviews by the school's top-tier scholars on ABC News.

The university's global influence in sharing Christ's gospel expanded dramatically. From Bulus Galadima, provost of Nigeria's largest evangelical seminary; to students at Torch Trinity in Seoul, Korea; to Jenny Salt, dean of students at Sydney Missionary and Bible College in Australia; to Greg Pritchard, founder of the European Leadership Forum; to Michael Oh, executive director/CEO of the Lausanne Movement; to Matt Bennett, founder of the Christian Union; to Julius Kim, president of The Gospel Coalition; to Don Sweeting, president of Colorado Christian University,

Trinity graduates served the Lord faithfully as evangelical missionaries, pastors, evangelists, apologists, educators, business leaders, and humanitarian workers throughout the world.

In 1996, TIU began the academic year with 1,250 undergraduates in the college and 1,784 students at TEDS. When President Waybright learned, to his surprise, of the school's debt, he was glad to know that Chancellor Meyer had launched a twenty-million-dollar centennial campaign called "Celebrating a Century, Entrusted with the Future."[1] The campaign fit well with Trinity's 1997 centennial—a marker of God's faithfulness to the school's one hundred years of educating men and women to live for Jesus Christ and to carry the gospel to the world.

President Waybright held an MDiv from TEDS and a PhD in New Testament from Marquette University. He drew heavily from his years of pastoral experience in Wisconsin, California, and Illinois, as well as his service as board chair of the Evangelical Free Church Mission. He knew the EFCA well and enjoyed immediate rapport with the college and divinity school boards, which soon merged into the university's board of regents.

Gregory Waybright, president of TIU

President Waybright embraced Kenneth Kantzer's guiding vision that Trinity was a "love gift to the global church," entrusted with the gospel. Trinity was not specifically a Reformed, Lutheran, Arminian, Anglican, Anabaptist or Pentecostal school. Rather, it was a broadly confessional, evangelical university welcoming students from diverse theological traditions. It affirmed the EFCA's Statement of Faith. As an evangelical school, TIU would be a place to train minds *and* nurture souls.[2] President Waybright invited well-respected Free Church leader Milo Lundell to become the executive administrator.[3] Nigel Cameron, Meyer's protégé, served as senior vice president/provost.[4]

VISION OF TIU AS A CHRISTIAN UNIVERSITY

Kenneth Kantzer dreamed of Trinity as a university in which students would be trained well to take the gospel of Jesus Christ to the world.[5] Academic rigor and orthodox faith were to be at the university's core.[6] TIU would not be an ivory-tower think tank uninterested in the concerns of public policy, business, and media, or aloof to the postmodern culture that was abandoning the idea of objective truth. Instead, it was envisioned that TIU students in every school and field of study would be trained to think biblically and integrate such thinking in all realms of knowledge and life, engaging society with scriptural truth.[7]

President Waybright believed too that Trinity as a Christian university was needed as much as ever. He declared:

> With the ongoing degeneration of the secular academy into relativism, institutions such as ours offer a healthy and meaningful alternative. There is a standard. Truth may be found and explored. It is the immutable truth of our Creator God. And the framework of such objective truth, far from being destructive, is freeing, providing a yardstick against which our culture's trends may be measured. It is this niche—high caliber academic training in the context of objective truth—we seek to fill.[8]

This vision was to be implemented throughout the school, and Nigel Cameron played a vital role.[9] For him, most universities had become almost hopelessly secular.[10] In contrast, at TIU the divinity school would provide a center for theological thought and scholarship. The university in all its parts would contribute to and apply evangelical thought and scholarship in the disciplines, thereby preparing pastors, counselors, missionaries, attorneys, teachers, scientists, corporate leaders, businessmen and businesswomen, physicians, and public servants.

Nigel Cameron

TEDS OF TIU

In 1996, with a new university structure in place, TIU needed a single university calendar. To sync schedules, TEDS moved from its ten-week terms to fifteen-week semesters. Rolfing Library received the college's collection. Dean Bing Hunter emphasized Christian spirituality within the community. Hunter soon welcomed Stephen P. Greggo to the counseling department.

Faculty wives regularly gathered for prayer and fellowship, led by Marie Tiénou and in time by Jules Cole, the wives of professors Tite Tiénou and Graham A. Cole. They, along with women from local churches, continued to minister at the Clothes Horse, where students could pick up free clothing, food, and kitchenware and be greeted with a caring welcome. Area churches in Illinois from Christ Church, Lake Forest, to EFCA churches in Libertyville, Lincolnshire, and Arlington Heights generously provided the items. Heartwarming stories from the Clothes Horse abounded about students finding just the right household utensil, a chair, or clothing at just the right time for themselves, or clothes or toys for their children. The White Horse Inn served as a favorite campus eatery where students and faculty could munch on a Reformation Luther or Zwingli burger, relax, have camaraderie, and share more than a few laughs. Seminary students continued to play in spirited intramural volleyball, soccer, and basketball tournaments. They also loved on a few occasions to challenge an aging faculty to a basketball or volleyball game.

In the same year, the Association of Theological Schools approved the PhD in intercultural studies, which replaced the doctor of missiology, and the next year approved the PhD in educational studies, which replaced the doctor of education.[11] Now with two new PhD programs alongside the PhD in theological studies, TEDS ranked among the world's largest institutions to offer theologically based PhD-level research.

In 1997, several new faculty were added at TEDS. Tite Tiénou joined the mission and evangelism department, James Moore began as associate academic dean, Doug Sweeney arrived from Yale to teach church history, and Marty Crain and Peter Cha joined the practical theology department.[12] In the following year, Phil Sell joined the educational ministries department, K. Lawson Younger arrived to teach Old Testament with a specialization in the ancient Near East, Steven C. Roy taught biblical and systematic theology, and David Pao joined the New Testament department.[13] In addition, Kevin Vanhoozer returned after seven years on the faculty of the University of Edinburgh, Scotland.

During this time, when Hunter hosted a prospective faculty member for an interview, as they were walking across campus, they met Paul Feinberg, the beloved professor of theology who was known to dress casually.[14] On this warm summer day, Feinberg was wearing a T-shirt, cutoff jean shorts, and flip-flops. After a friendly exchange, the prospective faculty member turned to Hunter and said, "So I am guessing there is no faculty dress code at TEDS," to which the dean replied, "Yes, you are correct. There is no faculty dress code here." Feinberg used to greet some of his male colleagues with "Hey, Brother ..." He and his brother John, both excellent theologians, often engaged in gospel missionary work overseas.

Other TEDS faculty were soon added. In 1999, Ben Mitchell became assistant professor of bioethics; Greg Scharf—well-known within the EFCA—joined the practical theology department; James Hoffmeier, a specialist in ancient Near Eastern studies and archaeology, came to teach Old Testament and Semitic languages; and Robert Priest arrived to teach mission and intercultural studies.[15]

In July 2000, Dean Hunter resigned as dean at a time when the MDiv program was in need of review. Harold Netland stepped in to serve as interim dean, doing so with skill and grace. In the fall of that year, H. Wayne Johnson began as dean of chapel, having served previously with the EFCA Mission in Singapore, and Scott Manetsch joined the church history department.[16]

In the same year, Marty Crain took over as director of the doctor of ministry program.[17] Among the DMin students to graduate that year was Lazarus Chakwera, a leader of the Assemblies of God of Malawi. After graduation, he lectured on theology and entered politics as the Malawi Congress Party leader. In 2020, Chakwera was inaugurated as the sixth president of the Republic of Malawi.[18]

TEDS's search for a new dean culminated with the announcement that Tiénou would be installed as academic dean and senior vice president of education, which took place on April 2, 2002.[19] After receiving a PhD from Fuller Theological Seminary, Tiénou had served as president and dean of the Faculté de Théologie Evangélique de l'Alliance Chrétienne in Abidjan, Côte d'Ivoire. In the same year, Dean Tiénou welcomed Graham Cole of Australia to the faculty to teach in the area of systematic theology.

Dean Tiénou sought to prepare students for the *global* church, emphasizing that "the student is the school's primary client" and "faculty is the curriculum." Tiénou insisted on the same high academic standards for all students, whether master's or doctoral. Under his leadership, the faculty began a review of the MDiv to build on its strengths and to make the program more effective at preparing students for ministry in contemporary contexts.[20] With the new curriculum in place, Wayne Johnson became director of the MDiv program. To underscore the importance of spiritual formation, *advisee* groups of students were renamed *formation* groups and met weekly with a faculty member to foster growth in biblical wisdom and interpersonal relationships. They discussed ministry issues and prayed together.[21] They enjoyed dining with each other.

Dean Tite Tiénou

In 2001, TEDS finalized an agreement with the EFCA to fund a professor of mission.[22] In the following year, Craig L. Ott, a veteran missionary and professor of mission in Germany, assumed the EFCA International Mission Chair, teaching courses at TEDS while spending a portion of his time with the EFCA International Mission.[23] In 2003, Dean Tiénou welcomed Keith Bjorge as assistant professor of pastoral counseling and psychology. The following year Thomas H. McCall came as assistant professor of biblical and systematic theology, and James F. Plueddemann arrived from Wheaton College and took up the role of professor of mission and intercultural studies.[24]

ALUMNUS AND FACULTY STORY
Craig Ott, in His Own Words

My story and Trinity's influence on my life and ministry is perhaps illustrative of many others. Having grown up in an atheist home, life seemed utterly meaningless when at a young age I lost my father. I became a "weekend hippie" and occupied myself playing in rock bands. But during college I was swept up in the Jesus movement of Southern California and came to faith in Jesus Christ. Soon I sensed God's call to prepare for ministry.

Craig Ott

Upon arriving on the Trinity campus in 1974 to begin my MDiv studies, I met TEDS student body president Bruce Fleming (MDiv, ThM), who had just returned from attending the historic Lausanne Congress on World Evangelization. A call was issued there for the development of theological education in Africa, Asia, and Latin America. Among other efforts, we initiated a book drive collecting theological books from TEDS students that would be sent to the library of the soon-to-be-established Faculté de Théologie Evangélique de Bangui (FATEB), one of the first graduate-level theological schools in Francophone Africa. A few years later Bruce would become the academic dean at FATEB. A few decades later, when giving lectures at FATEB, I was delighted to pull a book from the shelf in the library to find it was one donated by a TEDS student as part of our book drive.

Like so many other Trinity students, Bruce and I both met our wives at TEDS, Joy Elasky Fleming and Alice Krupp Ott, who were among the first TEDS women MDiv graduates. Both also went on to earn academic doctorates in theology. Today Alice is affiliate professor of history of mission and world Christianity at TEDS.

Countless TEDS students have caught the vision for world missions and gone on to make contributions great and small. Alice and I served for twenty-one years as church planters and theological educators in Germany.

Just prior to completing my PhD at TEDS in 1991, we witnessed the fall of the Iron Curtain and the increased freedoms for mission and evangelism in Eastern Europe. Numerous Trinity graduates followed a call to minister in those countries. We had the privilege of coaching missionaries and consulting with national church leaders during those exciting days of transition and opportunity.

The education of international students is one of the most significant chapters of Trinity's story. For example, one of my classmates, Edward Muhima Bakaitwako (MDiv), went on to earn a PhD at Northwestern University and return to Uganda, where he followed in the footsteps of Bishop Festo Kivengere, the "Billy Graham of Africa." Edward became a gifted international evangelist and bishop in the Anglican Church of Uganda. TEDS educated two of Korea's most influential missiologists. David Tai Woon Lee (DMiss) became director of the Global Missionary Training Center in Seoul Korea. Steve Sang Cheol Moon (PhD) became executive director of the Korea Research Institute for Mission. Their teachings and writings have not only helped fuel the remarkable Korean missions movement, but have significantly influenced the broader world of missions, giving leadership in the World Evangelical Alliance and the Lausanne Movement.

In 2002 Alice and I returned to the States, and I took up my current position as professor of mission and intercultural studies at TEDS, occupying the ReachGlobal Chair of Mission. This position was created to better bridge mission practice and mission teaching by allowing me to give 25 percent of my time to international ministry. I've had the joy of ministering in over forty countries, much of which involves training and consulting with emerging mission movements from countries such as mainland China and India. Missions today is truly from everywhere to everywhere. Many TEDS graduates are similarly involved in missionary mobilization in such locations. Others are pioneering work in some of the world's most difficult and dangerous places for ministry, such as Iraq and North Korea.

One TEDS graduate whom I have recently had the joy of mentoring is Manuel Scott (MDiv). Manny grew up in poverty amid gang violence in the inner city of Long Beach, California, in an unstable home with abuse, alcoholism, and drug addiction. After dropping out of high school, Manny met Jesus Christ on a park bench. When he returned to school, he had the good fortune of being in a high school class with teacher Erin Gruwell, who took a creative approach to reaching and teaching teens who seemed unreachable and unteachable. Manny became one of the original "Freedom Writers" described in Gruwell's book and a character in the Hollywood film *Freedom Writers*. After his dramatic turnaround, both academically and spiritually, he graduated from the University of California, Berkeley and then came to TEDS. Today Manny is a sought-after public speaker who has energized more than two million educators, students, and leaders worldwide with his authentic, inspiring messages of hope.

He is currently completing his PhD at TEDS, continuing to hone his skills in empowering students and teachers, and cultivating intercultural competence so needed in our conflicted society.

Countless other stories could be told of TEDS alumni, not all as dramatic as Manny's, but no less significant in God's kingdom and the advancement of the gospel. My own story from the streets of Hollywood to the halls of Trinity is but another stone in the beautiful mosaic of Trinity's legacy—a mosaic that is still being crafted to God's glory through so many lives entrusted with the gospel.[25]

TRINITY COLLEGE OF TIU
ACADEMIC, COMMUNITY, AND SPIRITUAL LIFE

In 1997, a high retention rate meant that 93.6 percent of college students who were expected to return did so. This positive factor, plus a new financial aid package, led to a doubling of new student inquiries and a 20 percent increase in enrollment. Donna Pederson, academic dean of the college, worked with the faculty to establish additional academic majors in pre–physical therapy and communication, and a minor in bioethics.[26] Moreover, the athletic training program received accreditation from the Commission on Accreditation of Allied Health Programs and the National Athletic Trainers Association, placing Trinity among an elite group of Christian schools qualified for the National Athletic Trainers Association exam.[27]

After forty-six years of teaching at Trinity, the much-respected Morris Faugerstrom retired from the music department.[28] In 1996, Paul J. Satre joined the music department, and two years later, Harvard PhD Chrystal

HoPao came to teach biology. In the following year, Jeanette Hsieh came from Wheaton College to take up the reins as dean of the college.

In 1999, Dr. Hsieh welcomed three new faculty members: Bradley J. Gundlach as assistant professor of history with specialization in B. B. Warfield; Chris Firestone, who taught philosophy; and Don Hedges, who joined the music department.[29] In 2000, Daniel Song'ony became assistant professor of business, and in the following year, Karl J. Glass came as associate professor of health science.[30]

With an increase in enrollment by nearly two hundred students in fall 1998, the traditional undergraduate student body was the highest in numbers on the Bannockburn campus since 1979, putting strains on the dining hall, classrooms, and residence halls.[31] In 2002, President Waybright reported, "We were at our housing capacity in the fall and temporarily housed seventeen students in Woodfield Suites for the first two weeks of school."[32] The administration and regents set out to explore a campus master plan and options for needed residence hall space, leading to a quiet phase of a $20 million capital and endowment campaign that began in 2003.[33] In the following year, TIU broke ground for a new residence building—named Trinity Hall. It opened to students in 2006.[34]

Academics kept pace. The college honors program, designed for students who excelled academically, had sixty students enrolled in courses. The program drew students because of the competitive Kantzer-Ruud Scholarship, which awarded full and partial tuition to fifty-three top students.[35] With the vision of TIU firmly in mind, faculty members such as Firestone mentored students to think Christianly in formulating scholarly arguments.[36] This bore immediate fruit: at the Midwest Regional Meeting of the Evangelical Theological Society, three of the four students in the undergraduate writing competition were from Trinity College.

A Trinity education that integrated Christian faith and scholarship was seen in the lives of alumni. For example, Sarah Fowler McCammon, who completed her BA in 2003 and was awarded the Lincoln Laureate, worked as a correspondent for National Public Radio, focusing on political and cultural divides in America, including abortion, reproductive rights, and religion.[37] Wilfredo "Choco" De Jesús, who graduated from Trinity College in 1999, became pastor of New Life Covenant Church in Chicago the following year. Since then, the church has grown to a weekly attendance of seventeen thousand globally through multiple campuses and ministries, reaching disenfranchised people including the homeless, prostitutes, drug addicts, and gang members. In 2013, Pastor "Choco" was named as one of *Time* Magazine's one hundred most influential people.[38]

In 1997, the college organized its academic departments into eight schools with twenty-nine undergraduate majors.[39] In the same year, under the guidance of Dr. Joyce A. Shelton, a microbiologist, and Richard Thompson, an Abbott Laboratories biochemist, TIU students extracted antimicrobial peptides secreted from the skin of frogs, potentially useful in formulating a new antibiotic. This collaborative research program was one of the first at Trinity College that demonstrated the commitment of the science faculty to the idea that undergraduate research experience contributes significantly to students' future success in scientific fields.

In addition to the college honors program, athletics and extracurricular activities challenged students to grow socially, physically, and spiritually.[40] Chapel services led by worship teams provided regular times for sharing testimonies, exposition of the Scriptures, and prayer. In chapel, Mel Svendsen, vice president for student life, and Hutz Hertzberg, university chaplain, challenged the Trinity community, students and faculty alike, to pursue lives of Christian discipleship evidenced by humility, repentance, and wholeness. In addition, weekly small group Bible studies and the University Day of Prayer encouraged students and faculty members to follow Christ through the power of the Holy Spirit.

F.A.T. Thursday gathering (*Trinity Magazine*)

In addition to these ministries, Thursday evening gatherings, known affectionately as "F.A.T. Thursday" (Faithful, Available, Teachable), brought spiritual renewal to the Bannockburn campus.[41] Dean Hsieh reported:

> Signs of spiritual renewal are evident on our campus that cross the boundaries of undergraduate, graduate, and divinity school students. Every Thursday evening a group of university students join together to praise the Lord and to encourage each other in their spiritual walk. ... This group grew out of five weeks of special prayer meetings at the end of spring 2000 semester which was the result of undergraduate athletes who were challenged by a speaker to spend more time in prayer. Since its inception in the fall, [the group] has grown to a weekly attendance of 200 students with both College and TEDS students in leadership roles.[42]

These gatherings continued for years. They helped nourish spiritual vitality in the Trinity community.[43]

FEATURED FACULTY

Samir Massouh—Adapted from a Tribute by Alumnus Derek Torres[44]

Samir Massouh was a man small in stature but great in faith. Few people have made as lasting an impact on my life as he has. I ended up taking nine classes with him in college. Samir was a Lebanese immigrant, a Vietnam US Army veteran, an educator, and a man of God.

Samir was a graduate student in philosophy at the University of California, Santa Barbara, but once Jesus got hold of him, he decided to pursue an MA in Old Testament at TEDS,

Samir Massouh in early career

where he came to know and was mentored by Walt Kaiser. He continued on for the MDiv and joined the TEDS faculty as an instructor of Old Testament and Semitic languages. In 1988, following a stint as an assistant pastor in Wisconsin, Samir joined the faculty of Trinity College, where he affected the lives of students over the next thirty years. Just about every Trinity College student took Introduction to the Old Testament with him. Besides many upper-level courses in his specialty, he also taught Christ and Culture, History of the Middle East, and Introduction to Christian Thinking and Living. Samir was a connoisseur of classical music and a devotee of art history. He faithfully attended Trinity women's soccer games and loved to joke with students and encourage them.

Samir Massouh in late career

If anyone was to hear the words from Jesus, "Well done, good and faithful servant," it would be Samir. He liked to say he was Darth Vader, but in reality he was Yoda. His humility shined from him, but he was a staunch defender of the faith and taught his young padawans dutifully.

Trinity College athletes made their mark too, with victories celebrated nearly yearly. For example, in fall 1998, the women's soccer team claimed a national championship, and in the same year, the men's basketball team finished third in the nation in the NCCAA.[45] In 2000, Dean of Students William Washington reported that for the second consecutive year, the women's soccer team was the NAIA Region VII champion.[46] In fall 2001, the Trinity Trojans football team, led by coach Andrew Lambert, finished the season with a record of 8–3, receiving an invitation to the NCCAA Victory Bowl.[47]

1997–1998 Women's soccer team

In each of these achievements, Trinity athletes and coaches demonstrated Christian character in their conduct both on and off the court or field. TIU athletics were not merely competitive but the means for coaches to encourage students to follow Jesus Christ.[48] For instance, Coach Lambert's coaching philosophy was that winning games was less important than the team's spiritual growth in Christ.

Masaki Matsumoto, who came to TIU on a football scholarship, played as a fullback and participated in F.A.T. Thursday gatherings. Matsumoto received his BA in 2006, and after graduate studies he began his first teaching job at a high school in Los Angeles, where he also coached football. Previously, not only did the high school's football team struggle with wins and losses, but the players struggled with the challenges of broken homes, drugs, and gang pressures. Despite these challenges, Matsumota turned the team around, along with the students' lives. In light of his accomplishments, beginning in 2016, he was three times honored as *Los Angeles Times* coach of the year and was featured on ESPN's E60.

Student athletes also combined athletics and scholarship. For example, Brian K. Hagedorn, who played baseball at Trinity and graduated with a BA in 2000, went on to study at Northwestern Law School and in 2019 was named a justice of the Wisconsin Supreme Court. Melissa Erickson, a captain of TIU's women's soccer team, graduated in 1999 with a BA in biology before attending Rush Medical School and becoming a fellow at the Mayo Clinic. She then became an orthopedic spine surgeon at Duke University Hospital.[49]

2005–2006 Trinity football players in a prayer huddle. Left to right: John Bear, Robbie Shomaker, Jon Lehman, and Masaki Matsumoto.

Students engaged also in service-learning opportunities off-campus. For the academic year 1996–1997 President Waybright reported:

> Trinity summer Missions '96 sent nine students to five countries: Belize, the Ukraine, Romania, Turkey, and Kazakhstan where they participated predominately and respectively in native children's camp ministry, evangelistic athletic programs, orphanage emotional and medical care, covert evangelism, and TESL. Christmas Break Outreach Trips '96 sent (approximately) 30 students to four locations: New York City, New Orleans, Atlanta, and Urbana, where they participated predominately and respectively with a rescue mission, an EFC inner city plant, a multicultural awareness conference, and a global missions conference. Spring Break outreach trips '97 sent 55 students to four locations: Philadelphia, North Carolina, Houston, and Laredo, TX, where they participated predominately and respectively with an inner-city Hispanic church ministry, United World Mission, Habitat for Humanity, and a local church sponsored vacation Bible school.[50]

Whether through academics, athletics, service-learning experiences, or other extra- and cocurricular activities, Trinity College lived out its vision of "forming students to transform the world through Christ."[51]

TRINITY GRADUATE SCHOOL

A strategic element of the vision of TIU was to establish a graduate school. Kenneth Kantzer served as the founding academic dean.[52] In 1996, at the EFCA conference, delegates approved plans to launch Trinity Graduate School (TGS).

The next year the school accepted its first students into four MA programs, which included bioethics, counseling and psychology, faith and culture, and interdisciplinary studies, each having a core in Bible and doctrine.[53] Soon added were the masters of education and master of arts in teaching, designed for students with a bachelor's degree to become certified for teaching in schools.[54]

Kenneth Kantzer, 1990s

The MA in bioethics was offered in the modular format, allowing physicians, nurses, lawyers, public policymakers, pastors, and educators to complete the program without having to leave their jobs or relocate to Chicagoland. An example of one such student was Nancy Jones. She completed an MA in bioethics in 2002 after earning a PhD in biochemistry at Wake Forest University School of Medicine.[55] She has served as a science policy fellow for the National Institutes of Health.[56]

THE CENTER FOR BIOETHICS
AND HUMAN DIGNITY

The first center at TIU was the Bannockburn Institute for Christianity and Contemporary Culture, mentioned in chapter 5.[57] In 1993, Nigel Cameron invited a dozen leading Christian bioethicists to assess the state of bioethics.[58] As a result, the center was organized under the leadership of Dr. John Kilner, with a view to impact the world with resources from a Christian perspective, analyzing challenges in the field of bioethics, critiquing prominent secular approaches, and providing credible Christian alternatives.[59] Such challenges included genetics, end-of-life decisions, abortion, reproductive technologies, and health care delivery.[60] The first conference was held in 1994, and ever since, annual conferences have featured a stellar roster of speakers, including British Minister of Health Brian Mawhinney, US Surgeon General C. Everett Koop, US Senator Sam Brownback, Director of the National Institutes of Health Francis Collins, and scientists from NASA, MIT, and the Human Genome Project.[61]

In 1995, the center released its first of over twenty books, titled *Bioethics and the Future of Medicine*.[62] It also produced the first Russian-language medical ethics textbook based on biblical principles and developed training seminars in Russia and Ukraine.[63] As the work grew larger in the sphere of bioethics, by 2002, the institute's

John Kilner

board decided to change the name officially from the Bannockburn Center to The Center for Bioethics and Human Dignity (CBHD).[64] The center has published the newsletter *Dignitas* and the *Ethics & Medicine* journal to serve members and a wider audience, including pastors and congregations.

In conjunction with CBHD's annual conferences, TGS has offered modular courses in bioethics taught by conference speakers such as Edmund Pellegrino, director of the Kennedy Institute of Ethics at Georgetown University, and Stanley Hauerwas, the Gilbert T. Rowe Professor of Theological Ethics at Duke Divinity School.

Spokespeople of CBHD, such as Kilner, C. Ben Mitchell, and Nigel Cameron, had opportunities to address the American Medical Association, US congressional committees, and global audiences through media such as ABC, CBS, NBC, Fox, and PBS.[65] Kilner discussed the first cloning of human beings in embryonic form on CNN, at a health-related gathering with President George W. Bush at the White House, and in strategizing sessions with the US Presidential Council on Bioethics.[66] In light of its leading role, CBHD was invited to assist US Congressman W. Curtis

John Kilner speaks in the Kantzer Lecture Hall

Weldon draft legislation that banned human cloning, taken up by the US Congress in 2001–2002.[67]

In 2007, Mitchell was appointed director of CBHD, and Kilner continued to serve as senior scholar of the center.[68] Among its academy of fellows was Patrick T. Smith, who completed an MDiv at TEDS in 2001. After doctoral studies, his work at Harvard Medical School led to a post as associate research professor of theological ethics and bioethics at Duke Divinity School and senior fellow at the Kenan Institute for Ethics.[69]

TRINITY LAW SCHOOL IN SOUTHERN CALIFORNIA

In 1995, Trinity began discussions with Simon Greenleaf University in Anaheim, California, about the possibility of a merger, giving TIU a West Coast campus.[70] Founded in 1980 as the Simon Greenleaf School of Law by former TEDS professor John Warwick Montgomery, the merger came in 1998 when the school was renamed Trinity Law School (TLS).[71] With Trinity's evangelical ethos, the school maintained its founding vision to integrate Christian faith, theology, and apologetics with law and human rights.[72] Following the merger, Trinity invested heavily in hiring full-time faculty. Myron Steeves, a graduate of Georgetown University Law Center, taught law, and Francis J. Beckwith taught human rights. Winston Frost followed Shannon Verleur as dean.[73]

Through the work of Waybright, Meyer, and Cameron, TIU provided the support and funding necessary for the law school to obtain

Trinity Law School

accreditation that previously had not been possible for the fledgling school. In 1999, TLS was accredited by the Committee of Bar Examiners of the State Bar of California.[74] With this accreditation, enrollment reached ninety full-time students, nearly doubling from the previous year. In addition, TLS moved to a location near the judicial courts in Santa Ana.

The school added to the faculty Kevin P. Holsclaw. In 2001, when, Barry Beitzel—then provost of TIU—found it necessary to intervene over allegations of academic dishonesty by Frost—in a highly publicized case— Holsclaw assumed the role of interim dean and later was appointed Dean.[75]

In addition to awarding the juris doctor, students were encouraged to spend an extra year to complete an MA in faith and culture, which provided additional theological and philosophical underpinnings for law and justice. An important part of TLS has been its summer program in Strasbourg, France, where students hear lectures by international scholars on human rights from a Christian perspective.

Holsclaw, who earned a JD from Pepperdine Law School and an MA in faith and culture from TGS, served as dean until 2005, when Daniel Lungren, US Congressman, appointed him as his chief legal counsel.[76] Donald McConnell was installed as dean in 2005, having taught at the school since 1988.[77]

In 2007, TLS reached an enrollment of 194 students. Nevertheless, the challenge remained for graduates to increase the passage rate among the twenty schools accredited by the State Bar of California, one of the most difficult bar exams in the country.[78]

Throughout the years, TLS has hosted events related to law, human rights, and justice. For example, in 2008, the school hosted a conference titled "God and Governing," with a forum that included Os Guinness, Dallas Willard, and David Wells.[79]

Trinity Law School students, 2014

Among adjunct professors of TLS is Sarah Sumner, who earned a PhD in theological studies from TEDS and served as dean of A. W. Tozer Theological Seminary in Redding, California, before becoming president of Right On Mission.[80] Kelli Marsh, an alumna of TLS who holds a JD, has worked at the Church Law Center of California in Santa Ana and served as president of the Christian Legal Society of Orange County Chapter.

TIU—FLORIDA REGIONAL CENTER

Kenneth Kantzer's vision for Trinity included gospel witness in the Hispanic world. In 1996, the South Florida campus, led by Joseph Hassey, academic dean, launched a new major in health and wellness management, and an MA in counseling psychology.[81] In the following year, the campus enrolled over three hundred students in programs of all levels, with a diverse student body composed of 20 percent Anglo, 30 percent African American, and 50 percent Hispanic, including many first-generation college students.[82]

In 2000, the campus was renamed Trinity International University–Florida Regional Center. Vickie Perea joined the TIU leadership team to head its operations. Approximately one hundred of the three hundred students were enrolled in the MA in counseling and psychology and MA in religion programs.[83] While 2001–2002 was the last year of the traditional undergraduate program, the nontraditional undergraduate program, called EXCEL, and the graduate programs continued.[84] In 2002, the campus relocated to the north Dade area.[85]

In addition to the school, a prominent component of Trinity in Florida was the Christian radio station WMCU (Spirit FM 89.7). This 100,000-watt station had an estimated 130,000 listeners per week.[86] In 2007, the board of regents deemed it prudent to sell the station to a nonprofit broadcast company for $20 million, pending approval of the FCC. Although longtime supporters of the station were deeply disappointed with the sale, the university's financial strength was bolstered, along with Trinity's ability to focus on its academic mission.[87]

In 2005, Kevin Meyer became executive director of the Florida Regional Center. In the following year, the campus relocated from North Miami to Davie in southwest Broward County.[88] This location made classes more accessible to the target population of south Florida.[89]

TIU'S DIVISION OF OPEN STUDIES

The Division of Open Studies in Bannockburn provided higher education in nontraditional ways such as EXCEL in Florida and distance education courses at the graduate level. The undergraduate program was known by the acronym REACH—Relevant Education for the Adult Christian. In 1999, eight hundred students enrolled for credit through all nontraditional programs, with a 65 percent increase the following year.[90] Moreover, the Division of Open Studies launched an urban site on Chicago's south side, offering a nontraditional undergraduate program with a major in Christian ministries.[91]

A second nontraditional offering in the Division of Open Studies led to a bachelor's degree with a major in elementary education, designed for students who wished to obtain teacher certification for employment in public schools. The REACH to Teach program came under the college's education department, which provided supervision to assure compliance with standards of the Illinois State Board of Education.[92]

In addition, TIU's Division of Open Studies managed between seven to eight extension sites in the Midwest, offering classes taught by TEDS professors.[93] Understanding the Old Testament and Understanding the New Testament, the first two online courses, were developed as part of Trinity's initiative to use internet technology for remote learning.[94]

With the internet and other advancements in technology, the Rolfing Library catalog went fully online, enhancing student and faculty research. In addition, plans were developed to expand computer labs and add course management systems as well as classroom video projection.[95] In an initiative led by Steve Geggie, senior vice president of information technology, the university created a new platform for its website called MyTrinity, later MyTIU.[96] This website allowed students to access email, campus news, course registration, academic resources, and campus services from any location.[97]

TRINITY FUND

While the vision of TIU as a Christian university was an inspiring concept, the way it came together was described by some as "trying to put pieces of a puzzle together." After the merger of the college, Florida campus, and TEDS came the new graduate school, the law school in California, and the small campus on Chicago's south side.[98] TIU had become a complex entity in ways that were perhaps more opportunistic than organic.[99] This meant that faculty and administrators from different campuses did not know one another well. Some wondered, "Have we tried to do too much with too little?"

As a tuition-dependent university, TIU faced financial challenges, and the administration recognized that its institutional endowment was meager, even paltry in comparison to other Christian colleges and universities.[100] The economic roller coaster that followed the attacks of September 11, 2001, showed this to be the case more than ever.[101] While a Trinity education was highly valued, students increasingly looked at the cost and decided they could not afford what the school offered, leading some to drop out, attend part time, or enroll in a program elsewhere. Since, by design, no student paid 100 percent of the cost of a Trinity education, financial backing from alumni, churches, friends, and foundations was more necessary than ever. In light of financial obstacles, President Waybright appealed to the EFCA to pray for and fund the school sacrificially, saying: "TIU does not accept government funds except those given to our students. TIU with its stand on inerrancy, the exclusive claims of Christ, salvation by grace through faith in Jesus alone, and similar core theological distinctives, is too 'conservative' to receive funding from some foundations and corporations. Thus, we rely upon our people—those to whom we are accountable—to stand with us."[102]

In addition, President Waybright worked with the EFCA Board of Directors and General Conference to reform the selection of the school's board of regents. This enabled him to recruit those who had not only wisdom but the gift of trusteeship and financial resources.[103] The Advancement Office was tasked with the goal of raising $2.2 million annually in unrestricted funds for operational purposes needed for scholarships, academic programs, salaries, library resources, and special programs.[104] This became known as the Trinity Fund.

As well as funding the EFCA International Mission Chair, William Hamel, president of the EFCA, committed funds from the EFCA President's Office to support TEDS faculty professional development.[105] In a reciprocal act in 2006, TIU's Office of Church Partnerships initiated a financial aid program for the children of EFCA pastors.[106]

While these undertakings demonstrated the partnership between the EFCA and TIU, faculty and administrators' expectations were not always met, perhaps because they underestimated the voluntary nature of local congregations of the EFCA to support the school financially. As much as the denomination's leadership may have wanted to see every EFCA congregation support the school, it could not demand that they do so.

The EFCA and TIU fostered mutual goodwill and good communication through events such as EFCA Week, held annually at Bannockburn. There were also cordial gatherings of TIU administrators and faculty members along with district and national leaders of the EFCA.[107] Intentional collaboration in student ministerial formation was enhanced by pastoral internships for Trinity students made available at campuses of Orchard Evangelical Free Church in Arlington Heights, Illinois, under Pastor Colin Smith, as well as pastoral residencies provided at Christ Community Evangelical Free Church in the Kansas City area under Pastor Tom Nelson, and internships at First Evangelical Free Church of Wichita, Kansas, directed by Lead Pastor Josh Black. Many EFCA church members faithfully supported Trinity over the years in creative and generous ways, and especially through prayer. EFCA administrators such as Greg Strand and Fritz Dale, among others in the EFCA home office, did so as well. Both faithfully prayed for spiritual revival throughout the EFCA, Trinity, and the nation.

RODINE GLOBAL MINISTRY BUILDING

In 2000, a lead gift set in motion the building of the Rodine Global Ministry Building, named for the EFCA mission director, H. G. Rodine.[108] The new academic building, located in the wooded area just east of Olson Chapel, was designed to be twenty thousand square feet, with two eighty-seat classrooms, four twenty-four-seat seminar rooms, a small conference room, twelve faculty offices, a missions research room, and an office suite for the EFCA, as well as Hinkson Hall, a large conference room that could accommodate two hundred people.[109]

In a groundbreaking service in May 2001, Carl F. H. Henry offered a dedicatory prayer that was surely needed and answered.[110] After land was cleared of trees, a type of endangered species of frog was discovered, and construction was delayed for nine months.[111] Despite the setback, all the money pledged, totaling $3.5 million, came in before the project was completed. Through the efforts of Carl Johnson and the Advancement

Groundbreaking ceremony for the Rodine building. On the far left is Lyle Erstad, longtime head of facility services at Trinity. In the middle are President Waybright, Milo Lundell, and Carl Johnson.

Office, the project was completed on time. Classes were first held in the Rodine building in January 2003.

Carl Johnson joined TIU's Advancement Office in 1998 after having served on the board of regents. When he retired as a metallurgical engineer and manager from Sundstrand Corporation, he worked to create TIU's Strategic Plan. At a board meeting in February of that year, President Waybright asked him to consider working for the university to raise money to carry out the plan. Johnson turned down the offer at the time, but a mission trip changed his mind. While in Uzbekistan, he met with TEDS graduate Keith Dunn and his wife, Molly, who were serving as teachers. Dunn shared with Johnson and others how TEDS's mission and evangelism faculty had prepared him for work in the Muslim world. After Carl met a young Uzbek who planned to remodel a section of his parents' home for space to teach the Uzbek language to missionaries and businesspeople coming to Uzbekistan, and after observing firsthand how God had used the Dunns, the Lord changed Johnson's mind about the offer to work at TIU. When he next spoke to President Waybright at an EFCA conference and heard that the offer was still open, he decided to join the Advancement Office, beginning a second career that has lasted over twenty years.

HENRY CENTER FOR THEOLOGICAL UNDERSTANDING

The Henry Center for Theological Understanding—named for Carl F. H. Henry, theologian and visiting professor at TEDS—began in 2000 as the Center for Theological Understanding, under the direction of Doug Sweeney.[112] It was initiated by Dr. D. A. Carson, President Waybright, and Dean Tiénou with the vision to bring the academy and church together, drawing top evangelical scholars to Trinity to advance biblical and theological scholarship, and to equip pastors further to engage the Scriptures for ministry.[113] Richard Borst and board member Edward Hearle gave some of the earliest monies to fund the initiative. In 2005, an anonymous donor pledged $2 million to a project that did not materialize, and so Waybright recommended to the donor that the gift be directed to the center in Carl Henry's name. The donor agreed enthusiastically. The Henry Center for Theological Understanding was born.[114]

In 2006, the Henry Center provided startup financial support for a group of pastors, as part of a faculty initiative led by Carson, along with Tim Keller of New York.[115] The initiative, originally called "The Pastors' Colloquium" and aimed at revitalizing confessional evangelicalism, led to the first conference and website of The Gospel Coalition.[116] By 2007, the Henry Center expanded its global impact to Hong Kong and Nairobi, Kenya, providing opportunity for ministers, professionals, and academics in various fields to work collaboratively with seminary faculty engaged in biblical and theological reflection.[117]

STUDENT DIVERSITY

TIU's theological vision of diversity is rooted in the Scriptures. President Waybright often cited Revelation 5:9: "because you [Jesus Christ] were slain, and with your blood you purchased for God persons from every tribe and language and people and nation" (NIV).[118] Ever since the school was founded in 1897, Trinity has been dedicated to the Great Commission, to "make disciples of all nations" (Matt 28:19).[119] EFCA President William Hamel worked to foster this diversity at TIU as well as within the denomination, whose tagline was "multiplying transformational churches among all people."[120]

President Waybright's dedication to diversity was recognized in 2006, when the school received the Racial Harmony Award from the Council for Christian Colleges and Universities.[121] The award recognized the school's sensitive handling of a racial threat on campus that required the evacuation of students of color.[122] Some Trinity faculty members, among others, sheltered students in their homes. Following the incident, President Waybright honored Wesley Smith, a senior majoring in chemistry and member of the football team, for his exceptional leadership in calming fellow students and urging them to trust in the Lord. Smith received the Presidential Award.

President Waybright's dedication to diversity was seen also in his intentional recruitment of students, administrators, and faculty from various backgrounds.[123] For instance, Watson Jones III came to Trinity and completed a BA in 2006 and an MDiv in 2010, working in the Multicultural Development Office.[124] Since then he has served as senior

Watson Jones III preaches in chapel as 2018 alumnus of the year

pastor of Compassion Baptist Church in Chicago, contributed articles to The Gospel Coalition, and has taught homiletics at Trinity.

In 2001, TEDS had 137 international students from approximately forty countries, adding a rich, cross-cultural dimension to classrooms and student life. Among the students in academic doctoral programs, 36 percent were internationals.[125] After graduation, mody returned to their home countries to assume leadership roles in church denominations, mission organizations, and Bible colleges and theological seminaries.[126] As a service to the students, the International Students Office provided them and their families with an orientation program, assistance with arrangements for household items and furniture, and a monthly dinner fellowship.

Dean Tiénou was eager for TEDS to be a school that not only *taught* about global theology but *engaged* in global theology.[127] Thus, in 2004, a consultation titled "Doing Theology in a Globalizing World" was held to honor Distinguished Professor of Mission and Anthropology Paul Hiebert.[128] Hiebert's impact was felt at many levels, formal and informal, academic and relational. Sometimes the impact was numerical. One of his students, Jae Hoon Lee, received a ThM in 2008 and serves as senior pastor of Onnuri Community Church of Seoul, Korea, a congregation with over seventy thousand members.

When Dean Tiénou and Robert Priest received $20,000 grants from the Wabash Center and the EFCA, they conducted a series of activities involving TEDS students and faculty as well as participants from the EFCA's Urban and Intercultural Mission to address issues of "Race and Ethnic Relations in Theological Education."[129] Moreover, Trinity College undergraduates were offered two courses that explored culturally based differences in communication styles and lifestyles with an emphasis on overcoming cultural barriers and mechanisms of discrimination.[130]

UNIVERSITY DEVELOPMENTS

At TEDS, Dean Tiénou saw an increase in student enrollment at the seminary after several years of slight decline. In 2004, there were 1,424 students, with 356 in the MDiv program. In the following year, the new MDiv curriculum was in place, with required courses in biblical theology, worship, leadership, and society.[131]

Steve Greggo, director of the Counseling Center, expanded its scope of ministry to address community needs such as psychological assessment and spiritual mentoring.[132] James Hoffmeier taught a course on Egypt and the Bible for undergraduate and graduate students that included a hands-on archaeology experience in Egypt.[133] Additionally, faculty members ministered in Australia, Côte d'Ivoire, France, Hong Kong, India, Romania, Singapore, Switzerland, Sudan, and Ukraine, with a profound influence in shaping the global evangelical church.[134]

Prompted by the accreditors at the Association of Theological Schools and the Higher Learning Commission, another development came with program assessment. More attention was given to course outcomes, grading rubrics, and student assessments. Perry Downs, associate dean of assessment, led efforts in preparation for the 2009 decennial visits, and Joyce Shelton succeeded him the following year, being appointed university assessment officer and chair of the Institutional Effectiveness Committee, designed for a university-wide program assessment in preparation for the following accreditation visits.[135]

Other university developments included the Trinity Society of Women, which was organized to encourage female students through its mentoring program, informal lunches, prayer meetings, and guest speakers on campus.[136] The MA in Christian studies, later named the MA in theological studies, was introduced for students who wanted academic training in Bible, theology, and historical studies, in preparation for parachurch and church staff positions.[137] In fall 2006, Dana M. Harris joined the TEDS faculty in the New Testament department.[138] The seminary also moved to a block schedule, designed to reduce the number of times that students had to travel to campus. In addition, a combination of weekend, evening, and modular courses made theological education more accessible to those living in the Chicagoland area.[139]

In 2006, Rolfing Library ren-ovated space in its lower level for archival use made possible by a gift of $25,000 from the estate of Gleason Archer, professor emeritus, and others.[140] With this gift, TIU archives welcomed researchers to view its rare book collection, TIU institutional archives, and papers of Carl F. H. Henry, Wilbur Smith, and Kenneth Kantzer.[141]

Dana M. Harris,
New Testament

In 2006, Felix Theonugraha, a graduate of the MDiv program, became TIU associate dean of stu-dents. When the student government hosted a comedy night, Theonugraha, known for his sense of humor, was asked to participate in a competition to deliver the "Worst Two-Minute Sermon." He preached from Genesis 22 and used the text of Abraham sacrificing Isaac for a message on "wise parenting." His obvious but satir-ical twisting of the text vividly showed how *not* to handle Scripture. The audience roared with laughter.[142]

TRINITY COLLEGE HIGHLIGHTS

The academic year 2003–2004 was a new highwater mark in enrollment for the college. At the same time, the school offered a generous financial aid plan to students of EFCA congregations. This again encouraged Free Church people to send their children to Trinity as they had done decades earlier.[143] However, when it was determined that this generous financial aid plan was not sustainable, it ended abruptly, leaving, in some cases, siblings of TIU students without comparable financial aid packages. Soon the college's enrollment trend started downward.[144] Many Free Church families who wanted their children to have a Trinity education at the college could not afford the tuition unless their children qualified as honors students. Thankfully for a few, four new $16,000 scholarships and eight $8,000 scholarships were available.[145]

During this period, Trinity College athletic teams continued winning championship seasons. For example, in 2004, the men's soccer team won the NCCAA's North Central Regional crown and placed third at the NCCAA National Tournament.[146] The women's volleyball team was named CCAC regular-season and tournament champions, and the women's soccer team was named NCCAA's national champions. In the fall of 2005, Trinity's women's soccer team (20–6–1) finished as national runner-up at the NCCAA Tournament in Kissimmee, Florida, and won the CCAC.[147]

New faculty were added at the college. In 2003, Karen A. Wrobbel came as assistant professor of education after serving for twenty-two

Women's volleyball

years as a missionary educator.[148] The next year, Sylvie T. Raquel began as assistant professor of New Testament.[149] Wendy L. Martin joined the business department as chair in 2006.[150] In the following year, three new faculty were added: Laurie Matthias and Peter Wright in education, and Greg Carlson in Christian ministries.

An example of Trinity's unique vision as a Christian university was seen in Sid Yeomans, a lecturer in business who developed a course in operations management that integrated Christian faith with concepts for directing and controlling processes to convert resources into goods and services.[151]

2005–2006 Concert Choir, with director Paul Satre

College students participated in a variety of theatrical and musical performances. In 2000, the Trinity Symphonic Band, under the direction of Thomas Hunt, toured Europe, and Paul Satre directed the choir.[152] Kristin Lindholm directed Trinity College students in a production of *Antigone*, with audience discussion led by Professor Harold Baxter following the play. In 2002, students performed in the debut of an original script of *Alice in Wonderland* adapted from the novel, and in 2004, Lindholm directed a performance of the Shakespeare pastoral comedy *As You Like It*.[153] In the same year, Don Hedges directed *Jane Eyre* (Caird/Gordon) in a joint production of the music and English departments. In the following year, he directed the opera *Gianni Schicchi* by Puccini and in 2007 directed the musical *Camelot* (Lerner/Loewe).

Trinity was also ready to respond in Christian love and service to people of the Gulf Coast following the devastation of Hurricane Katrina in 2005.[154] To bring relief to those affected, 103 students, staff, and faculty joined Urban Impact of the EFCA for four days in New Orleans, Louisiana.[155] Organized into teams, this group from TIU helped remove debris, mud, and ruined contents from people's homes. The following year, another group returned to begin the reconstruction of homes.

After Greg Waybright served for twelve years as president of TIU, he accepted a call to serve as senior pastor of Lake Avenue Church in Pasadena, California.[156] At Trinity, he was deeply appreciated for his pastoral approach, heart for global mission, and spirited chapel sermons. Students and faculty valued his personable, relational approach while respecting his commitment to the Scriptures and scholarship. Much to his credit, in 2005, *The Princeton Review* recognized Trinity College as "A Best Midwestern College," and in 2007 Trinity earned a ranking among "America's Best Colleges" by *U.S. News & World Report.*[157]

Following his departure, Jeanette Hsieh, who had been promoted by this time to executive vice president/provost, stepped in to serve as TIU's interim president.[158] Dr. Hsieh served in this role for eighteen months, communicating with grace and knowledge all that was happening on each of the campuses.

The economic downturn of 2007 and 2008 hit hard, affecting the American and global economies, adding stress to the university's finances, and worsening the decline in student enrollment. Despite this, TEDS hired Elizabeth Yao-Hwa Sung to teach systematic theology, and the following year, John M. Monson came from Wheaton College to teach in the Old Testament and Semitic languages department.

MOSAIC MINISTRY

The idea for a new ministry called Mosaic came in the spring of 2008 at a TEDS faculty workshop led by Dr. Bruce Fields.[159] The idea initially was to provide a welcoming haven for African American, Latino and Latina, and Asian students to discuss issues that were particularly significant to their churches and communities.

In 2009, the Mosaic formation group began. It was a multiracial group that pursued the biblical vision of reconciliation—first with God through

Mosaic gathering led by Peter Cha

Christ, and then with one another (2 Cor 5:18–19). Peter Cha provided leadership with support from John Woodbridge, Tite Tiénou, and Dana Harris. Soon, other students, including Anglos, expressed their interest to join Mosaic, hoping to engage in conversations around themes of reconciliation.[160]

With increased interest and growth, the Mosaic Gathering, under the leadership of Daniel Hartman, was launched to meet weekly. Soon the group acquired a larger meeting space, allowing more students to participate. They were joined by staff, other faculty members, local pastors, and lay leaders, some eighty to one hundred people every week. A student leader of Mosaic was Charlie Dates, who became senior pastor of Chicago's Progressive Baptist Church, having completed his MDiv and PhD at TEDS.

FEATURED FACULTY
Bruce Fields

Dr. Bruce L. Fields began his career at Trinity College in 1988 teaching New Testament and theology, and then joined the TEDS faculty, where he served as associate professor of biblical and systematic theology and chair of the biblical and systematic theology department. In addition to teaching, he coached TIU women's and men's tennis, as well as men's basketball.

Prior to Trinity, he served for six years on the staff of Cru, then known as Campus Crusade for Christ. There he served in a variety of roles, including

Athletes in Action—having played basketball earlier at the University of Pennsylvania—the Indian ministry in Colorado, and staff at the University of Michigan. He was first introduced to TEDS through Walter Kaiser's Old Testament survey course in summer 1973. Fields earned his MDiv and ThM at TEDS before completing his PhD in New Testament at Marquette University.

In addition to his expertise on the Epistle to the Philippians, Fields's well-known book *Introducing Black Theology* addressed the interface between Black theology and the evangelical church. At TIU, he cochaired the committee that produced the university's statement "A Biblical Theological Foundation of Racial Reconciliation."

Former student and professor of Wheaton College Vincent Bacote spoke of Fields's visionary nature, saying of him, "He began to convene fellow African American theologians and pastors to consider together how to be people of evangelical conviction while paying greater attention to the questions of justice and flourishing often unaddressed in white evangelical institutions and communities."

In 2019, Fields was present at Trinity for the inaugural Bruce Fields Racial

Bruce Fields

Reconciliation Award, which celebrates his compassion, conviction, and contributions toward racial reconciliation. Years earlier he said, "I am a theologian for the church. I visit the academy for wisdom and insight when it can be found. My burden, however, is the church and that which strengthens the church, equipping it for all realms of needed ministry."[161]

Fields and his wife, Mary, loved to attend athletic events in which their talented children and grandchildren participated. A talented musician, Fields also loved to play the bass. Fields loved the gospel of Jesus Christ.

PRESIDENT CRAIG WILLIFORD

In 2009, Craig Williford came from Denver Seminary to become the four-teenth president of TIU.[162] He was a TEDS alum himself, having earned a PhD in educational ministries in 1995. Williford came with impressive entrepreneurial skills, arrived with many good ideas, and was willing to try new things.[163] In 2010, he hired Robert Herron as academic dean of the college, David Hoag as director of advancement, and in 2011, Myron Steeves was appointed dean of the law school.[164] Moreover, Paige Cunningham, an attorney who had earned an MA in bioethics at TGS, became the executive director of CBHD.[165]

Inauguration of Craig Williford as
president of TIU (*Trinity Magazine*)

President Williford set in motion a series of projects, including class-room renovations and technology upgrades. With a push from the dean's office and college faculty, he launched the University Student Success Center—later rebranded the Thrive Center—in an effort to support students who were underprepared academically at the time of admission.[166] New programs were launched, including an undergraduate program in graphic design, an MDiv with pre-seminary honors, and a master of education.[167]

However, these projects were set in motion at the end of the economic recession that continued to plague the school financially.[168] In order to avoid declaring financial exigency, one program each at the college and graduate school was closed by administrative fiat, and the tenured faculty members associated with the programs were terminated at the end of the 2011–2012 academic year. To further reduce the size of the faculty, a generous retirement incentive was offered that led to the retirement of seven full-time faculty members. At the divinity school, there was a 10 percent pay cut for some faculty members. Moreover, retirement benefits for all university employees were no longer matched generously, as they had been up until that time.[169]

Waybright Center

Despite the challenges to Trinity's operating budget, in 2010, the school completed its largest and most successful capital campaign ever, raising more than $21 million.[170] The centerpiece of the campaign was construction of the Gregory L. Waybright Student Life Center, named in honor of the former president.[171] The campaign began with a lead gift of $1.3 million for a new student life center and cafeteria. The family who gave the gift added an additional gift to qualify as lead donor for the building. Within the Waybright Center is the Hawkins Dining Hall, named for this family.[172]

After reviewing all nontraditional programs in preparation for the new strategic plan, President Williford and the board of regents cast a vision to develop an array of online courses and to offer new online programs.[173] While other schools had entered the world of online education much earlier, TIU was dedicated to making courses and programs of the highest quality across all delivery platforms, saying, "a Trinity course is a Trinity course."

When Dean Herron found himself in a difficult position between the president and the college faculty, he departed. Jeanette Hsieh took up the reins a second time as dean of the college and graduate school and as interim co-provost, despite her plans to retire.[174]

In addition to President Williford's entrepreneurial skills as a strategic planner, he was a fundraiser. Thirty million dollars, the largest single gift in Trinity's history, was given by Susan Stover, a member of the board of regents, to fund five endowed chairs and other projects such as online course development.[175] Her family had given generously to Trinity for years, having known Waybright as their pastor in Wisconsin.[176] Their generosity continued with Williford as president.

President Williford developed a partnership with the Oikonomia Network, an organization dedicated to the integration of work, economics, discipleship, and the local church.[177] With the additional funding to TIU came some relief for meeting operating expenses, and so, in 2012, TEDS added several new faculty members, including Joshua Jipp in New Testament, Donald Guthrie in educational studies, Eric Tully in Old Testament, David J. Luy in systematic theology, and William Donahue in pastoral theology.[178] Kevin Vanhoozer returned to TEDS from Wheaton College for what was described as his "third coming."[179] The college added Martha Shin and Darryl Reynolds in business, Brian Reichenbach in music, Paul Worfel and Ruby Owiny in education, Brandon Waybright and Julia Wright Peterson in graphic design, and Aaron Smith in health sciences. At TLS, Adeline A. Allen became associate professor, teaching Contracts and Tort Law.

The commitment of the science faculty to undergraduate research experience led Chrystal HoPao in 2010 to develop a collaboration with the Chicago Botanic Garden, where she utilized her knowledge of genetics to participate in a populations genetic research project. This partnership involved six of Trinity College's best students in research and led to summer internships too.[180]

While President Williford had support of the board of regents and the EFCA and moved TIU forward, his strategic plan lacked ownership by many of the faculty. When the TEDS Faculty Senate articulated some of their concerns in a letter to him and copied leaders of the board of regents, the latter asked President Williford to go on sabbatical. In February 2013, he announced that he would be stepping down as president of TIU at the end of the academic year. At the time of his departure, the university enrolled approximately twenty-seven hundred students.[181]

The board of regents asked Neil Nyberg, who was a member of the board, a graduate of Trinity College, and a retired vice president and chief ethics and compliance officer of Kellogg Company in Battle Creek, Michigan, to serve as interim president beginning in 2013.[182] During his tenure, Nyberg helped to form a budget advisory task force composed of representatives from across the Deerfield campus, which helped TIU improve its financial position, and an enrollment task force, chaired by Karen Wrobbel, to address the enrollment challenges. Moreover, he held a faculty workshop that dealt with conflict resolution, matters of mismatched expectations, and the characteristics of a good president. When he completed his successful interim presidency, he was elected by the board of regents to serve as chair.

Jeanette Hsieh, while continuing to serve as dean of the college and TGS, held the Susan B. Stover Chair for Leadership in Christian Higher Education. At Hsieh's retirement, she was honored by the board of regents as provost emeritus and credited as one of the forces that held the school together throughout the years.[183]

Jeanette Hsieh

Jeanette L. Hsieh (EdD) began at Trinity in 1997 as professor of education, and then was dean of the College and Graduate School, before her appointment in 2004 as executive vice president/provost. Prior to her work at Trinity, she was on the faculty of Judson College, serving as the director of teacher education, and then was chair of the education department at Wheaton College.

At TIU, Hsieh's style of leadership brought administration and faculty together as she emphasized collaboration and consensus. Dean of Students William Washington recalled: "When

I met Dr. Hsieh, I could tell right away that Trinity was in for a treat. She had a compelling mission to enhance and build up the College. She had a wealth of knowledge and experience she had built up at Judson and Wheaton where she had faithfully served, and a sense of what it took to unify people in a common purpose."

Since 2004, Hsieh filled several important leadership roles at critical junctures in the school's history. In 2007, she was named interim university president. In 2009, she resumed her position as executive vice president/provost. In 2012, she became dean of the College and Graduate School. In 2014, she became co-provost and senior vice president for academic affairs and dean of Trinity College and Trinity Graduate School. Along with her husband, Ted, Dr. Hsieh had a particular interest in the advancement of the gospel in China. She and Ted also visited Indonesia to learn more about a remarkable evangelical educational ministry in that largely Muslim nation.

President David Dockery, recognizing her invaluable service to Trinity as a university, wrote, "It would not be an overstatement to say that Dean Hsieh's willingness to wear

Jeanette Hsieh

many administrative hats, her dedication to do whatever has needed to be done, her sensitivity to provide caring, people-focused leadership for faculty, staff, and students in both good and bad times, and her genuine commitment to exemplify Trinity's distinctive Christ-centered mission have literally been the glue to bind this institution together for the twenty-first century."

In recognition of her years of outstanding leadership to TIU, the endowed Jeanette L. Hsieh Chair of Educational Leadership was given in her honor. Upon her retirement, she received the title of provost emerita and dean emerita.[184]

PRESIDENT DAVID S. DOCKERY

In 2014, David S. Dockery was elected unanimously by the board of regents as the fifteenth president of Trinity. Holding a PhD from the University of Texas, Dockery previously served as president of Union University in Tennessee, coming to TIU with a sterling reputation. He was not only an experienced administrator but a respected theologian and gifted scholar, having authored or edited thirty-five books.[185]

President David S. Dockery

President Dockery laid out a strategic plan called Heritage & Hope: Trinity 2023, outlining several growth initiatives.[186] He implemented strategies to halt the college's decline in enrollment and raise its caliber of education, with hopes of increasing the college honors program. He brought a team with him from Union that included Mark Kahler in marketing, Jon Dockery in business services, and Rich Grimm in enrollment, and appointed Tom Cornman as dean of the college and graduate school and chief academic officer.[187] He welcomed Graham Cole as academic dean of TEDS.

President Dockery began immediately by making improvements to the appearance of the campus and repurposed the bookstore as a welcome center for admissions—the Norton Center, in honor of Will Norton, former Trinity president, who at the age of one hundred attended the dedication.[188] President Dockery instituted Founders' Day to remind students, faculty, and donors of Trinity's rich heritage and God's faithfulness.[189] At the same time, a major project of history between the EFCA and TIU digitized the denomination's periodicals, Trinity's yearbooks, and photo collections, making them accessible on the internet through Rolfing Library's website.

Besides a scholar and administrator, President Dockery showed that he was skilled in public relations and worked through issues like one would expect of a Southern Baptist gentleman trying to get TIU back on an even keel. During his tenure, the partnership with the EFCA was strengthened. With an eye for detail as well as seeing the big picture, he noticed that the official governance structure of the university was faulty, and so he worked skillfully with EFCA President Kevin Kompelien and the EFCA board of directors to correct this to the benefit of both parties.[190] President Dockery's vast experience in Christian higher education and his ties to evangelical networks proved to be a tremendous resource.

President Dockery was known to affirm faculty and staff at every level. He communicated through campus updates about Trinity's "wins," whether in athletics, academics, new faculty books, or grants for the academic centers.[191] Conversely, he did not want the school to be discouraged by setbacks or losses.

Among the wins were the thirty wins of the men's basketball team in the 2016–2017 season, when the Trojans shared the CCAC regular season title and advanced to the quarterfinals of the NAIA Division II Men's Basketball National Championships.[192] In 2015, Trinity's women's soccer team won the CCAC championship tournament against Olivet Nazarene, ending with a regular season record of 13–4–3. This made Coach Patrick Gilliam, after his twentieth season at TIU, the second-winningest coach in the NAIA and led to his induction into the NCCAA Hall of Fame.[193]

2016–2017 Men's basketball team

Other wins included receiving the gift of Camp Timber-lee in East Troy, Wisconsin, which for decades was associated with the EFCA. In 2014, the John and Susan Woodbridge Reading Room was dedicated in Rolfing

Library, named in honor of John Woodbridge, the longest-serving faculty member in Trinity's history.[194] In 2015, the Center for Transformational Churches was established with funding from the Kern Family Foundation.[195] Additionally, TEDS expanded its reach to Korea when Marty Crain and Steve Kang launched the Korean-language DMin program after working tirelessly with the Korean government's department of Culture.[196] The Christmas Concert performed by Trinity College's Concert Choir and Symphonic Band continued the annual tradition for students, families, donors, and friends of the university to celebrate the birth of Jesus Christ.

Dedication of the John and Susan Woodbridge Reading Room.
Left to right, Neil Nyberg, Susan Woodbridge, John Woodbridge.

Added to the list of wins during President Dockery's presidency was the discipline-specific accreditation of the TEDS mental health counseling program by the Counseling and Related Educational Programs.[197] In 2016, TLS ranked third on the National Jurist's list of "Most Devout Christian Law Schools," and in the following year launched its masters in legal studies program, which well exceeded the administration's expectations for enrollment.[198] The Henry Center received a grant of $3.4 million from the Templeton Religion Trust for a project titled "Evangelical Theology and the Doctrine of Creation."[199] Trinity's gymnasium was remodeled, owing to a generous gift from Mr. and Mrs. Henry Van Dixhorn. Mr. Dixhorn was a Trinity regent and former Trinity College basketball coach.

In partnership with the Wisconsin department of corrections and under the leadership of Dean Cornman, Trinity College established a partnership and enrolled inmates at Waupun Correctional Institution in a new bachelor of biblical studies program.[200] Cornman also encouraged the science faculty to develop a new major in computer science and an emphasis in data analytics, hiring Daniel Ayala to supervise the program. New faculty were added too, including Ryan Wilkinson in health sciences, Julia Wright Peterson and Taek Kim in graphic design, and Joshua Held in English.

In 2014, just prior to President Dockery's arrival as the new president, Tite Tiénou decided it was time to end his role as dean at TEDS and return to research, supervising doctoral students, and devoting time to the launch of a new academic center, the Paul Hiebert Center for World Christianity and Global Theology.[201] Tiénou was succeeded in the dean's office by Graham Cole, who returned to TEDS after teaching at Beeson Divinity School.[202] Cole was both an experienced and able administrator and a respected scholar and writer. He soon welcomed new faculty members, including James Arcadi, and several TEDS alumni, such as Jules Martinez in systematic theology, Michelle Knight in Old Testament

D. A. Carson

and Semitic languages, Lucas O'Neill in pastoral theology and homiletics, and Madison Pierce in New Testament.

In 2016, much-beloved Grant Osborne retired from TEDS after thirty-nine years of teaching, just two years before his passing to glory.[203] Among other professors who retired from TEDS was D. A. Carson, described as "one of the last great Renaissance men in evangelical biblical scholarship."[204] In addition to authoring and editing over sixty books, Carson served as president of The Gospel Coalition and appeared in media such as ABC News's *20/20* and *Nightline* to discuss certain claims regarding the historical Jesus.[205]

Trinity was taking significant strides forward when the school was shocked to learn that on March 6, 2017, Dockery experienced a near-fatal heart attack, followed by a life-saving heart procedure.[206] While he recovered slowly and became increasingly stronger, knowing that his stamina would not return to his former prodigious work level, he decided it was best to plan for his transition from the role of president. The board of regents began the search for his successor and named him chancellor in honor of his five fruitful years at the helm.[207]

David Dockery passes the baton of the presidency to Nicholas Perrin

In June 2019, Dr. Nicholas Perrin was elected as the sixteenth president of TIU. Perrin came from Wheaton College, where he held the Franklin S. Dyrness Chair of Biblical Studies and served as dean of Wheaton Graduate School. He wasted little time before stepping into his new position, steering TIU into its next chapter. He was installed formally as president on October 24, 2019.

Perrin's inaugural theme of "God so loved the world" (John 3:16) was warmly appreciated by the Trinity community. Perrin's understanding of Trinity as a Free Church school and his commitments to gospel proclamation and the school's statement of faith regarding Scripture were likewise welcomed.[208] In addition, he advocated ethnic diversity, the fostering of a culture of mentorship on all campuses, and the recognition of the Lord's faithfulness to Trinity. Early on Perrin called on Trinity's faculty, board, and staff to pray for the Lord's blessing on the school.

The Partnership between TEDS and Korea's Torch Center for World Missions (1990–2021), by Peter Cha[209]

In 1990, President Ken Meyer learned about the ministry of Torch Center for World Missions (TCWM) in South Korea, particularly the center's efforts to provide continuing theological education for Korean pastors and to mobilize Korean churches for the task of world evangelization. President Meyer reached out to Chairwoman Hyung Ja Lee of TCWM to explore different ways that TCWM might collaborate with TEDS, initiating a three-decades-long international partnership between the two organizations. She said: "I have no doubt that God's amazing providence and grace will continue to be with us all as the Torch Center

Chairwoman
Hyung Ja Lee

The Lee International Center at TEDS

for World Missions and Trinity partner together with trust and love."

In 1992 and 1993, TCWM implemented a pilot program that invited TEDS faculty members to Korea to teach weeklong courses for Korean pastors. Representing different disciplines, eight faculty members (Ken Kantzer, Walter Kaiser, John Woodbridge, Ted Ward, Nigel Cameron, Mark Senter, Charles Sell, and Paul Cedar) offered courses in which several hundred pastors participated. The great success of this two-year project played a critical role in cementing the partnership between TEDS and TCWM and in raising the visibility of TEDS in Korea during the 1990s.

Yoon Hee Kim (TEDS PhD),
president of Torch Trinity Graduate University

Then, in 1997, TCWM and TEDS collaborated to establish an international (English-speaking) seminary in Seoul, Korea, called Torch Trinity Graduate School of Theology (TTGST). From its beginning, many TEDS faculty members regularly taught there as visiting faculty members while Meyer, soon after retiring from Trinity International University, served as the second president of TTGST. Since then, as the school grew and offered a growing number of programs at master's and doctoral levels, many TEDS alumni have served as its regular faculty members and administrative leaders. Recently, the school renamed itself as Torch Trinity Graduate University and installed Dr. Yoon Hee Kim (TEDS PhD in Old Testament) as its sixth president.

In 2015 TCWM and TEDS began to explore the possibility of starting a TEDS doctor of ministry program in Korea. The TCWM leadership felt there was a growing need for a quality theological education program that would further equip Korean pastors to think biblically and missionally as their culture and society faced significant changes and challenges. In 2016, TEDS and TCWM received the approval of the Association of Theological Schools and the South Korean government to begin a new doctor of ministry that would be taught by TEDS faculty members and TEDS alumni who are teaching or pastoring in Korea. The program grew quickly, graduating seventeen students in May 2019.

TEDS was relatively little known in Korea until 1990. Today, partly due to the partnership between TEDS and TCWM, TEDS is widely recognized in Korea as a leading, global evangelical school that has produced many gifted and dedicated Korean theologians and pastoral leaders. At the same time, due to the fruitfulness of this international partnership, TEDS has become more international in understanding its calling and mission. God has used this strategic, cross-cultural partnership to help Trinity to more fully and intentionally embrace its middle name, Trinity *International* University.

THANKSGIVING TO THE LORD

The year was 1897. The Evangelical Free Church Swedes in Chicago who launched Trinity could have scarcely imagined all the wonderful ways the Lord would use the school during the next 125 years. After all, the beginnings of Trinity were really quite humble. Moreover, Trinity experienced significant obstacles and wrenching setbacks. But in his mercy, God graciously blessed the school as an evangelical, Christ-centered, and Bible-based learning community. In the span of its history Trinity has prepared nearly thirty thousand alumni for Christian service and mission around the world.

Many international and American students have been attracted to the school by professors who write books and lead the fields in which they study and perform. Hundreds of thousands know the work of D. A. Carson, Kevin J. Vanhoozer, and John Woodbridge. Others have been mentored by outstanding teacher-scholars such as Craig Ott, Bradley Gundlach, Joyce Shelton, Scott Manetsch, Myron Steeves, Deborah Colwill, Peter Cha, Kristin Lindholm, Paul Bialek, K. Lawson Younger, Donald Guthrie, Steve Greggo, Chrystal Ho Pao, Karen Wrobbel, Harold Netland, and Dennis Magary. These are only some of the most experienced professors. Many younger faculty, whether in Illinois, Florida, or California, are following in their footsteps.

Undoubtedly the prayers of Trinity friends worldwide, EFCA supporters and board of regents members (Peter Etienne, Judy Bradish, Neil Nyberg, Bill Kynes, Bob Kleinschmidt, Martin Klauber, Howard Dahl, Quintin Stieff, among many others), and faculty members, students, and staff explain in the greatest measure the reason that Trinity, after 125 years, still remains resolutely committed to its motto, "Entrusted with the gospel." No doubt this resolution exists against overwhelming human odds. This is a divine providential blessing for us to genuinely celebrate. This is a gracious divine blessing for which to give grateful thanks to the Lord.

May we be inspired in our own Christian lives by the Trinity story of God's faithfulness. And may we pray for God's continued blessing on Trinity and the school's graduates wherever they might serve him in the future. To our faithful and loving God be all glory and honor, now and forever. Amen.

Chapter 7

Thanksgiving to the Lord for His Great Faithfulness

John D. Woodbridge

After the children of Israel miraculously passed over the Jordan River on dry land, the Lord told Joshua to charge a man from each of the twelve tribes to gather a stone from the river bed. Joshua then took the stones and built a memorial of thanksgiving for the providential care of the Lord for his people. Joshua indicated he wanted children of future generations who inquired about the meaning of the stones to learn about the Lord's divine intervention. This intervention permitted the children of Israel to cross over the Jordan River (Josh 3–4).

The Trinity story does not include any event nearly parallel to the crossing of the Jordan River by the children of Israel, but it certainly includes inspiring evidence of the Lord's faithfulness to the school. Nor does the Trinity campus have a stone memorial of thanksgiving to the Lord. But the school's history has certain foundational themes running through it. They help explain the school's evangelical vitality at its 125th anniversary. Hopefully future generations will find these themes of remembrance from the Trinity story not only illuminating but inspiring.

As noted throughout this volume, these themes of remembrance include the following:

1. The Lord has been faithful to care for Trinity even in seriously trying circumstances, including financial shortfalls and spiritual failures.

2. Trinity's relationship with the EFCA has often provided stabilizing theological ballast and material resources to both Trinity and the EFCA. The school is deeply rooted in the EFCA and remains the EFCA's love gift to the evangelical world.

3. Trinity affirms the Protestant *solas* and is committed to a gracious and generous evangelical orthodoxy.

4. Trinity understands the vital importance of prayer for spiritual revivals and the outpouring of the Holy Spirit.

5. Trinity's motto, "Entrusted with the gospel," has not been a tip of the hat to Christ's Great Commission. Rather, on occasion it has served as an inspirational reminder for the school's students and faculty to engage in passionate Christian evangelism.

6. Holy Scripture is the verbally inspired, inerrant word of God. It should inform the school's teaching about personal salvation and Christian living, issues related to love of neighbor, ethics and social justice, creation, evangelism, and worldview formation.

7. The promotion of world-class scholarship and the pursuit of personal piety and care for neighbors are not incompatible endeavors.

8. We all stand before the cross as sinners in need of a Savior, whatever our race, ethnic, and socioeconomic position. In time Trinity promoted racial diversity.

9. The Trinity story is amplified by the stories of thousands of Trinity grads who have served the Lord faithfully throughout the world and often at great personal sacrifice.

10. The Lord's faithfulness during the school's history should solicit our thankfulness and heartfelt gratitude.

As David Gustafson, himself a Swede, observed, the Swedes in Chicago who founded the school in 1897 could have hardly envisioned all the ways the Lord would use Trinity during the next 125 years. Despite obstacles and setbacks, God has enormously blessed the school as an evangelical learning community. Trinity has to date prepared nearly thirty thousand alumni for Christian service in the United States and around the world.

Afterword

S ome institutions are founded by farsighted planners who, gifted not only with an entrepreneurial spirit but with great organizational anticipation, chart out a careful path that proves stable for a long time.[1] Of course, history is messy, and unexpected turns inevitably demand modifications in one's long-term plans. The essays in this book, however, demonstrate that Trinity cannot legitimately lay claim to that sort of steady vision, tweaked from time to time by the pressures of the day. Rather, our messy history bespeaks the kindness of God at many turning points in which things could have gone another way—in which, institutionally, we scrabbled our way to the next step on short notice and then looked around in time to observe that God had been kind to us again. Yet, ironically, a handful of enduring priorities can be discerned across the twelve-and-a-half decades of our history. Perhaps it will not be thought inappropriate to use this afterword to tease out some of the lessons to be learned in the rearview mirror. After all, if this book is a collection of essays about our history, then what comes afterward must surely say something about the future—about what comes next.

SHIFTING PRIORITIES AND STABLE VISION

In what David Gustafson calls the "humble beginnings" of Trinity, there was no heraldic declaration that the goal was to establish a world-class Christian university. Rather, there was a ten-week Bible course held in the basement of a local church largely made up of Swedish immigrant evangelicals responding to a felt need. This developed into the Swedish Bible Institute of Chicago. Even when it merged with the Norwegian-Danish Bible Institute, there was no move toward an institution providing liberal arts education in the Christian tradition: the goal was to provide adequate theological training for the pastors and other Christian leaders needed by Scandinavian immigrant evangelicals. Swedish evangelical Baptists merged with Norwegian-Danish Evangelical Free Lutherans on the assumption that Scandinavian blood is thicker than baptismal water. The educational institution was eventually renamed Trinity College and Trinity Evangelical Divinity School, serving in the first instance the denomination that had come to be called the Evangelical Free Church of America. The "Free" component of the name arose out of the fact that the Norwegian contingent of these believers were "free Lutherans"—that is, they did not spring from the Norwegian state church in Norway, but were independent Lutherans, "free" Lutherans.

The three-and-a-half decades that began around 1960 brought about half a dozen significant changes to Trinity, changes that attested or contributed to Trinity's shifting educational priorities: (1) Especially under the leadership of Kenneth S. Kantzer and of many who followed him, there was a concerted effort to pursue excellence—that is, not only orthodoxy and faithfulness, but academic excellence. (2) As it was with the mothering denomination, so also with the college and divinity school: whereas the names of faculty and students alike had at one time been overwhelmingly Scandinavian, by the end of the twentieth century Trinity reflected a diversity of names that left those with Scandinavian roots in a small minority. These shifts in Trinity's demographics were the result not only of Scandinavian evangelicals reaching beyond their cultural immigrant bubbles, but also of the rising number of international students enrolling on campus (often about 25 percent)—itself the product, in part, of Scandinavian American missionaries serving around the world. (3) Coincidentally, Trinity's numbers grew rapidly, partly owing to the impact of the baby boom bubble passing through the national population, and partly owing to the large vision of several Trinity administrators. Moreover, the rising numbers led to multiple campuses and extension sites, and eventually some digital distance learning. They also left space in the curricula for (4) new programs. Thus began the expansion from Bible courses, to theology and pastoral training, to Christian liberal arts, all well beyond the vision of 1897. Doubtless some of the impetus for these shifts came from the rising levels of education in the nation. There was a time when a bachelor's degree in theology would make the minister one of the most educated persons in the congregation, and in some rural settings that remains true. But where the minimum expected level of training is the MDiv, which is granted by a seminary, then even while Trinity College retained a strong emphasis on Bible and theology, fewer of its graduates headed directly toward vocational ministry, and more headed toward teaching, administration, business, advanced education, and more. The same realities spawned several centers, such as the Center for Bioethics and Human Dignity, whose conferences and publications exert far-reaching influence. The work of the Center for Bioethics and Human Dignity soon led to the establishment of a master's in bioethics in Trinity Graduate School. None of this, of course, had been anticipated by the founders. (5) Such developments also led to the decision to take on the law school in California. Once again, Trinity did not plan in advance to build a law school, still less to choose that it be located in California. The opportunity arose, and the board and administration saw it as a good next step. (6) Similarly, these developments led to various structural changes. As Brad Gundlach has shown, when Trinity College became focused on providing a Christian liberal arts education, for a while it thought its Free Church connection too restrictive and withdrew to become an independent institution. For various reasons, some time later it rejoined the Trinity complex. Neither move was enshrined in the Trinity DNA. Again, when Trinity reorganized itself as Trinity International University, it was not so much the fruit of long-term planning as a step that seemed to reflect what Trinity had become.

In sum, the route to Trinity's present status is not so much a well-designed superhighway as a leisurely romp through the woods. Yet it is a romp singularly blessed by God. Trinity has exercised an influence far greater than anyone might have guessed from the smallness of the denominations that gave it birth.

Having scanned the shifting priorities that stand out in Trinity's history, it would nevertheless be a mistake to ignore elements of the stable vision that shaped that history. Quite a few could be enumerated; I choose three.

First, Trinity has never abandoned its doctrinal commitments, including its high view of Scripture. This steadfastness has manifested itself in at least two ways. On the one hand, when the leaders of the Free Church decided, during the last quarter century, to examine its startlingly simple (some might venture "simplistic") statement of faith, the result of several years of study, discussion, and debate was a more detailed, more polished, and more robust document pretty much in the same direction as that of the original. On the other hand, Trinity owes its allegiance to surprisingly broad streams of confessional strength. As David Dockery comments in the foreword, "Recognizing their place as heirs of the sixteenth-century Reformation, pietism, Puritanism, as well as the Awakenings, the men and women of Trinity have been shaped by the great historic Christian confessions and the larger evangelical tradition." To say it in a slightly different way: on the one hand, Trinity and its parent denomination have clung to certain nonnegotiable commitments, not least the truthfulness of Scripture; on the other hand, they have allowed—indeed, fostered—a certain degree of flexibility that reflects the diversity of their mixed cultural and ecclesiastical heritage. Quite remarkably, this "theological triage" (as some have started to label it) has so far proven remarkably stable.

Second, even Trinity's humble beginnings were motivated by a desire to reach and train believers, and grow. Obviously, if the love of growth is nothing more than the love of big numbers, without a concomitant commitment to the gospel in all the ways it works out in the world, then growth becomes a seductive mistress. But conversely, if an educational institution such as TIU loses its passion for outreach, it is announcing its incipient decline. In Trinity's case, the long-standing commitment to evangelize, reach out, plant churches around the world, and teach has largely endured and was also tied to:

Third, Trinity has a deep commitment to the local church, and especially to the EFCA. And yet, ironically, this commitment took on a peculiarly expansive form. Most institutions of higher learning that are tied to a denomination demand that their full-time faculty belong to a denominationally affiliated local church and that a minimum percentage of the student body must spring from that heritage too. There may be sound reasons for these requirements, but from the early 1960s on, Trinity has followed another course. Faculty members are expected to be active Christians who are tied to a local church and who can sign the statement of faith, but that church does not have to be part of the EFCA. There is no denominational restriction on the students. Inevitably, some people have objected that the

EFCA is spending too much of its resources on the training of the young people of other groups. But history has shown that this policy has actually attracted people to the EFCA, in line with the immaculately archaic wording of the wisdom of Proverbs 11:24: "there is that scattereth, and yet increaseth" (KJV). In any case, Trinity has been shaped by allegiance to the local church in general, and the EFCA in particular, while retaining a surprisingly catholic view of the church.

UNYIELDING COMMITMENTS
TO SHAPE THE FUTURE

So what comes *after* the history of Trinity laid out in this volume? What comes afterward? At the risk of turning a reflective afterword into an intrusive sermon, I shall venture five priorities that Trinity will do well to pursue unflaggingly.

First, maintain the confessional center. This is more challenging than it looks. It is one thing to require faculty and administrators to sign on to the statement of faith; it is another to find faculty and administrators who really do love the gospel and cherish the truthfulness of Scripture. Lecturers and professors know that students do not learn most of what we teach them; rather, they learn what we are excited about. If you assume the gospel but get excited by (say) the best cultural pundits of the age (e.g., Charles Taylor, Douglas Murray, Christopher Caldwell, Thomas Sowell, and many others), your students will learn to become cultural commentators without any deep passion for the gospel itself. To assume the gospel is not the same as loving to talk about it and discerning how it works in Scripture and how it addresses men and women in their highly diverse cultures; to sign a pledge about Scripture is not the same thing as reading Scripture meditatively, studying it faithfully, and talking about it incessantly. Of course, this presupposes a thoughtful commitment to theological triage, as Gavin Ortlund has nicely argued.[2] It also presupposes working with students to teach how to engage with others—winsomely, with acute listening and integrity, and without fear, defensiveness, or arrogance.

Second, maintain a theological/visionary leadership. Just over twenty years ago, James Tunstead Burtchaell published his long (888 pages) and carefully researched study of the steps that numerous Christian colleges have taken in their move from some kind of confessionalism to some brand of secularism.³ Among his many insightful observations, one concerns us here. Most of the relevant colleges were begun by visionary pastors/theologians/scholars. Once the institution became large enough, however, the chief officers needed to possess administrative, financial, and legal skills, so eventually the board started to look not for a pastor/theologian/scholar to serve as president but for a scholar/lawyer/administrator or an administrator/fundraiser. It was not as though the candidate disavowed the institution's historic vision, of course—but that vision was no longer what got them out of bed in the morning. So by all means hire accountants, enrollment experts, and other competent administrators, but make sure the persons in charge at the top of the administrative heap are those with the deepest and most thoughtful loyalty to the founding vision.

Third, along the same line, but worth bringing up as an additional point, maintain leadership that is transparently devoted to prayer and to candid dependence on God. Not only is a life of prayer contagious, but it fosters humility and dependence on God, rather than projecting omnicompetence. At the risk of a personal story, I recall the time when the president of a small Christian university that was facing dire financial and other challenges gathered the faculty. He candidly laid out the challenges and led the faculty in prayer shaped by the example of Jehoshaphat: "We do not know what to do, but our eyes are on you" (2 Chr 20:12).

Fourth, maintain absolute probity in all financial matters. This is no more than another element of Christian commitment. For example, money that is pledged and raised for Project X must not be funneled off, without permission and agreement, to Project Y. Little will more quickly squander, among constituents, an institution's reputation for integrity than slightly shady financial dealings.

Finally, maintain the clarity that sees a college, seminary, or university is above all an educational institution. It is not a church, though ideally it fosters excellent relationships with local churches and, where the churches have a strong emphasis on teaching, it shares some of the church's goals. It is not a counseling center, though ideally it provides wise counsel to students who need it (and more than ever do, during the current pandemic). It is not a restaurant, though the best college cafeterias win well-deserved awards for their fare. It is not an evangelistic center, though I have seen many students during the course of their studies become more adept in talking to others about their faith in the Lord Jesus, while sometimes faculty/student teams have been known to plant churches. A flourishing Christian university may *do* all of these things, and more, but in the first instance it is an *educational* institution, so it is committed to training people how to think. And it is a *Christian* educational institution, so it is less concerned to demonstrate that faculty and students are woke (people who study ancient texts are rarely snookered by the faddish) and more concerned to demonstrate that they are awakened.

D. A. CARSON, emeritus professor of New Testament,
Easter 2022

Postscript

The Trinity Story Going Forward:
The Question for the Future

The Trinity story is a kind of extended miracle story. The far-ranging scope of the institution's influence—quite apart from the depth of its impact on the church, the academy, and society—has been extraordinary. Of course, Trinity's impressive track record does not ensure its ongoing significance for the future: past performance is no guarantee of forthcoming results. That said, there is good reason to believe that the university will continue to exert a powerful and broad-shaping influence in the years to come. In fact, given the challenges facing the church today, the need for a Trinity education has never been greater.

As these pages have labored to show, the Trinity story is firmly rooted in the story of the Scandinavian Free Church. From the nineteenth-century down to the present day, this movement has retained both an inimitable simplicity and an enduring vitality. Its legacy is best epitomized in and explained by the refrain, *"Var står det skrivet?"* ("Where is it written?"). When it came to Free Church communities debating issues of doctrine and practice, the question "Where is it written?" was *the* question that repeatedly came to the fore. "Where is it written?" marked the beginning of every theological dialogue; it also marked the end. In the Free Church movement, the word of God, contained in the Scriptures, would always have the first word and the last word.

For these same communities, the heart of that word was always understood to be the gospel. This is simply a matter of sound biblical theology. The gospel is the climax of the scriptural story; the sum and substance of the Scriptures is encapsulated in the gospel. Nor is there any contradiction between the diversity of special revelation and the singularity of the gospel. Just as the Law and the Prophets testified to Jesus Christ, so too this same Christ, crucified and risen, now stands as the singular fulfillment of the whole of Scripture. In this sense, Jesus *is* the gospel.

In order to elaborate on this profound truth, Luke the Evangelist tells a now-familiar story about two sisters who host Jesus in their home. In a well-meaning effort to serve the master and his disciples, the (presumably) older sister Martha busies herself with what she perceived to be needful, all the while fretting aloud to Jesus because her younger sister Mary was not helping. For her part, Mary is simply sitting at Jesus's feet, listening to the teacher and being formed by him through his word. In the end, in an unexpected response to the complaining sister, Jesus vindicates Mary. Whereas Martha had allowed herself to become distracted by "many things," the younger sister had somehow come to recognize the simple truth that only "one thing" was needful: listening to the word of Jesus.

In reprimanding Martha and affirming Mary, Jesus catches us by surprise because most readers of this story are disinclined either to doubt the older sister's intentions nor to shake the impression that the younger sister *is* in fact shirking her responsibility. And yet in Jesus's eyes Martha's behavior was as problematic as Mary's was commendable. In focusing on the "one thing," Mary had secured her irrevocable inheritance; meanwhile, her sister, in allowing herself to be distracted by "many things," had unwittingly allowed herself to drift from Jesus's aims. Martha *thought* she was discharging the gospel mission through her activism, but for Jesus true activism must start with the word of God as its point of departure. This is not to say that service to others is a bad thing (if we go that route, we would have a hard time explaining the immediately preceding parable of the good Samaritan!) but rather that the whole of the Christian life must be made to rest on the gospel as it is revealed in the Scriptures. "Where is it written?"

By God's grace, Trinity has remained faithful to the "one thing" of the gospel for 125 years now. This legacy is a gift from God and should not be taken for granted. This historical trajectory has not necessarily been the norm for historically Christian institutions. Today, tragically, there exist far too many seminaries and colleges that originally had Christ-honoring aims at their founding only to drift over time, eventually losing most or all trace of the evangelical conviction that helped give them birth. Were we to delve into the historical particulars of each of these post-evangelical institutions, I am all but certain that we would discover that each decisive shift away from the gospel was occasioned by the best of intentions. For all we know, when those advocating for a functional redirection of the mission appealed to other stakeholders, they did so on the basis of a legitimate need, perhaps even with echoes of Martha's accusation: "Don't you care ... ?"

History proves how astonishingly easy it is for institutions of Christian higher learning to become distracted by any number of many things, once they've taken their focus off of the one thing. I am convinced, and all the more so as broader evangelicalism seems to be undergoing its own reshaping, that if Trinity has any hope of moving forward with its mission into the future, it must do so while remaining firmly planted at Jesus's feet. As this institution continues to educate men and women to engage in God's redemptive work through a critical engagement with culture, may it ever do so with the stubborn longing of Mary in its heart and the insistent question of our forebears in its mouth: "Where is it written?"

Trinity's historical commitment to being informed and shaped by the word of God has at least three important implications for future prospects. First, as long as the body of Christ fights to retain its gospel focus in the midst of competing agendas and even other gospels emerging from within its own walls, the church will continue to benefit from a steady influx of Trinity-educated believers. This is simply because Trinity has historically valued the integration of Christian faith and Christian vocation, orthodoxy (right doctrine) and orthopraxis (right action), and these habits of integration will remain critical as the church of the future discerns the proper relations between the one gospel and the many ways that the gospel can take practical form.

Second, with its internationally recognized faculty, Trinity will continue to give—from the halls of the academy to the pavement of the marketplace—supporting witness to the Free Church voice in affirming an orthodox faith while remaining relatively flexible on issues that have historically divided believers. With various camps presently taking on harder edges beneath the broader evangelical tent, the Free Church refrain of "Where is it written?" provides a pair of guardrails that discourage, on the one side, the local church's all-too-common tendency to squelch good-faith attempts to reason together about disputable issues, and, on the other side, the equally common move of loading secondary convictions with a doctrinal payload they cannot reasonably bear.

Third, with the number of Christian converts continuing to outpace the number of qualified teachers and pastors across the world, now more than ever the global church is calling for exactly the kind of pastors, ministry leaders, and theological educators that Trinity has been known to produce. If there's something that the ends of the earth need now more than baptized converts, it's disciples whose leaders have trained them to ask "Where is it written?"

Thanks to the efforts of its contributors and editors, this book has admirably described Trinity's past. It is a book that has answered many of our questions as to how Trinity came to be, how it came to progress in its journey, and how it came to the place where it is today. But behind and underneath this amazing story is a central preoccupying question: "Where is it written?" If Trinity has any hope of continuing its mission that it took up so many years ago, it must continue to occupy itself with exactly that same question. By God's grace, Trinity has remained faithful to the word of God; by God's grace, too, Trinity will continue to remain faithful. When the sequel to this book is written 125 years from now, may it also tell a story of men and women who, having chosen the one thing, lived and taught as those entrusted with the gospel.

NICHOLAS PERRIN, president of Trinity International University,
Maundy Thursday 2022

Notes

1. Calvin B. Hanson, *The Trinity Story* (Minneapolis: Free Church Press, 1983), 14–15.
2. M. W. Montgomery, *A Wind from the Holy Spirit in Sweden and Norway* (New York: American Home Missionary Society, 1885), 84.
3. David M. Gustafson, *D. L. Moody and Swedes: Shaping Evangelical Identity among Swedish Mission Friends, 1867–1899* (Linköping: Linköpings Universitet, 2008), 67–91.
4. H. Wilbert Norton, et al., *The Diamond Jubilee Story of the Evangelical Free Church of America* (Minneapolis: Free Church Publications, 1959), 61.
5. Frederick Hale, *Trans-Atlantic Conservative Protestantism in the Evangelical Free and Mission Covenant Traditions* (New York: Arno, 1979).
6. Norton et al., *Diamond Jubilee Story*, 138–39.
7. E. A. Halleen, et al., *The Golden Jubilee of the Swedish Evangelical Free Church: Reminiscences of Our Work under God. 1884–1934* (Minneapolis: Swedish Evangelical Free Church, 1934), 14.
8. John Carlstig, *Gustaf F. Johnson: Mannen med det brinnande hjärtat* (Jönköping: SAM Förlaget, 1965), 20.
9. Carlstig, *Gustaf F. Johnson*, 20.
10. Norton et al., *Diamond Jubilee Story*, 149.
11. Halleen et al., *Golden Jubilee*, 36–38.
12. David M. Gustafson, "P. J. Elmquist: Founding President of the Swedish Bible Institute of Chicago, 1897–1908," *Swedish-American Historical Quarterly* 68.1 (January 2017): 11–47.
13. David M. Gustafson, "The 1884 Boone Conference of the Free Mission Friends: Founding of the EFCA or Theological Discussion?" *Trinity Journal* 34 (Fall 2013): 276.
14. See: Philip J. Anderson, "Education and Identity Formation among Swedish-American Mission Friends: The Case of Ansgar College, 1873–1884," in *Scandinavian Immigrants and Education in North America*, ed. Philip J. Anderson, Dag Blanck, and Peter Kivisto (Chicago: Swedish-American Historical Society, 1995), 58–59.
15. Ernst W. Olson, ed., *History of the Swedes of Illinois*, part 1 (Chicago: Enberg-Holmberg, 1908), 280.
16. G. A. Young, Frank W. Anderson, and E. A. Halleen, *Minnen och Bilder: Från Svenska Ev. Frikyrkans Predikantförening, 1894–1919* (Chicago: Swedish Evangelical Free Church Ministerial Association, 1919), 32.
17. *Chicago-Bladet*, 29 June 1897, 1; Halleen et al., *Golden Jubilee*, 33.
18. *Chicago-Bladet*, 29 June 1897, 1.
19. *Svenska Bibel-Institutet i Chicago: Redogörelse, från dess början i form af kortare kurser åren 1897, 1898 och 1901 och sedan dess första läsår 1902–1903 till och med dess andra läsår 1903–1904* (Chicago: J. V. Martenson, 1904), 9.

20. "Skol- och Bibel-Kurs," *Chicago-Bladet*, 14 September 1897, 1.

21. "Skol- och Bibel-Kurs," 1.

22. *Svenska Bibel-Institutet i Chicago: Redogörelse, 1903–1904*, 8–9.

23. Della Olson, *A Woman of Her Times* (Minneapolis: Free Church Press, 1977), 74, 79.

24. Nathaniel Carlson, *Sixty Years in Gospel Song, Music and Testimony* (Robbinsdale, MN: Osterhus, 1955), 12.

25. Olson, *Woman of Her Times*, 79.

26. Carlson, *Sixty Years in Gospel Song*, 12–13.

27. Carlson, *Sixty Years in Gospel Song*, 20–21.

28. Norton, et al., *Diamond Jubilee Story*, 201, 283; *The Evangelical Beacon*, 8 July 1975, 13.

29. Olson, *Woman of Her Times*, 74, 79.

30. *Chicago-Bladet*, 2 August 1898, 2.

31. Roy A. Thompson, "Trinity Is 70," *Evangelical Beacon*, 24 October 1967, 4.

32. *Svenska Bibel-Institutet i Chicago: Redogörelse, 1903–1904*, 14–15.

33. *Svenska Bibel-Institutet i Chicago: Redogörelse, 1903–1904*, 15.

34. *Svenska Bibel-Institutet i Chicago: Redogörelse, 1903–1904*, 15–16.

35. *Svenska Bibel-Institutet i Chicago: Redogörelse, 1903–1904*, 16.

36. *Svenska Bibel-Institutet i Chicago: Redogörelse, 1903–1904*, 17.

37. Letter from J. Elmquist, G. A. Young, and John Martenson, 20 March 1905, Archives, Trinity International University, Deerfield, Illinois.

38. Letter from Elmquist, Young, and Martenson, 20 March 1905, 20.

39. Letter from Elmquist, Young, and Martenson, 20 March 1905, 24.

40. Calvin B. Hanson, *What It Means to Be Free: A History of the Evangelical Free Church of America* (Minneapolis: Free Church, 1990), 84.

41. J. Elmquist, "Det svenska bibelinstitutet i Chicago," *Chicago-Bladet*, 15 July 1902, 1.

42. Josephine Princell, *Memoirs of J. G. Princell*, trans. David M. Gustafson (Chicago: Frisk Collection of Covenant Literature, North Park University, 2012), 16.

43. Olson, *History of the Swedes*, 271–72.

44. *Svenska Bibel-Institutet i Chicago: Redogörelse, 1905–1906*, 5, 23.

45. *Svenska Bibel-Institutet i Chicago: Redogörelse, 1905–1906*, 35–46.

46. *Chicago-Bladet*, 20 October 1908, 8.

47. For Karl Newquist, see Young et al., *Minnen och Bilder*, 43.

48. Thompson, "Trinity Is 70," 4.

49. Halleen et al., *Golden Jubilee*, 126, 269–70.

50. *Evangelical Beacon*, 25 January 1972, 13.

51. Mel Larson, *117 Ways to the Mission Field* (Moline, IL: Christian Service Foundation, 1957), 201.

52. *Evangelical Beacon*, July/August 2003, 28–29.

53. David M. Gustafson, "Evangelical Convictions in Response to Liberal Theology: The Bible Institute and Academy of the Norwegian-Danish Evangelical Free Church, 1910–1949," *Trinity Journal* (Spring 2019): 37–63.

54. Arnold T. Olson, *The Search for Identity* (Minneapolis: Free Church, 1980), 80.

55. A. C. McGiffert Jr., *No Ivory Tower: The Story of the Chicago Theological Seminary* (Chicago: Chicago Theological Seminary, 1965), 59.

56. R. Arlo Odegaard, *With Singleness of Heart: Pioneers and Pioneering for Christ in Home Mission Fields* (Minneapolis: Free Church, 1971), 89.

57. McGiffert, *No Ivory Tower*, 146.

58. Frederick Hale, "Norwegians, Danes and the Origins of the Evangelical Free Tradition," *Norwegian-American Studies* 28 (1979): 82.

59. A. D. Hartmark, "The Norwegian-Danish Evangelical Free Church Movement" (MA thesis, Minnesota Bible College, 1944), 83.

60. Hartmark, "Norwegian-Danish Evangelical Free Church Movement," 76, 94.

61. *Compass 1942* (Minneapolis: Trinity Seminary and Bible Institute, 1942), 43.

62. Aarsrapport for De Evangeliske Frikirkeforeningers Aarsmöder, Milwaukee, 22 May 1909, 67–70.

63. Norton et al., *Diamond Jubilee Story*, 88.

64. Norton et al., *Diamond Jubilee Story*, 88.

65. Odegaard, *With Singleness of Heart*, 437.

66. *Compass 1948* (Minneapolis: Trinity Seminary and Bible Institute, 1948), 48. *Compass* was the school yearbook.

67. *Compass 1942*, 43.

68. Arnold T. Olson, *Believers Only: An Outline of the History and Principles of the Free Evangelical Movement in Europe and North America Affiliated with the International Federation of Free Evangelical Churches* (Minneapolis: Free Church Publications, 1964), 302.

69. "Missionary Murdered," *Malaya Tribune*, 12 February 1918, 5.

70. H. W. Norton, ed., *The Diamond Jubilee Story of the Evangelical Free Church of America* (Minneapolis: Free Church Publications, 1959), 82, 96.

71. *Evangelisten*, 24 September 1913; *China and the Gospel: An Illustrated Report of the China Inland Mission 1919* (London: China Inland Mission, 1919), 3; Marshall Broomhall, *By Love Compelled: The Call of the China Inland Mission* (London: China Inland Mission, 1947), 62.

72. C. T. Dyrness, "Hedningenmissionen: Et Sorgens Budskab," *Evangelisten*, 27 February 1918, 4.

73. "Missionary Murdered," 5.

74. Mary Taylor, Geraldine Guinness, and Shu-ming P'u, *With P'u and His Brigands* (London: China Inland Mission, 1922), 64; James C. Hefley and Marti Hefley, *By Their Blood: Christian Martyrs of the Twentieth Century* (Grand Rapids: Baker Books, 2004), 49.

75. *Den Kristelige Talsmand* 49, no. 16 (18 April 1918), 248 (8).

76. Josephine Princell, *Alliansmissionens tjugufemårsminnen, 1891–1916* (Chicago: Skandinaviska Allansmissionen, 1916), 230; O. C. Grauer, *Fifty Wonderful Years: Scandinavian Alliance Mission 1890–1940, Missionary Service in Foreign Lands* (Chicago: Scandinavian Alliance Mission, 1940), 76, 78.

77. Dyrness, "Hedningenmissionen: Et Sorgens Budskab," 4.

78. David V. Martin, *Trinity International University, 1897–1997: A Century of Training Christian Leaders* (Deerfield, IL: Trinity International University, 1997), 41.

79. Odegaard, *With Singleness of Heart*, 445.

80. This statement was condensed from a conference lecture delivered in Detroit, Michigan. L. J. Pedersen, "Our Free Churches," *Compass 1942*, 31.

CHAPTER 2: ON THE MOVE TO MERGER (1916–1960)

1. Claudia Goldin and Lawrence F. Katz, "Human Capital and Social Capital: The Rise of Secondary Schooling in America, 1910–1940," *Journal of Interdisciplinary History* 29.4 (1999): 685.

2. Norton et al., *Diamond Jubilee Story*, 89.

3. *Compass 1942*, 43.

4. Norton et al., *Diamond Jubilee Story*, 89.

5. *Compass 1942*, 9; *Evangelical Beacon*, 16 October 1962, 3.

6. Norton et al., *Diamond Jubilee Story*, 90.

7. *Compass 1948*, 48.

8. Norton et al., *Diamond Jubilee Story*, 107.

9. *Compass 1942*, 44.

10. Norton et al., *Diamond Jubilee Story*, 107–8.

11. Odegaard, *With Singleness of Heart*, 501.

12. L. J. Pedersen, *Our Evangelical Free Churches* (Chicago: Evangelisten, 1933), 9.

13. *Compass 1948*, 48; Odegaard, *With Singleness of Heart*, 566.

14. *Evangelical Beacon*, 24 May 1949, 5.

15. Odegaard, *With Singleness of Heart*, 495.

16. Norton et al., *Diamond Jubilee Story*, 114.

17. Odegaard, *With Singleness of Heart*, 500–501.

18. *Compass 1948*, 48; Odegaard, *With Singleness of Heart*, 503.

19. The seminary degree led to a diploma or the bachelor of theology. A. D. Hartmark, "Sketches of the Restoration Movement and the Norwegian Danish Evangelical Free Church Movement: Their Comparison" (MA thesis, Minnesota Bible College, 1944), 77.

20. Also called Northwestern Evangelical Seminary and Bible Training School, where Dr. W. B. Riley was president; today University of Northwestern, St. Paul. *Compass 1942*, 47.

21. *Compass 1943* (Minneapolis: Trinity Seminary and Bible Institute, 1943), 35.

22. *Evangelisten*, 5 July 1941, 2.

23. T. B. Madsen, "The New Name for the Bible School," *The Evangelist* 11.7 (July 1941): 5.

24. Olson, *This We Believe: The Background and Exposition of the Doctrinal Statement of the Evangelical Free Church of America* (Minneapolis: Free Church Publications, 1933), 133.

25. Madsen, "New Name," 5.

26. Olson, *This We Believe*, 132.

27. Madsen, "New Name," 5.

28. Odegaard, *With Singleness of Heart*, 507.

29. Quoted in full from *The Compass 1944, Trinity Seminary and Bible Institute of Minneapolis, Minn.* (Minneapolis: Evangelisten, 1944), 12.

30. "Early Beginnings," unpublished paper, cited in Martin, *Trinity International University*, 4.

31. *Evangelical Beacon*, 6 July 1948, 1

32. Norton et al., *Diamond Jubilee Story*, 182.

33. Halleen et al., *Golden Jubilee*, 270.

34. *The Christian Workers Magazine* 17.2 (October 1916), 143; *Chicago-Bladet*, 6 July 1948, 3; Gene A. Getz, *MBI: The Story of Moody Bible Institute* (Chicago: Moody Press, 1969), 82.

35. Note that some sources incorrectly state: "Gustav Edwards, a former missionary to China who was home studying at Chicago Theological Seminary and Wheaton College, was called to head the Bible Institute of the Swedish Evangelical Free Church." Norton et al., *Diamond Jubilee Story*, 184; Hanson, *Trinity Story*, 26; David V. Martin, *Trinity International University, 1897–1997: A Century of Training Christian Leaders* (Deerfield, IL: Trinity International University, 1998), 32.

36. *The Fireside 1928* (Chicago: Free Church Academy, 1928), 15.

37. *Chicago-Bladet*, 6 July 1948, 3; *Fireside 1930* (Chicago: Free Church Academy, 1930), 10.

38. *Evangelical Beacon*, 6 July 1948, 1; Norton et al., *Diamond Jubilee Story*, 182.

39. The Moody Bible Institute of Chicago Bulletin, 1916–1917, June 1916, 34; Getz, *MBI: The Story of Moody Bible Institute*, 100.

40. Moody Bible Institute Bulletin, Catalogue Number 1926/27, 4.

41. Olson, *Woman of Her Times*, 74.

42. Norton et al., *Diamond Jubilee Story*, 185.

43. *Evangelical Beacon*, 6 July 1948, 1; 17 August 1948, 6; Norton et al., *Diamond Jubilee Story*, 185.

44. Norton et al., *Diamond Jubilee Story*, 182.

45. *Fireside 1933* (Chicago: Bible Institute and Academy, 1933), 48.

46. *Evangelical Beacon*, 10 December 1940, 4.

47. *"A Book of Remembrance": Dedicated to the Memory of Axel Leonard Wedell* (Chicago: Free Church, 1940), 20; Hanson, *Trinity Story*, 31.

48. Norton et al., *Diamond Jubilee Story*, 182.

49. Halleen et al., *Golden Jubilee*, 34.

50. Halleen et al., *Golden Jubilee*, 271.

51. *"Book of Remembrance,"* 20; Norton et al., *Diamond Jubilee Story,* 182.

52. 1927/28 Catalog, 10, cited in Hanson, *Trinity Story,* 34.

53. Martin, *Trinity International University,* 48–53.

54. Swedish Evangelical Free Church Yearbook 1931 (Minneapolis: Swedish Evangelical Free Church, 1931, June 1931), 91, cited in Martin, *Trinity International University,* 48.

55. From September 1916 to December 1933, 594 students had been enrolled in the Swedish Free School, and 209 had graduated with diplomas from Moody Bible Institute and/or the Free Church's Bible Institute and Academy. Halleen et al., *Golden Jubilee,* 274.

56. The academy had always been controversial within the Swedish Free Church. Norton et al., *Diamond Jubilee Story,* 182. Also see Swedish Evangelical Free Church Yearbook, 90, cited in Martin, *Trinity International University,* 49.

57. Martin, *Trinity International University,* 49.

58. 1939 EFCA Yearbook, 12, 26, 65; Martin, *Trinity International University,* 49.

59. 1940 EFCA Yearbook, 61.

60. *"Book of Remembrance,"* 25.

61. *Evangelical Beacon,* 10 December 1940, 7; 1941 EFCA Yearbook, 54.

62. *Evangelical Beacon,* July 1941, 6.

63. Fenggang Yang, *Chinese Christians in America: Conversion, Assimilation, and Adhesive Identities* (University Park: Pennsylvania State University Press, 1999), 61, 77.

64. Ted Choy and Leona Choy, *My Dreams and Visions: An Autobiography* (Paradise, PA: Ambassadors for Christ, 1997).

65. Yang, *Chinese Christians in America,* 64–65.

66. 1942 EFCA Yearbook, 54.

67. 1943 EFCA Yearbook, 134–35.

68. Hanson, *Trinity Story,* 36.

69. Martin, *Trinity International University,* 51.

70. *Evangelical Beacon,* 27 June 1944, 7. See also *Evangelical Beacon,* 14 March 1950, 7.

71. *Evangelical Beacon,* 27 June 1944, 7.

72. After the annual meeting in June 1944, at Jersey City, NJ, the official name became "The Evangelical Free Church Association of North America." Hartmark, "Sketches," 80.

73. Norton et al., *Diamond Jubilee Story,* 122–23.

74. *The Fireside 1942* (Chicago: Evangelical Free Church Bible Institute and Seminary, 1942), 13. Steelberg's dissertation is titled, "An Analysis and Evaluation of Missionary Education Materials of the Evangelical Church in the Light of the Doctrinal Standard of That Church."

75. *Evangelical Beacon,* 14 March 1950, 7.

76. David J. Hesselgrave and Ed Stetzer, eds., *Missionshift: Global Mission Issues in the Third Millennium* (Nashville: B&H Academic, 2010), 259–60.

77. Norton et al., *Diamond Jubilee Story,* 123.

78. Norton et al., *Diamond Jubilee Story,* 123.

79. *Evangelical Beacon,* 22 March 1949, 2. See also *Evangelical Beacon,* 16 November 1948, 7; Hanson, *Trinity Story,* 64.

80. *Evangelical Beacon,* 16 November 1948, 7.

81. *Evangelical Beacon,* 16 November 1948, 7.

82. *Evangelical Beacon,* 9 December 1947, 16.

83. *Evangelical Beacon,* 9 December 1947, 16.

84. 1948 EFCA Yearbook, 28.

85. *Evangelical Beacon,* 28 September 1948, 6; 16 November 1948, 7; 7 May 1949, 4; 1949 EFCA Yearbook, 40.

86. "Dr. Ludwigson to Head United Free Church School," *Evangelical Beacon,* 16 November 1948, 7.

87. *Evangelical Beacon,* 30 August 1949, 9.

88. *Evangelical Beacon,* 16 November 1948, 7; 1949 EFCA Yearbook, 41.

89. *Evangelical Beacon,* 16 November 1948, 7.

90. Hanson, *Trinity Story*, 49.

91. *Fireside 1949* (Chicago: Free Church Seminary and Bible Institute, 1949), 8.

92. *Evangelical Beacon*, 26 June 1951, 4. Ludwigson's inauguration was postponed until 1951. *Evangelical Beacon*, 19 June 1951, 4; 1951 EFCA Yearbook, 5.

93. *Fireside 1949*, 7.

94. *Evangelical Beacon*, 30 August 1949, 9.

95. *Evangelical Beacon*, 8 November 1949, 5. This report further stated: "In the old Bible Institute course, the name of which has been changed to Bible College ... there are enrolled six men and sixty-three women. In the Seminary there are thirty-two men and one woman. In our newly added two-year Junior College course with a Bible major, there are twenty-six men and four women enrolled."

96. 1949 EFCA Yearbook, 40.

97. *Evangelical Beacon*, 20 September 1949, 5.

98. 1950 EFCA Yearbook (covering the Merger Conference as well as the Annual Conference), 255; Hanson, *Trinity Story*, 61.

99. *Evangelical Beacon*, 16 August 1949, 2.

100. *Evangelical Beacon*, 8 November 1949, 5; 1950 EFCA Yearbook, 134. The new building was dedicated on Sunday, 28 May 1950. See *Evangelical Beacon*, 6 June 1950, 6.

101. *Evangelical Beacon*, 24 January 1950, 7.

102. *Evangelical Beacon*, 24 January 1950, 7.

103. *Evangelical Beacon*, 26 June 1951, 3.

104. *Evangelical Beacon*, 16 November 1948, 7.

105. *Evangelical Beacon*, 16 November 1948, 2.

106. *Evangelical Beacon*, 28 February 1950, 15.

107. Wes Carlson, "My Impressions of the Day of Prayer at Trinity," *Evangelical Beacon*, 28 February 1950, 15.

108. C. R. Ludwigson, "School News," *Evangelical Beacon*, 7 March 1950, 4.

109. *Evangelical Beacon*, 7 March 1950, 4.

110. *Trinitarian 1950* (Chicago: Trinity Seminary and Bible College, 1950), 10.

111. Marge Anderson, "God Working at Trinity," *Evangelical Beacon*, 28 February 1950, 15–16.

112. *Evangelical Beacon*, 12 December 1950, 13.

113. *Evangelical Beacon*, 13 February 1951, 6.

114. *Evangelical Beacon*, 13 February 1951, 6.

115. Hanson, *Trinity Story*, 59, 65.

116. 1950 EFCA Yearbook, 135.

117. 1954 EFCA Yearbook, 77.

118. 1951 EFCA Yearbook, 43. "George Tweed, a student at Trinity, was designated by the school to act as group leader and he arranged to have various Free Church pastors and faculty members as special speakers." "Dedication Events and History: Evangelical Free Church of Libertyville, Illinois, October 5–12, 1958." Archives, CrossLife Evangelical Free Church, Libertyville, IL.

119. *Evangelical Beacon*, 1 June 1954, 5.

120. *Trinitarian 1951*, 53; *Trinitarian 1952*, 19.

121. Hanson, *Trinity Story*, 57.

122. Hanson, *Trinity Story*, 63.

123. Hanson, *Trinity Story*, 68.

124. Hanson, *Trinity Story*, 69.

125. 1959 EFCA Conference Report.

126. Hanson, *Trinity Story*, 79.

127. Hanson, *Trinity Story*, 80.

128. Hanson, *Trinity Story*, 80.

129. Calvin B. Hanson, *The Trinity Story*, Heritage Series, 1884–1984 (Minneapolis: Free Church Press, 1983), 6:80–82.

130. *Evangelical Beacon*, 22 March 1960, 6–7.

131. Hanson, *Trinity Story*, 80–84.

Chapter 3: A Gift to Evangelicalism (1963–1974)

1. These details are reported in a letter from Wilbert Norton to Kenneth Kantzer, 17 June 1963, TEDS dean file.

2. Martin, *Trinity: Entrusted with the Gospel*, 64.

3. Oral interview with Milo Lundell, 6 February 2014.

4. Martin, *Trinity: Entrusted with the Gospel*, 68–69.

5. Martin, *Trinity: Entrusted with the Gospel*, 65. See also 1958 EFCA Yearbook, 120; 1960 EFCA Yearbook, 111.

6. The problem of indebtedness is a recurring theme in President Norton's annual reports to the EFCA Conference. In his 1958 report, for example, Norton reports Trinity's debt at more than $44,000. 1958 EFCA Yearbook, 121.

7. Seminary enrollment figures were as follows: 58 students (1959–1960), 44 students (1960–1961), 42 students (1961–1962). 1960 EFCA Yearbook, 111; 1961 EFCA Yearbook, 122.

8. 1959 EFCA Yearbook, 117.

9. *Evangelical Beacon*, 10 October 1961, 10.

10. See the student testimonials in *Evangelical Beacon*, 19 January 1960, 7–9; 26 January 1960, 5–7.

11. Oral interview with Howard Matson, 23 January 2014.

12. 1959 EFCA Yearbook, 16, emphasis added.

13. See President Arnold T. Olson's description of the Sunset property in *Evangelical Beacon*, 16 February 1960, 2.

14. Mrs. Pearl Nielsen Krause, letter to the editor, *Evangelical Beacon*, 12 April 1960, 4.

15. *Evangelical Beacon*, 31 May 1960, 8.

16. 1960 EFCA Yearbook, 18.

17. 1963 EFCA Yearbook (page M13) reports that this decision was taken at the previous year's annual conference.

18. 1960 EFCA Yearbook, 111–12. In January 1962, the Trinity Advancement Committee voiced similar concerns: "Trained theological students are needed to fill the gap in our rapid growth." See *Evangelical Beacon*, 16 January 1962, 13.

19. Oral interview with Clayton Lindgren, 31 January 2014.

20. 1961–1962 Trinity Seminary Catalog, 22.

21. *Evangelical Beacon*, 20 November 1962, 8.

22. See 1962 EFCA Yearbook, 111; 1963 EFCA Yearbook, R44.

23. 1962–1963 Trinity Seminary Catalog Supplement, 14.

24. Reports on the progress of the Trinity Advancement Campaign appeared regularly in the *Evangelical Beacon* during these years. The 22 October 1963 edition of the *Beacon* (p. 8) reports that $618,050.10 had been raised. "Of this amount, $485,447.30 has been pledged by the Free Churches. One hundred fifteen Trinity Alumni have pledged $30,144.00."

25. For a brief biography of Kenneth Kantzer, see the Festschrift published in his honor by John D. Woodbridge and Thomas E. McComiskey, eds., *Doing Theology in Today's World* (Grand Rapids: Zondervan Academic, 1991), 495–505. See also autobiographical comments in Kantzer's article, "Why I Chose the Ev. Free Church," *Evangelical Beacon*, 7 July 1964, 6–7.

26. Kenneth and his wife, Ruth (Forbes) Kantzer, were married in September 1939 and became parents of two children, Mary Ruth (born in 1942) and Dick (born in 1947).

27. "An Interview with Kenneth S. Kantzer," in Martin, *Trinity: Entrusted with the Gospel*, 142, 144.

28. "An Interview with Kenneth S. Kantzer," in Martin, *Trinity: Entrusted with the Gospel*, 141–57.

29. Kantzer, "Why I Chose the Ev. Free Church," 6–7. This article is based on the address that Kantzer delivered to the annual conference of the EFCA at Winona Lake, Indiana, June 1964.

30. In the course of his career, Kantzer articulated his doctrine of inerrancy in a variety of brief essays; he was also an author and one of the original signatories of the Chicago Statement on Biblical Inerrancy in 1978. For the Chicago Statement, see library. dts.edu/Pages/TL/Special/ICBI_1.pdf. Also see Kantzer's essays, "Evangelicals and the Doctrine of Inerrancy," in *The Foundations of Biblical Authority*, ed. James Montgomery Boice (Grand Rapids: Zondervan, 1978), 147–56; and "Why I Still Believe the Bible Is True," *Christianity Today*, 7 October 1988, 22–25.

31. In an address in the early 1990s, Kantzer noted: "Trinity's confession of faith, its doctrine and theological basis is broadly ecumenical and represents what Christians and evangelicals have believed down through the centuries. We are truly ecumenical, but unlike many ecumenists in our day, we really do believe our ecumenical heritage, and we want to keep and build on it." TEDS dean file, "Address Regarding Trinity University," 3.

32. Writing to Kantzer on 17 June 1963, H. Wilbert Norton comments, "I have sensed an increasing consciousness of God's guidance in our decisions, tentative though they have been, and of His approval of the plans you have presented for Trinity Theological Seminary." TEDS dean file.

33. Kantzer to H. Wilbert Norton, Harry Evans, and Arnold T. Olson, 1 June 1963, TEDS dean file.

34. These stipulations appear in an untitled, typed memo, written somewhat later by Kantzer, which begins with the sentence, "The following items were agreed to but I do not find them spelled out in these letters." TEDS dean file. For more on these provisions, see "Interview with Kenneth S. Kantzer," 144–47.

35. The American Association of Theological Schools (AATS) was the precursor of today's Association of Theological Schools (ATS).

36. Kantzer states, "The effect of this was to preclude the possibility that the school would become a dispensational school of the Dallas type." TEDS dean file, Kantzer memo.

37. Kantzer to President Arnold T. Olson, 12 June 1963, TEDS dean file.

38. Kantzer, "Why I Chose the Ev. Free Church," 7.

39. 1963 EFCA Yearbook, M12–M13.

40. Rev. Ted Olson, then serving an EFCA church in Rockford, Illinois, recalls first hearing Kantzer's statement from an enthused delegate returning home from one of these early annual conferences. Oral interview with Rev. Ted Olson, 22 January 2014. A version of this statement appears in the 1964–1965 TEDS Catalog, 21–22.

41. 1963 EFCA Yearbook, R44.

42. The details of the convocation that follow are described in the *Evangelical Beacon*, 15 October 1963, 2–3.

43. Liefeld and Perry joined the faculty for the spring semester.

44. New faculty additions are listed by President Norton in his annual report to the general conference. See 1964 EFCA Yearbook, 20.

45. *Evangelical Beacon*, 7 July 1964, 7.

46. Oral interview with Howard Matson, 23 January 2014.

47. Oral interview with Clayton Lindgren, 31 January 2014.

48. 1965–1966 TEDS Catalog, 17.

49. See the entry on Carl F. H. Henry in *Dictionary of Christianity in America*, ed. Daniel Reid et al. (Downers Grove, IL: InterVarsity Press, 1990); also Gregory Alan Thornbury, *Recovering Classic Evangelicalism: Applying the Wisdom and Vision of Carl F. H. Henry* (Wheaton, IL: Crossway, 2013).

50. *Evangelical Beacon*, 4 November 1985, 18.

51. Video interview with Walter and Olive Liefeld, 10 February 2014.

52. *Evangelical Beacon*, 24 April 1979, 12.

53. On this, see George Marsden, *Reforming Fundamentalism* (Grand Rapids: Eerdmans, 1987), 208–19. Historian John Woodbridge notes that TEDS with its explosive growth was "linked at the hip to Fuller" in the 1960s. Oral interview, 6 February 2014.

54. *Evangelical Beacon*, 19 January 1965, 4.

55. See 1970 EFCA Yearbook, 233; 1967 EFCA Yearbook, 203.

56. Oral interview with John Woodbridge, 6 February 2014. Similarly, in one of his reports, President Evans assured delegates at the EFCA annual conference that "we are still more deeply interested that these [students] are also men and women of the Spirit rather than merely able people of academic achievement." 1966 EFCA Yearbook, 198.

57. Board chairman Harry Evans summarized these decisions in his letter to board members on 16 February 1964. See Wilbert Norton's file.

58. In a document titled "For the Record" (17 April 1964), President Norton provided a lengthy self-defense and stinging rebuke of the board's methods. See Wilbert Norton's file. See also Martin, *Trinity: Entrusted with the Gospel*, 76–77.

59. *Evangelical Beacon*, 4 July 1967, 19.

60. See the chart in Scott Manetsch, "Trinity Evangelical Divinity School, the Early Years" (unpublished booklet, 2014), 13, TIU Archives.

61. *Evangelical Beacon*, 1 August 1967, 11.

62. See, for example, 1971–1972 TEDS Catalog, 184.

63. Oral interview with John Woodbridge, 6 February 2014.

64. *Trinity Today*, January 1971.

65. These descriptions are drawn from oral interviews with Duane Elmer (29 January 2014), Greg Scharf (30 January 2014), Barry Beitzel (3 February 2014), and John Woodbridge (6 February 2014), and the video interview with Walter and Olive Liefeld (10 February 2014). For reflections on Wilbur Smith, see the dedicatory preface to Kenneth Kantzer, ed., *Evangelical Roots* (Nashville: Thomas Nelson, 1978), 11–14. The author's personal recollections are included as well.

66. Richard Boldrey, in *Evangelical Beacon*, 19 January 1965, 9.

67. Written statement of Duane Elmer, given to author on 1 February 2014 and used with permission. Elmer graduated from TEDS with an MA in New Testament in 1969. The book in question is John Baillie, *The Idea of Revelation in Recent Thought* (New York: Columbia University Press, 1954).

68. The college buildings included a dormitory, a classroom/office building, and a food service/student union building.

69. *Evangelical Beacon*, 20 December 1966, 14.

70. For an artist's drawing and description of the Peterson building, see *Evangelical Beacon*, 4 August 1964, 11. The building was 128 feet long by 40 feet wide and was constructed at a cost of $75,000.

71. 1969 EFCA Yearbook, C–44.

72. *Evangelical Beacon*, 10 September 1968, 15.

73. *Evangelical Beacon*, 1 August 1967, 10. In 1967, the generous gift of a house closed the financial gap in the last weeks of the fiscal year. See 1968 EFCA Yearbook, 188.

74. 1967 EFCA Yearbook, 205. These 136 congregations encompassed around one-third of all EFCA members.

75. *Evangelical Beacon*, 26 September 1967, 15.

76. *Evangelical Beacon*, 19 January 1965, 4.

77. Monies raised by the United Development Crusade were designated for the construction of the EFCA headquarters building (12.5 percent), as well as college buildings at Trinity Junior College in British Columbia (16.5 percent) and Trinity College and Trinity Evangelical Divinity School (71 percent).

78. See *Evangelical Beacon*, 29 August 1967, 14.

79. See *Evangelical Beacon*, 4 July 1967, 8; 13 February 1968, 17.

80. *Evangelical Beacon*, 6 May 1969, 16.

81. See the fuller version of the story of Rolfing Library in chapter 4.

82. *Evangelical Beacon*, 4 August 1964, 11; 1 February 1966, 15; 31 January 1967, 10.

83. *Evangelical Beacon*, 19 January 1965, 9.

84. 1971 EFCA Yearbook, 233.

85. See *Trinity Today*, October 1971 and June 1974.

86. 1971–1972 TEDS Catalog, 50.

87. Oral interview with Greg Scharf, 30 January 2014.

88. Reminiscence of Martin Klauber, 13 February 2014.

89. *Trinity Today*, December 1971.

90. *Evangelical Beacon*, 7 August 1973, 19; 9 April 1975; 25 November 1975, 20.

91. *Evangelical Beacon*, 24 April 1979, 12.

92. Though students did not acquire formal credit for practical ministry assignments, TEDS catalogs during this period stated that "every student is expected to be engaged in some regular church work each weekend or during the week." See, for example, 1967–1968 TEDS Catalog, 31.

93. *Evangelical Beacon*, 13 February 1968, 17.

94. *Evangelical Beacon*, 14 January 1969, 8.

95. Those congregations were the Village Church of Lincolnshire and Christ Church of Lake Forest. Several decades later, TEDS faculty and students were also instrumental in the founding of CrossWay Church in Kenosha, Wisconsin.

96. In Mark Senter III, "Personal Memoirs," 4.

97. In Senter, "Personal Memoirs," 4. These discussions were usually led by Ray Bakke and Mac White, whom Senter calls "the blackest white man I ever met."

98. Oral interview with Perry Downs, 17 February 2014.

99. Oral interview with Perry Downs, 17 February 2014.

100. 1968 EFCA Yearbook, 188–89.

101. *Trinity College Digest*, 15 May 1970, 1.

102. This description of the People's Christian Coalition and its magazine comes from an article in the *Trinity Digest*, 10 December 1971.

103. Oral interviews with Greg Scharf (30 January 2014), Barry Beitzel (3 February 2014), John Woodbridge (6 February 2014).

104. *Evangelical Beacon*, 14 January 1969, 2.

105. Kenneth Kantzer to Robert Picirilli, 20 October 1971, in Kantzer Papers, TIU Archives.

106. Martin, *Trinity: Entrusted with the Gospel*, 83. In all, Trinity College and TEDS received $211,680 from the United Development Crusade—far less than projected. See *Evangelical Beacon*, 11 July 1972, 9.

107. *Evangelical Beacon*, 19 October 1971; 8 August 1972, 15.

108. See Martin, *Trinity: Entrusted with the Gospel*, 83–84.

109. *Evangelical Beacon*, 2 November 1971, 12.

110. *Evangelical Beacon*, 2 May 1972, 17.

111. *Evangelical Beacon*, 3 October 1972, 17; 28 November 1972, 18.

112. Martin, *Trinity: Entrusted with the Gospel*, 84.

113. "A Study for the Future of Trinity College and Trinity Evangelical Divinity School," cited in Martin, *Trinity: Entrusted with the Gospel*, 89–91.

114. Martin, *Trinity: Entrusted with the Gospel*, 90–91. At the time, Kantzer judged this to be "a short-sighted and dangerous move" (150).

CHAPTER 4: A CHRISTIAN LIBERAL ARTS COLLEGE (1957–1996)

1. Hanson, *Trinity Story*, 73. Hanson was for many years president of Trinity Junior College (now Trinity Western University) in Canada, and later an administrator at TEDS.

2. *Evangelical Beacon and Evangelist*, Trinity Sunday Issue, 22 January 1957: Roy A. Thompson, "Editorial," 2; Monroe Sholund, "Monroe Sholund Looks at Trinity," 6; Warren Franzen, "The Christian Teacher in the Public School," 7.

3. Hanson, *Trinity Story*, 73.

4. *Trinitarian 1966*, 24.

5. Dwight Fuller, "Trinity College Trains Missionaries," *Evangelical Beacon*, 21 January 1964, 6.

6. *Trinitarian 1957.*

7. *Trinitarian 1959.*

8. *Trinitarian 1961.*

9. *Trinitarian 1957.*

10. *Trinitarian 1961* and *1964*. For the book see Clyde S. Kilby, *Christianity and Aesthetics* (Chicago: InterVarsity Press, 1961).

11. *Trinitarian 1957.* Their outfits got more cheerleader-appropriate in coming years.

12. The 1958–1959 season included games versus Bethany, Northern Baptist Seminary, Garrett, Moody, Fort Wayne, Huntington, Grace, McCormick, E.T.S. North Park, Emmaus Bible, Spring Arbor, and Lakeland, with some repeats. *Trinitarian 1959.*

13. Joseph Swan, foreword to 1960 EFCA Yearbook, 3. For the inspiring early history of Trinity Junior College (now Trinity Western University), see Hanson, *Trinity Story,* esp. ch. 11.

14. Arnold T. Olson, EFCA President's Report, 1961 EFCA Yearbook, 33.

15. NAE Report, 1961 EFCA Yearbook, 160. Another National Association of Evangelicals initiative launched a three-pronged program against communism, and the Women's Fellowship of the National Association of Evangelicals called for "total abstinence as the only hallmark of evangelical Christian ethics." Three members of the National Association of Evangelicals executive board that year were EFCA men.

16. 1960 EFCA Yearbook, 17–18. The express purpose of the new commission was to "safeguard those principles and that spirit which must be continued if we are to justify our existence as an evangelical movement and if we are to have an educational program which has as its foundation the inspired Word of God, and its center loyalty to the Lord Jesus Christ." Olson tells the story in *Give Me This Mountain* (Minneapolis: privately published, 1987), 156.

17. Hanson, *Trinity Story,* 93.

18. Hanson, *Trinity Story,* 99.

19. Martin, *Trinity: Entrusted with the Gospel,* 69.

20. Olson, EFCA President's Report, 1963 EFCA Yearbook, R7.

21. Norton, TC/TTS President's Report, 1963 EFCA Yearbook, R47; Martin, *Trinity: Entrusted with the Gospel,* 76.

22. Norton, TC/TTS President's Report, 1963 EFCA Yearbook, R48.

23. *Trinitarian 1961.*

24. Hanson, *Trinity Story,* 113.

25. Norton, TC/TTS President's Report, 1963 EFCA Yearbook, R43–R51.

26. Olson, EFCA President's Report, 1963 EFCA Yearbook, R14–R15. Another revealing question was, "Can we use funds given for a capital expansion program to meet past and current deficits without so informing the people?"

27. Olson, EFCA President's Report, 1963 EFCA Yearbook, R15.

28. Harry Evans, "The Question Is This: Will the EFCA Rise to Its Greatest Missionary Opportunity in History?," *Evangelical Beacon*, 21 January 1964, 2–3; Ed Neteland, "The Assistant Dean of Trinity College Reports on the First Six Months," *Evangelical Beacon*, 21 January 1964, 3.

29. Recollections of Morris Faugerstrom and a letter from Neteland to Faugerstrom, quoted in Martin, *Trinity: Entrusted with the Gospel,* 78–79.

30. Norton, TC TEDS President's Report, 1964 EFCA Yearbook, 199. He cited "gratifying reactions to the new divinity school program" and proclaimed that "Trinity College stands poised for its greatest achievement in history," candidacy for accreditation.

31. Hanson, *Trinity Story,* ch. 16; interviews with Paul Satre and Lee Eclov, January 2021.

32. Edward Neteland, "Education with a Purpose at Trinity College," *Evangelical Beacon*, Annual Trinity Issue, 16 January 1968, 4. His prayer requests in this issue of the *Beacon* radiate a heartfelt warmth of devotion. "Please pray that God will speak to the faculty, administration, staff and students in such a way as to cause a revival in me, in us, and in God's work at Trinity."

33. *Trinitarian 1966*. Numbers are gleaned from the profiles given with the graduates' portraits. Some double-majored, hence the total of majors outnumbers the forty-two total graduating students.

34. *Trinitarian 1966*, 98.

35. Oral interview with Lee Eclov, February 2021. Eclov is the recently retired pastor of the Village Church of Lincolnshire, an EFCA congregation near the Trinity campus, and author of several books, including *Pastoral Graces: Reflections on the Care of Souls* (2012) and *Feels Like Home: How Rediscovering the Church as Family Changes Everything* (2019).

36. *Trinitarian 1966*. Unfortunately the library holdings of the *Digest* go back only to 1968, so the "headlines" in question are no longer available.

37. *Trinitarian 1968*, 116; *Trinitarian 1969*, 46. See also Karen Grigsby Bates and Shereen Marisol Maraji, "The Student Strike That Changed Higher Ed Forever," *Code Switch*, 21 March 2019, https://www.npr.org/sections/codeswitch/2019/03/21/704930088/the-student-strike-that-changed-higher-ed-forever.

38. Paul S. Johnson, *Trinitarian 1966*, 92.

39. Report of the Committee on Social Concern, 1967 EFCA Yearbook, 222, quoting David L. McKenna and James DeForest Murch from *Why—in the World?: A Symposium on the Dynamics of Spiritual Renewal*, ed. Harvey C. Warner (Waco: Word Books, 1965).

40. Report of the Committee on Social Concern, 1968 EFCA Yearbook, 205–8.

41. Olson, EFCA President's Report, 1968 EFCA Yearbook, 171.

42. Doran B. Morford '69, "New Dimensions," *Evangelical Beacon*, Annual Trinity Issue, 14 January 1969, 6.

43. Lynne Cartwright '69, "Inter-Varsity Coffee Houses," *Evangelical Beacon*, Annual Trinity Issue, 14 January 1969, 6. For several years not only college students but a new generation of young evangelical faculty had begun calling the church to social awareness and involvement. The year 1968 saw the publication of *Protest and Politics: Christianity and Contemporary Affairs*. The *Evangelical Beacon* brought this work to the attention of EFCA people in an apparently sympathetic news item. It reported that the authors of this volume were "young evangelicals, refusing to be categorized as doctrinaire political conservatives," and they were "displeased with the 'calloused indifference on the part of so many of our fellow evangelicals to the vital political, social, and economic problems of the day.'" The *Beacon* observed that these views were widespread among younger evangelicals, who "are warning their fellow believers that now is time to act to make the Christian faith relevant to the needs of our time." See "A Summons to Vigorous Action," *Evangelical Beacon*, Annual Trinity Issue, 14 January 1969, 20; Robert G. Clouse, Richard V. Pierard, and Robert D. Linder, *Protest and Politics: Christianity and Contemporary Affairs* (Greenwood, SC: Attic, 1968). Among the contributors to this volume was US Senator from Oregon Mark Hatfield.

44. Norman Geisler, "Interaction in the Classroom," *Evangelical Beacon*, Annual Trinity Issue, 14 January 1969, 32. He continues, "Granted that our task is to discover new and creative ways to communicate Christ to our contemporary age, we should not underrate the role of the student. They know more about this generation than do most adults. They *are* this generation. In order to profit most from their contribution our educational process must 'open up' so they may 'speak up' and tell us what this age is all about. And, as they relate the age to us, so we must relate the ageless to them. They can keep us geared to the times; we must keep them grounded in the truth."

45. Larry Zentz '61, "Trinity Students: Meaningful, Significant Interaction," *Evangelical Beacon*, Annual Trinity Issue, 14 January 1969, 5.

46. Richard Reigle, "Student Life at Trinity," *Evangelical Beacon*, Annual Trinity Issue, 13 January 1970, 12–13.

47. Evans, TC TEDS President's Report, 1968 EFCA Yearbook, 189–90.

48. Evans, "Is Trinity Going Liberal?," *Evangelical Beacon*, Annual Trinity Issue, 14 January 1969, 12.

49. J. Robert Christensen, "What Kind of Students Does Trinity Accept?," *Evangelical Beacon*, Annual Trinity Issue, 13 January 1970, 8.

50. Evans, TC TEDS President's Report, 1971 EFCA Yearbook, 235–36. It was called the "Save America Run." Many EFCA people made pledges. See "Brothers Run against Pollution," *Evangelical Beacon*, Annual Trinity Issue, 12 January 1971, 29.

51. "Band to Tour Midwest," *Evangelical Beacon*, Annual Trinity Issue, 13 January 1970, 9.

52. "Trinity Extends Its Ministries to Europe," *Evangelical Beacon*, Annual Trinity Issue, 23 January 1973, 5.

53. Galen Carey '76, "SMF Reaches Out," *Evangelical Beacon*, Annual Trinity Issue, 23 January 1973, 11.

54. This tribute was provided by Paul Satre (1972 Trinity College graduate), associate professor of music emeritus.

55. Evans, TC TEDS President's Reports: 1969 EFCA Yearbook, C-46; 1970 EFCA Yearbook, 215–18; 1974 EFCA Yearbook, 293.

56. Olson, *Give Me This Mountain*, 157–58. There was considerably more complexity to the crisis, including a clash of advancement philosophies between Evans and Olson. Hanson recounts it in *Trinity Story*, chs. 18–22.

57. Hanson, *Trinity Story*, chs. 19–20.

58. Hanson, *Trinity Story*, chs. 21–22; Arnold T. Olson, Carroll High, and Willard Vetter, "The Financial Crisis at Trinity," *Evangelical Beacon*, 16 November 1971, 11–12.

59. Alvin A. Anderson, "Divinity School, Yes," and M. D. Christensen, "Long Live Our Schools," *Evangelical Beacon*, Annual Trinity Issue, 11 January 1972, 16, 21.

60. Hanson, *Trinity Story*, ch. 23. Martin, *Trinity: Entrusted with the Gospel*, 89–91, gives a good summary of the McLean report and its adoption.

61. Evans, TC President's Report, 1978 EFCA Yearbook, 70c. Note how this ambition paralleled somewhat the Kantzer vision at TEDS. A later college catalog would label this the era of "New Horizons," when independence was "to allow the college to more effectively expand its ministry as an evangelical school." 1979–1980 Trinity College Catalog, 27.

62. Evans, TC President's Report, 1975 EFCA Yearbook, 287.

63. Evans, TC President's Report, 1976 EFCA Yearbook, 260.

64. Evans, TC President's Report, 1978 EFCA Yearbook, 70c.

65. Evans, TC President's Report, 1975 EFCA Yearbook, 290–92. Swindoll's address was titled "Calmness amid Chaos."

66. Evans, TC President's Report, 1981 EFCA Yearbook, 69a. Shea came into contact with the college when his son Ronald attended.

67. Morris Faugerstrom, music, hired 1952, PhD from Northwestern; Douglas Frank, history, 1969, PhD from SUNY-Buffalo; Kenneth Shipps, history, 1971, PhD from Yale; Joseph Alexanian, Bible, 1973, PhD from Chicago; Kevin Cragg, history, 1973, PhD from Michigan; William Moulder, Bible, 1975, PhD from St. Andrews; Mark Noll, history, 1975, PhD from Vanderbilt; William Graddy, English, 1975, PhD from Southern Illinois; Harold Johnson, math, 1977, PhD from California; Marion Schwartz, English, 1977, PhD from Princeton; Joel Carpenter, history, 1978, PhD from Hopkins; Patrick Sheehen, education, 1979, PhD from Case Western. No longer at the college in 1979 but there from 1970–1974 was John Woodbridge, later of TEDS, history, Doctorat de Troisième Cycle, University of Toulouse.

68. Interview with William Moulder, 12 November 2020.

69. Evans, TC President's Report, 1976 EFCA Yearbook, 262.

70. This tribute was provided by Dr. Joshua Held (Trinity College graduate 2009), assistant professor of English.

71. Evans, TC President's Reports: 1977 EFCA Yearbook, 253b–54b; 1979 EFCA Yearbook, 67a.

72. Interview with Moulder, 12 November 2020; Evans, TC President's Report, 1978 EFCA Yearbook, 71c.

73. *Trinitarian 1975*.

74. *Trinitarian 1975*, 29; 1979–1980 Trinity College Catalog, 25; interview with Moulder, 12 November 2020.

75. 1979–1980 Trinity College Catalog, 25–26.

76. Thomas McDill, EFCA President's Report, 1979 EFCA Yearbook, 12a.

77. Thomas McDill, EFCA President's Reports, 1980 EFCA Yearbook, 21a.

78. On these historical connections and divisions, see David R. Swartz, *Moral Minority: The Evangelical Left in an Age of Conservatism* (Philadelphia: University of Pennsylvania Press, 2012).

79. Evans, TC President's Report, 1979 EFCA Yearbook, 68a–69a.

80. Interview with Moulder, 12 November 2020. Interestingly, six years later the EFCA resolved that its churches should "develop ministry to the divorced," "recognize the gifts of ministry and provide for those who have been divorced opportunities to serve the Lord," and "radically deal with non-biblical prejudice surrounding divorce and seek the healing and full restoration of the divorced to the life and fellowship of the body." Resolutions, 1985 EFCA Yearbook, 14b.

81. Evans reported 807 students in his 1979 report to the EFCA (p. 67a); Kantzer reported a fall '83 head count of 511, FTE 430, dropping to FTE 369 in spring '84 (Kantzer, TC President's Report, 1984 EFCA Yearbook, 82b). Kantzer also reported that the number of supporting EFCA churches went from about 600 "formerly" (year not specified) to 169 in 1983 (p. 88b).

82. Martin, *Trinity: Entrusted with the Gospel*, 98–99. He submitted the resignation in January 1983, effective June 30.

83. Kenneth Kantzer, "Trinity College—Coming Home!," 1984 EFCA Yearbook, 82b.

84. Kantzer, TC President's Report, 1983 EFCA Yearbook, 101a–102a.

85. Ken Meyer, undated letter (1997) to Morris Faugerstrom, quoted in Martin, *Trinity: Entrusted with the Gospel*, 100–101.

86. Kantzer, "Trinity College—Coming Home!," 84b.

87. Thomas McDill, Challenge to the Conference, 1985 EFCA Yearbook, 5b.

88. Kantzer, "Trinity College—Coming Home!," 89b.

89. Kantzer, TC President's Report, 1983 EFCA Yearbook, 104a.

90. Kantzer, TC President's Report, 1983 EFCA Yearbook, 105a.

91. Meyer, TC TEDS President's Report, 1985 EFCA Yearbook, 66b; Craig Chapin, "New Discipleship Program at TEDS and TC Fosters Spiritual Growth, Mutual Concern," *Evangelical Beacon*, 20 January 1990, 23; Martin, *Trinity: Entrusted with the Gospel*, 106.

92. Meyer, TC President's Report, 1989 EFCA Yearbook, 79b; TC President's Report, 1991 EFCA Yearbook, 84b; interview with Lois Fleming, October 2020.

93. Meyer, TC President's Report, 1990 EFCA Yearbook, 129b.

94. "Trinity College: The Year in Review," *Evangelical Beacon*, 15 February 1988, 9; Meyer, TC President's Report, 1987 EFCA Yearbook, 93b; Meyer, "The President's Report," *Evangelical Beacon*, 15 February 1988, 8; Bob Moeller, "Trinity College: The Excitement Is Building," *Evangelical Beacon*, 20 February 1989, cover and 6.

95. Craig Chapin, "Preparing Students to Bring Christ to the Marketplace," *Evangelical Beacon*, 19 February 1990, 8.

96. Ken Meyer and James Westgate, "CMD Works to Train 'Shepherds' in Youth Ministries," *Evangelical Beacon*, 20 February 1989, 20–21.

97. Meyer, TC President's Report, 1987 EFCA Yearbook, 93b.

98. Meyer, TC President's Report, 1988 EFCA Yearbook, 96b; Morris Faugerstrom, quoted in Martin, *Trinity: Entrusted with the Gospel*, 107; Bob Moeller, "Debate Team among Best," *Evangelical Beacon*, 5 June 1989, 22.

99. Bob Moeller, "Chicago's 'Genuine Heroes' Given Recognition," *Evangelical Beacon*, 5 June 1989, 22.

100. Meyer, TC President's Report, 1988 EFCA Yearbook, 96b.

101. Pat Salmeri, "Trinity Launches Its First Football Season," *Evangelical Beacon*, 16 October 1989, 21.

102. *Trinitarian 1969*, 70–73.

103. NAE Report, 1985 EFCA Yearbook, 53b.

104. Resolutions, 1989 EFCA Yearbook, 16b–17b.

105. Resolution: "The 'New' Racism," 1992 EFCA Yearbook, 34b.

106. Martin, *Trinity: Entrusted with the Gospel*, 110–11; 1993 EFCA Report Book, 168b–69b.

107. 1993 EFCA Report Book, 152b.

108. Meyer, TC President's Reports, 1992 EFCA Yearbook, 99b, and 1994 EFCA Yearbook, 75b. Trinity had a long tradition of refusing federal money for fear of government encroachment on the freedom to offer a distinctively Christian education. For example, Norton warned in 1963, "Christian higher education faces its greatest challenge of history as the 21st century space-age culture dawns. With the federal government financing college and university education in an alarmingly increasing fashion, socialism emerges as the offspring of materialism wedded to irresponsibility." 1963 EFCA Yearbook, R42–R43. Again in 1967 the Free Church decided to refuse federal or state grants for its colleges—see foreword to 1968 EFCA Yearbook, 8. Evans warned the church that its refusal to accept government funding would spell financial trouble: TC TEDS President's Report, 1968 EFCA Yearbook, 187.

109. For example, the college gave $300,000 to TEDS "for unrestricted purposes" in 1990. The divinity school loaned the college a total of $1,430,000 (at 12 percent interest or one-half percent over prime) in 1983 and 1984. 1993 EFCA Report Book, 75b; 1985 EFCA Yearbook, 149b–150b.

110. Martin, *Trinity: Entrusted with the Gospel*, 116–17; Meyer, TIU President's Report, 1995 EFCA Yearbook, 121b.

Chapter 5: Decades of Consolidation (1975–1996)

1. *Evangelical Beacon*, 3 September 1974, 3.

2. *Evangelical Beacon*, 25 November 1975. The quoted description comes from the address of Dr. Robert A. Cook (president of The King's College) at Meyer's inauguration in November 1975. For another description of Meyer, see the statement by Joseph Horness Jr., "Kenneth M. Meyer," in Martin, *Trinity: Entrusted with the Gospel*, 92–93.

3. *Evangelical Beacon*, 25 November 1975.

4. 1984 EFCA Yearbook, 91b.

5. *Evangelical Beacon*, 1 August 1980, 15.

6. Compare 1974–1975 TEDS Catalog Supplement (p. 8) to 1978–1979 TEDS Catalog Supplement (p. 3). By 1979, the EFCA subsidy per student had decreased below $1,200 per year. See 1979 EFCA Yearbook, 46a.

7. *Evangelical Beacon*, 15 August 1582, 25.

8. *Evangelical Beacon*, 28 September 1976, 22.

9. See EFCA Yearbooks for 1975 (293), 1979 (45a–46a), 1984 (90b).

10. "Ten Year Projection," 10, TEDS dean file. Proposed concentrations within the PhD program in history and philosophy of religion included church history, systematic theology, and philosophy of religion. Proposed concentrations within the PhD in practical theology included Christian education, pastoral psychology, communication skills, Christianity and society, Christianity and Black studies, preaching, evangelism, and church administration.

11. "Ten Year Projection," 8, TEDS dean file.

12. See Senter, "Personal Memoirs," 3.

13. "Ten Year Projection," 15, TEDS dean file.

14. 1977–1979 TEDS Catalog, 168.

15. Oral interview with Howard Matson, 23 January 2014.

16. See 1978 EFCA Yearbook, 65c; *Evangelical Beacon*, 7 November 1978, 19.

17. *Evangelical Beacon*, 1 June 1985, 8.

18. Oral interview with John Woodbridge, 6 February 2014.

19. 1973–1975 TEDS Catalog, 73. See Kantzer's discussion of these curricular reforms in *Trinity Today* 1.6 (June 1971): 7.

20. *Evangelical Beacon*, 20 March 1976, 20.

21. In his report to the annual conference of 1977, President Meyer noted that faculty had recently taken a poll of graduates of the MDiv program. "A trend is evident in these returns, calling for a greater emphasis in the practical areas of ministry, to balance our excellent Biblical studies." 1977 EFCA Yearbook, 244b.

22. Reported by Senter, "Personal Memoirs," 8.

23. *Evangelical Beacon*, 15 June 1984, 17.

24. Summarized in *Trinity's Wellspring* 5.1 (Fall 1993): 11.

25. Oral interview with Perry Downs, 17 February 2014.

26. Video interview with Walter and Olive Liefeld, 10 February 2014.

27. Oral interview with Barry Beitzel, 3 February 2014.

28. Video interview with Walter and Olive Liefeld, 10 February 2014.

29. 1976 EFCA Yearbook, 250.

30. "Interview with Kenneth S. Kantzer," 154.

31. Oral interviews with Barry Beitzel, 3 February 2014; Perry Downs, 17 February 2014. Kantzer later met with the faculty member privately to discuss their differences and to inform him that such behavior would not be tolerated in the future.

32. Oral interview with John Woodbridge, 6 February 2014.

33. See *Evangelical Beacon*, 14 October 1975, 20.

34. *Evangelical Beacon*, 7 December 1976, 23.

35. The *Time* article from 9 October 1972 is described in the *Evangelical Beacon*, 26 June 1973, 4.

36. See *Evangelical Beacon*, 30 August 1977, 14.

37. *Evangelical Beacon*, 24 April 1979, 12.

38. *Evangelical Beacon*, 24 April 1979, 13.

39. *Evangelical Beacon*, 24 April 1979, 13.

40. Email correspondence with select TEDS faculty members, 19 June 2020.

41. *Evangelical Beacon*, 1 June 1983, 5.

42. *Evangelical Beacon*, 15 May 1983, 22.

43. For this dramatic story, see ch. 4 below and Martin, *Trinity: Entrusted with the Gospel*, 98–104.

44. Martin, *Trinity: Entrusted with the Gospel*, 101.

45. See https://www.biola.edu/talbot/ce20/database/ted-warren-ward#biography.

46. *Evangelical Beacon*, 1 June 1987, 11. Kenneth Meyer sounded a similar note in his address to the delegates of the EFCA national conference in 1989: "The professional masters' degrees, Master of Divinity, Master of Religious Education, etc., are still the core of our ministry. Our mission is to train pastors and missionaries." See 1988 EFCA Yearbook, 97b.

47. Archive of the TEDS Academic Doctorate Office. My thanks to Bryan Woods for providing this information.

48. Archive of the TEDS Academic Doctorate Office. Of these 127 students, 36 were international students, and three were female. My thanks to Bryan Woods for providing this information.

49. Statistical charts from TEDS catalogs, 1988–1996.

50. Mark Senter III describes the rocky beginning of Office of Extension and Continuing Education in a memo to Dean Bing Hunter dated 11 March 1999. Thanks to Emanuel Nayendov for making this document available to me.

51. *Trinity's Wellspring* 5.2 (Fall 1994): 11. These sites were in Colorado Springs, Colorado; Miami; Chicago (urban campus); Indianapolis; Akron, Ohio; Erie, Pennsylvania; Arlington, Virginia; Charlottesville, Virginia; Madison, Wisconsin; and Milwaukee.

52. *Trinity's Wellspring* 5.2 (Fall 1994): 10–11; *Evangelical Beacon*, November 1993, 26.

53. There were, of course, years that defied such approximations. For example, 65 percent of the students matriculating in the fall of 1975 had received their undergraduate training at secular academic institutions. See *Evangelical Beacon*, 14 October 1975, 20.

54. See "Preliminary Report of TEDS 2000" (May 1993), in Trinity President's Box 3 (1974/5–1995), folder 8, TIU Archives.

55. My thanks to TIU alumni director Garrett Luck for this information.

56. Senter, "Personal Memoirs," 1.

57. In 1976, President Meyer noted: "Last year, 19 percent of our graduating class reported that they entered the Seminary as members of a Free Church, but at graduation, 38 percent went into ministries of the EFCA." *Evangelical Beacon*, 30 March 1976, 19.

58. *Evangelical Beacon*, 1 August 1980, 15. See also *Evangelical Beacon*, 7 January 1975, 18.

59. Grant Osborne, "ABBA: A Brief History," *The Flame* 4.1 (January/February 2003): 1, in TEDS Box 12, folder 4, TIU Archives.

60. See *Trinity's Wellspring* 2.1 (Winter 1989): 10–11.

61. *Trinity's Wellspring* 2.1 (Winter 1989): 11.

62. Annual commencement bulletins, in TC & TEDS/TGS Graduation, Baccalaureate & Commencement file, TIU Archives.

63. 1965–1966 TEDS Catalog, 95–98.

64. 1975–1977 TEDS Catalog, 155–70.

65. *Evangelical Beacon*, 27 November 1979, 18.

66. The 1973–1975 TEDS Catalog states, "Trinity welcomes women students, whose applications are considered for any program offered by the Divinity School" (60).

67. Missiologist Ruth A. Tucker was the best known and most regular of these visiting professors. In the early 1990s, Judith Golz and Sandra Wilson frequently served as instructors in pastoral counseling and psychology.

68. Kantzer to Thomas A. McDill, 2 February 1987, in Kantzer Papers, TIU Archives. The context behind this letter is important: previously, Kantzer wrote an article for *Christianity Today* stating his support for women's leadership in local churches. Without Kantzer's permission, this article was subsequently published by the *Evangelical Beacon* on 3 November 1986 (8–10), causing a widespread protest among EFCA leaders and laypersons.

69. Anonymous letter to Kenneth Kantzer, in Kantzer Papers, TIU Archives.

70. Reported by President Meyer, in 1983 EFCA Yearbook, 107a.

71. Dean of the Chapel Hutz Hertzberg reported these remarkable events in a memo titled "God's Work at Trinity International University," 10 April 1995, Trinity Presidents' Box 3, folder 7, TIU Archives.

72. *Evangelical Beacon*, 1 June 1985, 8.

73. In 1988, more than two hundred faculty, staff, and students participated in this evangelistic event. See *Evangelical Beacon*, 18 April 1988, 22.

74. See, for example, 1988 EFCA Handbook, 97b.

75. Reminiscences of the author.

76. Thus, at the Urbana Conference in 1990, around fourteen hundred students requested information about the missions programs at TEDS. See *Trinity's Wellspring* 4.2 (Spring 1991): 9.

77. See *Evangelical Beacon*, 1 January 1995, 11.

78. Reminiscences of Miriam Stark Parent, email exchange, 6 July 2020. Used with permission.

79. The material in this paragraph is adapted from Senter, "Personal Memoirs," 5–6.

80. Oral interviews with John Woodbridge, 6 February 2014, and Perry Downs, 17 February 2014.

81. These biographical details are drawn largely from Andreas J. Köstenberger, "D.A. Carson, His Life and Work," in *Understanding the Times: New Testament Studies in the Twenty-First Century*, ed. Andreas J. Köstenberger and Robert Yarbrough (Wheaton, IL: Crossway, 2011), 349–69.

82. See the exchange of letters between Dean Kaiser and Kenneth Kantzer on this subject from 17 and 21 May 1990, in ADO Archives, PhD 1987–90.

83. Sailhamer described his methodology in his *Introduction to Old Testament Theology: A Canonical Approach* (Grand Rapids: Zondervan, 1995). For a helpful description of Sailhamer's method, see the review by Michael D. Prevett, https://jbtsonline.org/review-of-introduction-to-old-testament-theology-a-canonical-approach-by-john-h-sailhamer/.

84. See Martin, *Trinity: Entrusted with the Gospel*, 113–14. The preliminary report of the task force is found in Trinity Presidents' Box 3 (1974/5–1995), folder 8, TIU Archives.

85. See Murray Harris, *Raised Immortal: Resurrection and Immortality in the New Testament* (Grand Rapids: Eerdmans, 1983), 53–54.

86. The details of this controversy are described in "A History of the Norman Geisler/Murray Harris Issue," in Kantzer Dean's Office, box 5, TIU Archives.

87. See "History of the Norman Geisler/Murray Harris Issue."

88. *Christianity Today*, 5 April 1993, 62–66.

89. "History of the Norman Geisler/Murray Harris Issue."

90. "History of the Norman Geisler/Murray Harris Issue."

91. 1992 EFCA Yearbook, 101b.

92. See Martin, *Trinity: Entrusted with the Gospel*, 111–12.

93. For the conservative takeover of Southern Baptist Theological Seminary (Louisville, Kentucky), see Gregory Wills, *Southern Baptist Theological Seminary, 1859–2009* (New York: Oxford University Press, 2009), ch. 12. TEDS's role in training conservative students for ministry in the Southern Baptist Convention was significant. In 2020, David Dockery counted no fewer than 65 graduates of TEDS who were serving as pastors or professors in the SBC or in SBC-related colleges and seminaries. Private correspondence between Scott Manetsch and David Dockery, 28 November 2020.

94. *Trinity Wellspring* 6.1 (Spring 1996): 21.

95. See Martin, *Trinity: Entrusted with the Gospel*, 110–11.

96. *Evangelical Beacon*, August 1992, 26.

97. *Trinity's Wellspring* 5.1 (Fall 1993): 8.

98. Martin, *Trinity: Entrusted with the Gospel*, 116–17.

99. Martin, *Trinity: Entrusted with the Gospel*, 116.

100. 1993 EFCA Yearbook, 80b. See also Martin, *Trinity: Entrusted with the Gospel*, 116–17.

101. *Trinity's Wellspring* 6.1 (Spring 1996): 21.

102. Martin, *Trinity: Entrusted with the Gospel*, 117.

CHAPTER 6: TRINITY BLOSSOMS AS A CHRISTIAN UNIVERSITY (1996–2019)

1. 1996–1997 EFCA Yearbook, 129b; 1997–1998 EFCA Yearbook, 132b. Meyer focused much attention on the South Florida campus and Simon Greenleaf University. He finished his term as chancellor in 2007. *Trinity Magazine* (Winter 2008): 5; *Trinity Magazine* (Fall 2016): 42–43.

2. John Woodbridge, "Great Is Thy Faithfulness: A History of God's Providence Encourages Trinity's Ongoing Service," *Trinity Magazine* (Fall 2010): 20–22.

3. *Trinity Magazine*, 4 (Fall 2003): 5. See also "Milo David Lundell," *Trinity Magazine* (Spring 2015): 34.

4. TIU Institutional Self-Study, North Central Association/ATS, Bannockburn, Illinois, November 14–17, 1999, 1:39.

5. Kantzer held that TIU was a "uni-versity," not a "multi-versity" like most Western universities. For TIU, the unity was found in Jesus Christ. Greg Waybright, "A Word from the President: Christ-Centeredness," *Trinity Magazine* (Fall 2004): 2.

6. *Trinity Magazine* (Fall 2008): 31.

7. 1999–2000 Trinity Graduate School Catalog, 5.

8. "Multiplying Healthy Churches among All People," 1999 EFCA Report Book, 63.

9. 1996–1997 EFCA Yearbook, 131b.

10. 1997–1998 Trinity Graduate School Catalog, front page.

11. 1996–1997 EFCA Yearbook, 130b.

12. *Trinity Magazine* (Winter 2008): 17; 1997–1998 EFCA Yearbook, 132b.

13. Sell later joined the practical theology department, now known as the pastoral theology department.

14. For Feinberg, see "Dr. Paul Feinberg: August 13, 1939–February 21, 2004," *Trinity Magazine* (Fall 2004): 9.

15. "Multiplying Healthy Churches," 66. For Hoffmeier, see Oliver A. Hersey, "From the River of Egypt," *Trinity Magazine* (Spring 2018): 22–23.

16. 2001 EFCA Report Book, 75; *Trinity Magazine* (Spring 2005): 19. In 2000, Gene Swanstrom began as director of placement.

17. *Trinity Magazine* (Fall 2016): 9.

18. Damian Zane, "Lazarus Chakwera: Malawi's President Who 'Argued with God,' " *BBC News*, 29 June 2000, https://www.bbc.com/news/world-africa-53221035.

19. "The Window Is Open," *Trinity Magazine* 3 (Winter 2001): 10; 2002 EFCA Report Book, 67.

20. *Trinity Magazine* (Fall 2005): 7.

21. "Formation Groups," *Trinity Magazine* (Fall 2007): 6.

22. 2000 EFCA Report Book, 82.

23. 2001 EFCA Report Book, 75; *Trinity Magazine* 4 (Winter 2003): 4; 2005 EFCA Report Book, 67.

24. *Trinity Magazine* 4 (Fall 2003): 6.

25. Craig Ott (MDiv 1977, PhD 1991) is professor of mission and intercultural studies at TEDS, where he directs the PhD program in intercultural studies and occupies the ReachGlobal Chair of Mission.

26. Also in 1997, Trinity Graduate School launched its MA in bioethics, which allowed undergraduates with junior standing and excellent grades to begin the MA in bioethics while still in the BA program. Many premedical students chose this degree path, which was instrumental in their acceptance to medical schools.

27. *Trinity Magazine* (Spring 2004): 5; 2004 EFCA Report Book, 70.

28. Faugerstrom taught at Trinity from 1952–1998.

29. *Trinity Magazine* 3 (Winter 2001): 5.

30. For Daniel Song'ony, see *Trinity Magazine* (Fall 2004): 19.

31. "Multiplying Healthy Churches," 67.

32. 2002 EFCA Report Book, 66.

33. 2006 EFCA Report Book, 65. As of April 2008, contributions generated more than $17.25 million toward the goal of $20 million for the campaign. *Trinity Magazine* (Winter 2007): 14.

34. *Trinity Magazine* (Fall 2005): 5; *Trinity Magazine* (Winter 2007): 13; 2006 EFCA Report Book, 64.

35. 2001 EFCA Report Book, 73.

36. 2003 EFCA Report Book, 72.

37. Sarah McCammon, NPR, https://www.npr.org/people/448294256/sarah-mc-cammon. See also "2003 Outstanding Senior Award," *Trinity Magazine* 4 (Fall 2003): 7.

38. Rich Warren, "The 2013 Time 100," *Time*, 18 April 2013; *Trinity Magazine* (Fall 2015): 40.

39. 1997–1998 EFCA Yearbook, 133b.

40. TIU Institutional Self-Study 1999, 1:446.

41. Jon Watters, "Communing at FAT Thursday," *Trinity Magazine* 2 (Summer 2002): 4–5.

42. 1997–1998 EFCA Yearbook, 133b; 2001 EFCA Report Book, 73.

43. 2002 EFCA Report Book, 66.

44. Derek Torres (Trinity College graduate 2005, TEDS graduate 2010) shared on Facebook the original tribute from which this is adapted. Used with his permission.

45. "Multiplying Healthy Churches," 68. In the 1996–1997 season, the men's basketball team won the conference title and advanced to the NAIA Division II tournament, reaching the second round. 1996–1997 EFCA Yearbook, 130b.

46. 2001 EFCA Report Book, 74.

47. 2002 EFCA Report Book, 66; *Trinity Magazine* (Spring 2004): 6.

48. TIU coaches have used, for example, curriculum written by Scotty Kessler, director of the Robert Coleman School of Discipleship and the Wes Neal School of Sports Ministry.

49. "Melissa M. Erickson, M.D., Named as One of Becker's Spine Review '35 Female Spine Surgeon Leaders to Know,' " Duke Orthopaedic Surgery, https://ortho.duke.edu/latest-news/melissa-m-erickson-md-named-one-beckers-spine-review-35-female-spine-surgeon-leaders.

50. 1996–1997 EFCA Yearbook, 130b; 1997–1998 EFCA Yearbook, 135b–136b.

51. TIU Institutional Self-Study 1999, 1:28, 445; "Multiplying Healthy Churches," 63.

52. TIU Institutional Self-Study 1999, 1:7.

53. 1996–1997 EFCA Yearbook, 131b; 1997–1998 EFCA Yearbook, 134b. Despite the excitement for these programs, when enrollments fell short of projections, budgets had to be adjusted accordingly. The MA in faith and culture was changed later to the MA in communication and culture.

54. 2004 EFCA Report Book, 71.

55. "Dr. Nancy Jones: Contractor for the National Institutes of Health," *Trinity Magazine* (Fall 2008): 12–15.

56. Another example of a graduate of the MA in bioethics program at TGS is William P. Cheshire, professor of neurology at Mayo Clinic in Florida, where he chairs the Ethics Committee and leads the Program in Professionalism and Values.

57. The Bannockburn Institute, which developed several centers initially, engaged thoughtfully on several cultural issues. For instance, the institute held a major conference that produced a book titled *Telling the Truth: Evangelizing Postmoderns*, edited by D. A. Carson. In 2001, the institute produced a film on the life and writings of C. S. Lewis for PBS television. 1998–1999 TEDS Catalog, 26–27; "Multiplying Healthy Churches," 70; 2001 EFCA Report Book, 79; 2002 EFCA Report Book, 72.

58. "A Tale of Two Centers," *Trinity Magazine* (Winter 2008): 14.

59. John Kilner, CBHD History, lecture notes, 6, 9.

60. "Multiplying Healthy Churches," 70; 1995–1996 EFCA Yearbook, 121b.

61. Kilner, CBHD History, lecture notes, 11. In addition to this major annual event, the center held fifty conferences all over the US and in multiple other countries.

62. 1996–1997 EFCA Yearbook, 130b. John F. Kilner, Nigel M. de S. Cameron, and David L. Schweder Mayer, *Bioethics and the Future of Medicine: A Christian Appraisal* (Grand Rapids: Eerdmans, 1995). Other titles include *Bioethics: A Christian Approach in a Pluralistic Age* and *The Reproduction Revolution*. 2000 EFCA Report Book, 85.

63. 2000 EFCA Report Book, 85.

64. 2002 EFCA Report Book, 72.

65. *Trinity Magazine* (Winter 2005): 17; 2005 EFCA Report Book, 72.

66. 2002 EFCA Report Book, 72–73. On behalf of CBHD, Kilner was one of two North American representatives on the bioethics task force at the Lausanne World Evangelization Movement global gathering in Thailand. "Tale of Two Centers," 16.

67. 2002 EFCA Report Book, 72–73.

68. 2007 EFCA Report Book, 65.

69. In addition, other notable CBHD fellows who earned the MA in bioethics from TGS are Shari Falkenheimer, MD, PhD, and D. Christopher Ralston, PhD.

70. 1996/97 EFCA Yearbook, 131b.

71. TIU Institutional Self-Study 1999, 1:7; "Poised for the Public Square," *Trinity Magazine* (Winter 2006): 10. Simon Greenleaf was a nineteenth-century Harvard law professor who was an authority on the laws of evidence and wrote *The Testimony of the Evangelists: The Gospels Examined by the Rules of Evidence*. See John Warwick Montgomery, "Legal Reasoning and Christian Apologetics," *Christianity Today*, 14 February 1975; *Trinity Law Magazine* (Fall 2014): 2.

72. TIU Institutional Self-Study 1999, 1:449–50. For examples, see Stephen Kennedy, "What Is "Natural Law?," *Trinity Magazine* (Winter 2006): 14–15; Paul Hughes, "Biblical Diversity: Aids Justice Mission at TLS," *Trinity Magazine* (Spring 2011): 17.

73. When Verleur married John Spann, they joined the CIA. In Afghanistan, John was the first American killed (beheaded on television) during Operation Enduring Freedom. In 2002, Shannon was introduced by George W. Bush in his State of the Union address. See also "Widow of CIA Officer Shows Her Resolve," *Orange County Register*, 13 December 2001.

74. TIU Institutional Self-Study 1999, 1:7.

75. Todd Hertz, "Frost Fired as Dean of Christian Law School," *Christianity Today*, 1 August 2001. David Llewellyn was appointed dean in 2003 but resigned in 2004 to return to the classroom. "New Dean for Law School," *Trinity Magazine* 4 (Fall 2003): 4; "Trinity Law School," *Trinity Magazine* (Spring 2004): 5.

76. *Trinity Law Magazine* (Fall 2014): 50–51. Holsclaw remained associated with the school, serving on the advisory board and teaching as an adjunct professor. 2005 EFCA Report Book, 68.

77. *Trinity Magazine* (Winter 2005): 6. See also Donald R. McConnell, "Christians and the Government: Ten Suggestions," *Trinity Magazine* (Fall 2008): 25–27.

78. In 2003, 11 percent of the TLS graduates passed the California Bar Exam. In 2018, 44 percent of Trinity graduates taking the exam for the first time passed, as did 10 percent of those repeating the exam.

79. "God and Governing Conference," *Trinity Magazine* (Spring 2008): 6.

80. For Sumner, see "Dr. Sarah Sumner," *Trinity Magazine* (Fall 2004): 7.

81. 1996–1997 EFCA Yearbook, 130b.

82. 1997–1998 EFCA Yearbook, 133b–134b; "Multiplying Healthy Churches," 69; TIU Institutional Self-Study 1999, 1:450.

83. "Multiplying Healthy Churches," 69.

84. *Trinity Magazine* (Winter 2009): 20.

85. 2002 EFCA Report Book, 70.

86. *Trinity Magazine* 4 (Fall 2003): 9; "Multiplying Healthy Churches," 69.

87. "Trinity Sells Radio Station," *Trinity Magazine* (Winter 2008): 6; 2008 EFCA Report Book, 28; 2007 EFCA Report Book, 64. For TIU's mission and values, see TIU Accreditation Self-Study Report 2010: Presented to HLC and ATS, 11.

88. *Trinity Magazine* (Winter 2007): 11.

89. In addition, classes were held at Ft. Meyers. 2007 EFCA Report Book, 66.

90. 2000 EFCA Report Book, 85.

91. 2001 EFCA Report Book, 76.

92. 2005 EFCA Report Book, 66. For the history of REACH, see "The 25th Anniversary of REACH: Trinity's Adult Undergraduate Program," *Trinity Magazine* (Winter 2009): 18–21.

93. 2002 EFCA Report Book, 69.

94. "TEDS Classes Now Online," *Trinity Magazine* (Winter 2005): 4.

95. "Technological Advances," *Trinity Magazine* (Winter 2005): 17.

96. TIU Accreditation Self-Study Report 2010, 12.

97. *Trinity Magazine* (Winter 2007): 18.

98. In 2005 TIU, in partnership with New Life Celebration Church of God in Dolton, Illinois, opened a new facility for Trinity's South Chicago Regional Center that offered REACH and the MA in religion with an emphasis in urban ministries. The center was directed by Michael Reynolds. *Trinity Magazine* (Spring 2005): 5; (Fall 2005): 5; (Winter 2009): 20.

99. TIU Institutional Self-Study 1999, 1:448.

100. TIU Institutional Self-Study 1999, 1:453.

101. 2002 EFCA Report Book, 66.

102. 2000 EFCA Report Book, 79–80; see also 2001 EFCA Report Book, 80. Some foundations balked at funding TIU because the EFCA did not provide greater financial support to its own school.

103. TIU Accreditation Self-Study Report 2010, 11, 44.

104. 2003 EFCA Report Book, 75.

105. 2005 EFCA Report Book, 67; 2007 EFCA Report Book, 65.

106. One of TIU's values was church connectedness. The catalog states: "Our vision for serving the Church is a global vision, just as God's vision for his Church is global. A particular value affecting Trinity's work is to identify and meet the educational needs of the EFCA." Other values were Christ connectedness, comprehensive education, community, and cultural engagement. 2004–2005 TEDS Catalog, 11.

107. Despite such events, half of the pastors of the EFCA have come from other seminaries than TEDS. Some of the superintendents themselves are graduates of different evangelical seminaries and by geographic proximity tend to relate to other schools such as Gordon-Conwell in New England, Dallas Theological Seminary in Texas, and Talbot Theological Seminary in California.

108. Zach Kincaid, "Complete in Him: The Life of H. G. Rodine," *Trinity Magazine* (Summer 2003): 4–13; 2000 EFCA Report Book, 80.

109. 2001 EFCA Report Book, 78; Paul J. Maurer, "Steps towards Trinity's Tomorrow: The H. G. Rodine Global Ministry Building in Perspective," *Trinity Magazine* (Summer 2003): 23–24. For the story of Bud Hinkson, see Jon Hinkson, "Win, Build, Send: The Life of Bud Hinkson," *Trinity Magazine* (Summer 2003): 16–18. Arnold T. Olson died 25 July 2003. *Trinity Magazine* 4 (Fall 2003): 21.

110. One of the large classrooms in the Rodine Building is named after Carl F. H. and Helga Henry. Robert H. Krapohl, "The Life of Carl F. H. Henry," *Trinity Magazine* (Summer 2003): 14–15; (Fall 2003): 10.

111. Ron Friedman, "Sending Capacity: From Canton Rice Paddies to Trinity Wetlands," *Trinity Magazine* (Summer 2003): 19–20.

112. *Trinity Magazine* (Fall 2007): 8. At the very beginning it was called the "Center for Centers."

113. On 6 November 2000, Waybright announced the appointment of Sweeney as director of the new Center for Centers, and on 8 January 2001, a memo from Sweeney introduced the new name, Center for Theological Understanding.

114. *Trinity Magazine* (Winter 2008): 19. For more about Henry see "Trinity Remembers Dr. Carl F. H. Henry: January 22, 1913–December 7, 2003," *Trinity Magazine* (Spring 2004): 10; (Fall 2005): 2, 5; 2006 EFCA Report Book, 65.

115. "Leading in Christian Thought," *Trinity Magazine* (Winter 2007): 15. Separately, HCTU received $1.3 million from Walter and Darlene Hansen to endow annual TEDS's PhD fellowships and several international conferences. *Trinity Magazine* (Spring 2007): 5.

116. Although geographically originating at Trinity and funded by Henry Center resources, The Gospel Coalition is free from any institutional affiliation.

117. *Trinity Magazine* (Fall 2007): 8; (Winter 2008): 20; (Fall 2008): 8–9; (Winter 2008): 7; 2008 EFCA Report Book, 28.

118. Greg Waybright, "A Word from the President," 1997–1998 TEDS Catalog; TIU Institutional Self-Study 1999, 1:452.

119. TIU Accreditation Self-Study Report 2010, 34, 37.

120. "EFCA Week Explores Biblical Diversity," *Trinity Magazine* (Fall 2011): 4; "William 'Bill' J. Hamel," *Trinity Magazine* (Winter 2018): 36–37.

121. TIU Accreditation Self-Study Report 2010, 33.

122. Students were sheltered at the Village Church of Lincolnshire and various homes. In the highly publicized event, Jesse Jackson came to TIU to support the students. The racial threat was determined to be a faked hate crime by a disgruntled African American student writing threatening letters to other African American students on campus.

123. At the time, 31 percent of Trinity's undergraduates were minority students. Minority administrators—such as Jeanette Hsieh, William Washington, and Tite Tiénou—comprised 38 percent of Trinity's executive council. *Trinity Magazine* (Fall 2006): 5; (Spring 2015): 35.

124. "Unafraid," *Trinity Magazine* (Fall 2005): 14–15. In addition, among Hispanic students is Eric Rivera, who after completing the MDiv and a PhD in historical theology planted the Brook, an EFCA congregation in Chicago. He serves on the speaker team for Family Life's Weekend to Remember conferences.

125. "Multiplying Healthy Churches," 66.

126. 2000 EFCA Report Book, 82. For example, "Dennis Nyamieh Walker from Liberia, West Africa," *Trinity Magazine* 3 (Winter 2001): 11.

127. For example, see "The Church in a Different Context: Four International Trinity Students Discuss the Church and Effective Christian Leadership," *Trinity Magazine* (Fall 2004): 10–13. See also Jennifer L. Aycock, " 'No Mere Option': Rising to the Challenge of Multinational Classrooms," *Trinity Magazine* (Spring 2012): 24–27.

128. 2004 EFCA Report Book, 71; *Trinity Magazine* (Spring 2004): 7; (Winter 2005): 5. See "Dr. Paul Hiebert, 1932–2007," *Trinity Magazine* (Spring 2007): 10.

129. "Race and Ethnicity," *Trinity Magazine* 3 (Winter 2001): 6; 2002 EFCA Report Book, 68.

130. 2003 EFCA Report Book, 72. Race and Ethnic Relations was taught by Michael Reynolds, and Intercultural Communication was taught by Carmen Mendoza.

131. 2005 EFCA Report Book, 67.

132. 2003 EFCA Report Book, 74.

133. "A Bigger Picture of the World," *Trinity Magazine* (Fall 2004): 14–15; 2004 EFCA Report Book, 70.

134. TEDS's mission was stated as "to serve the church of the Living God by equipping servants for the work of the gospel of Christ worldwide." 2007 EFCA Report Book, 65.

135. TIU Accreditation Self-Study Report 2010, 12, 14.

136. 2004 EFCA Report Book, 73; 2008–2009 TEDS Catalog, 26.

137. 2006 EFCA Report Book, 63.

138. 2007–2008 TEDS Catalog, 38.

139. With the block schedule in place, a radio campaign promoted one-day-per-week courses and a free Metra shuttle for easy access to campus for Chicagoland commuters.

140. *Trinity Magazine* (Fall 2006): 5; "Dr. Gleason Archer: May 22, 1916–April 27, 2004," *Trinity Magazine* (Fall 2004): 9.

141. Since then, the papers of D. A. Carson have been added. EFCA-specific archive materials held at Bannockburn were transferred to the EFCA Archives in Minneapolis.

142. After completing the PhD in educational studies at TEDS, Theonugraha became TIU vice president for student life and university services and in 2019 became president of Western Theological Seminary in Michigan.

143. In 2004–2005, traditional undergraduate enrollment remained the same, with 823 students. With an additional 288 nontraditional adult students, the total undergraduate head count in Bannockburn was 1,111.

144. For all of TIU, the fall of 2005 had a total head count of 3,340 students enrolled, down from the previous year by 31. For the fall of 2006, TIU had a total head count of 2,855. 2006 EFCA Report Book, 65; 2007 EFCA Report Book, 65.

145. 2006 EFCA Report Book, 62.

146. 2005 EFCA Report Book, 69.

147. *Trinity Magazine* (Spring 2006): 7.

148. *Trinity Magazine* 4 (Fall 2003): 7.

149. *Trinity Magazine* (Winter 2005): 17.

150. 2006 EFCA Report Book, 61.

151. 2007 EFCA Report Book, 64.

152. 2000 EFCA Report Book, 83.

153. *Trinity Magazine* (Fall 2004): 17; (Spring 2005): 7.

154. *Trinity Magazine* (Winter 2006): 6, 21; 2007 EFCA Report Book, 66.

155. 2006 EFCA Report Book, 64.

156. *Trinity Magazine* (Spring 2007): 2; "Farewell to a President," *Trinity Magazine* (Fall 2007): 20–23; 2007 EFCA Report Book, 64, 67.

157. *Trinity Magazine* (Winter 2008): 2, 5; 2005 EFCA Report Book, 66; 2008 EFCA Report Book, 28.

158. *Trinity Magazine* (Spring 2007): 5; 2007 EFCA Report Book, 67; "Dr. Jeanette Hsieh Appointed New Executive Vice President," *Trinity Magazine* (Fall 2004): 5.

159. "The Mosaic of God's Kingdom," *Trinity Magazine* (Spring 2016): 25.

160. "Mosaic Ministries: Putting Reconciliation into Practice," *Trinity Magazine* (Fall 2017): 3. Under the broader theme of reconciliation, Mosaic addressed topics such as immigration reform, educational inequality, human sexuality, and the kingdom of God and politics.

161. "Remembering Bruce L. Fields," *Trinity News Room*, 23 April 23 2020; Vincent Bacote, "Remembering Bruce Fields, the Theologian," *Christianity Today*, 29 April 2020.

162. "You Are Invited to Meet the Willifords," *Trinity Magazine* (Fall 2009): 14–19; (Spring 2010): 10–11.

163. TIU Accreditation Self-Study Report 2010, 13.

164. For Steeves, see *Trinity Magazine* (Fall 2009): 8; (Fall 2010): 5; (Spring 2011): 17; *Trinity Law Magazine* (Fall 2014): 8.

165. "New Executive Director," *Trinity Magazine* (Fall 2009): 10; (Spring 2013): 16; (Spring 2016): 15.

166. *Trinity Magazine* (Spring 2012): 15; (Winter 2018): 4.

167. *Trinity Magazine* (Spring 2012): 6. One of the first professors of graphic design was Brandon Waybright. The graphic design major had been the longtime dream of Wayne Kijanowski, known by the Trinity campus for his standard greeting: "Welcome, friend!"

168. Craig Williford, "God-Given Dreams," *Trinity Magazine* (Fall 2011): 8.

169. An additional matter with TEDS was turning the White Horse Inn in the lower level of the Olson Chapel into classrooms. This loss of a place for informal fellowship over coffee or a meal hurt student and faculty morale.

170. "Campaign Update: TIU Transformation," *Trinity Magazine* (Winter 2008): 8–9.

171. *Trinity Magazine* (Spring 2009): 2, 10–11.

172. "Campaign Update: TIU Transformation," *Trinity Magazine* (Winter 2009): 12–13.

173. *Trinity Magazine* (Fall 2011): 4; For TIU's mission and values of the strategic plan, see TIU Accreditation Self-Study Report 2010, 3.

174. 2012–2013 TEDS Catalog, 5. See tribute to Jeanette Hsieh, *Trinity Magazine* (Spring 2015): 18, 20, 22. During this period, James E. Gruenewald and Julie West Russo joined the TEDS counseling department.

175. *Trinity Magazine* (Fall 2012): 4–5.

176. *Trinity Magazine* (Fall 2007): 9.

177. *Trinity Magazine* (Spring 2013): 5.

178. In 2014, Gustafson moved to the mission and evangelism department.

179. Vanhoozer served at TEDS 1986–1990, 1998–2009, 2012–.

180. *Trinity Magazine* (Spring 2010): 7.

181. *Trinity Magazine* (Spring 2013): 4–5.

182. "Trinity College 2005 Alumnus of the Year: Neil Nyberg (BA '74)," *Trinity Magazine* (Winter 2006): 23; (Fall 2007): 9.

183. *Trinity Magazine* (Spring 2015): 22.

184. *Trinity Magazine*, Spring 2015; Trinity College Academic Catalog, 2014–2015.

185. Mark D. Kahler, "David S. Dockery: 'Keep the Light Burning,' " *Trinity Magazine* (Winter 2018): 24–27.

186. *Trinity Magazine* (Winter 2014): 4–10; (Spring 2015): 4; (Fall 2015): 20–29.

187. "Dr. Tom Cornman: Dean of Trinity College and Trinity Graduate School," *Trinity Magazine* (Fall 2015): 16–17; (Spring 2015): 5.

188. *Trinity Magazine* (Spring 2015): 7; "Hugo Wilbert 'Will' Norton," *Trinity Magazine* (Spring 2017): 38.

189. *Trinity Magazine* (Spring 2015): 7; (Spring 2016): 12. See: Doug Sweeney, "The Trinity Story," *Trinity Magazine* (Spring 2017): 30–31; (Winter 2018): 8.

190. *Trinity Magazine* (Spring 2017): 4.

191. Mark D. Kahler, "20 Key Accomplishments of the Dockery Administration at Trinity," *Trinity Magazine* (Winter 2018): 18–23.

192. Greg Gorman, "From Worst to First: Trinity's Dramatic Basketball Transformation," *Trinity Magazine* (Spring 2017): 18–21. Compare previous winning years, *Trinity Magazine* (Spring 2015): 5; (Spring 2016): 6.

193. "Stellar Finish for Women's Soccer," *Trinity Magazine* (Spring 2016): 4; (Fall 2017): 11.

194. For a biographical sketch of John Woodbridge, see *Trinity Magazine* (Spring 2009): 8.

195. "Center for Transformational Churches," *Trinity Magazine* (Spring 2016): 16–17; (Spring 2017): 3.

196. *Trinity Magazine* (Spring 2016): 28–29.

197. Steve Greggo and Julie West Russo led in the accreditation process. David S. Dockery, Campus Update, February 3, 2017.

198. *Trinity Magazine* (Fall 2016): 6.

199. "The Creation Project," *Trinity Magazine* (Spring 2016): 18–19.

200. *Trinity Magazine* (Fall 2017): 6.

201. "Trinity Launches Hiebert Center for World Christianity and Global Theology," *Trinity Magazine* (Spring 2017): 5; (Fall 2017): 12, 14. For a tribute to Tite Tiénou see *Trinity Magazine* (Spring 2015): 19, 21, 23.

202. "Dr. Graham Cole: Dean of Trinity Evangelical Divinity School," *Trinity Magazine* (Fall 2015): 18–19; (Spring 2015): 5.

203. *Trinity Magazine* (Winter 2018): 38–39.

204. Andreas J. Köstenberger, "Getting to Know D. A. Carson," September 21, 2016, https://www.crossway.org/articles/the-life-and-lasting-legacy-of-d-a-carson/; Christine Meyers, "Nurturing the Whole Person," *Trinity Magazine* (Spring 2018): 26–27; Chris Donato, "Every Pulpit in Every Church," *Trinity Magazine* (Spring 2018): 24–25; (Fall 2016): 31; (Spring 2018): 16–20.

205. "Carson on ABC," *Trinity Magazine* (Fall 2006): 9. Carson addressed claims by James Tabor, author of *The Jesus Dynasty*.

206. David S. Dockery, Campus Updates, 17 March 2017.

207. *Trinity Magazine* (Spring 2018): 3.

208. "Where Is Trinity Headed? An Interview with President Perrin," TIU Publication (2020), 2.

209. Peter Cha is professor of church, culture, and society at TEDS.

AFTERWORD

1. A little of this essay overlaps with "A Biblical Theology of Education," prepared for a conference sponsored by the International Association of Christian Education, delivered in Fort Worth, Texas, on 3 February 2021.

2. Gavin Ortlund, *Finding the Right Hill to Die On: The Case for Theological Triage* (Wheaton, IL: Crossway, 2020).

3. James Tunstead Burtchaell, *The Dying of the Light: The Disengagement of Colleges and Universities from Their Christian Churches* (Grand Rapids: Eerdmans, 1988).

PASTORS CARE FOR A SOUL IN THE WAY A DOCTOR CARES FOR A BODY.

In a time when many churches have lost sight of the real purpose of the church, *The Care of Souls* invites a new generation of pastors to form the godly habits and practical wisdom needed to minister to the hearts and souls of those committed to their care.

"Pastoral theology at its best. Every pastor, and everyone who wants to be a pastor, should read this book."
—Timothy George, Founding Dean, Beeson Divinity School, Samford University; General Editor, Reformation Commentary on Scripture